THE FRANCHISE

SAN FRANCISCO GIANTS

A Curated History of the Orange and Black

ALEX PAVLOVIC

First Triumph Books paperback edition 2025

Library of Congress Cataloging-in-Publication Data available upon request.

This book is available in quantity at special discounts for your group or organization. For further information, contact:

Triumph Books LLC
814 North Franklin Street
Chicago, Illinois 60610
(312) 337-0747
www.triumphbooks.com

Printed in U.S.A.
ISBN: 978-1-63727-156-8
Design by Preston Pisellini
Page production by Patricia Frey

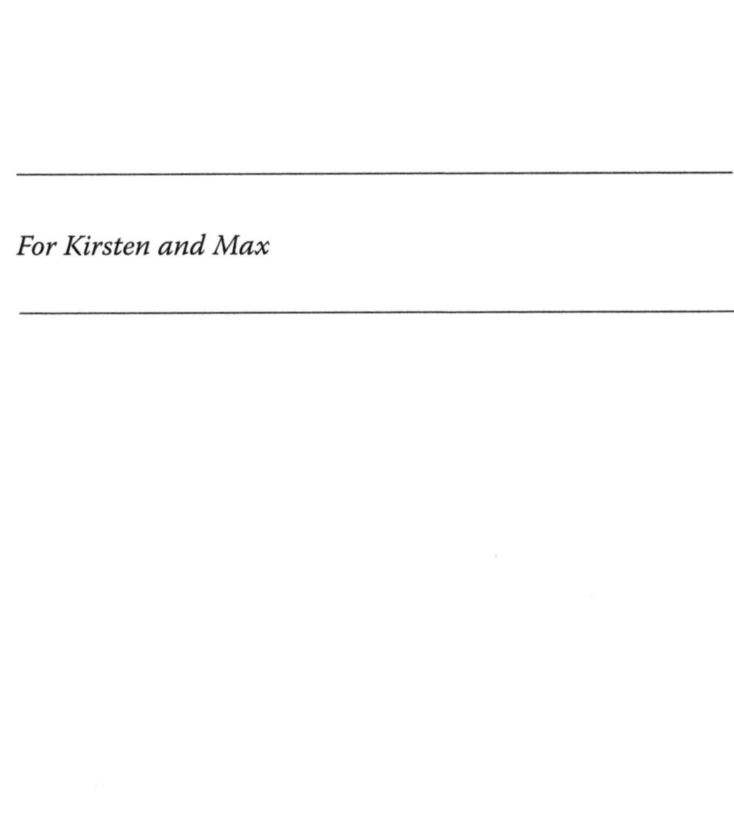

For Kirsten and Max

CONTENTS

Foreword

It was around midnight in Bakersfield when I got the call from assistant general manager Bobby Evans, who wanted to know how quickly I could get to Fresno. *It's midnight, and we're in Bakersfield,* I thought. *You tell me.* The question was Bobby's way of telling me I was headed to San Francisco and, for the first time, getting called up to the big leagues.

I was born a Giants fan and had always wanted to be their shortstop, following in the footsteps of Royce Clayton, Rich Aurilia, and others. Getting called up to the big leagues was a lifelong dream, but as I played for the San Jose Giants in May 2011, it wasn't something I thought was imminent. I was supposed to start the season in Triple A, but a broken finger set me back, and the Giants wanted me to first play in some A ballgames with the San Jose Giants. That's where I was when the big league club suffered injuries to Buster Posey, Mike Fontenot, and Darren Ford, leading to a series of call-ups.

My first call was to my future wife, Jalynne, who was at graduate school at Pepperdine but had come to the game with her parents. Then I called my parents, who knew early on that I only had one goal in mind.

I didn't even realize Bakersfield had an airport, but in the morning, I was on a flight to San Francisco. I got to Oracle

Park an hour before first pitch, and as soon as I walked into the clubhouse, I was greeted by Murph, who told me how excited he was to have me with the Giants. Murph had picked out No. 35 for me, which had been worn by two shortstops he loved watching. I still remember how excited he was to hand that jersey over. That was pretty cool for me, that a guy who had been doing it for as long as Murph was still excited about giving a rookie his new number.

That first day in the big leagues was such a rush. It was all about trying to figure out where my locker was and where I was supposed to be and what I was supposed to be doing, and I didn't end up getting into the game. At one point, Bruce Bochy told me I might pinch-run, but he ended up using backup catcher Chris Stewart. I don't remember who he ran for, but it couldn't have been someone very fast.

This was long before the lineup was texted to players a day in advance, so I wasn't sure if I would be playing the next day in Milwaukee. Second baseman Manny Burriss told me to make sure I got to the ballpark early just in case, so we took a taxi from the team hotel to Miller Park, making sure we arrived long before the team bus. When I walked into the clubhouse, I saw my name in the lineup, and that's when the butterflies hit. It was like, "Oh, this is actually real."

The first pitch I saw in the big leagues was a changeup from right-hander Shaun Marcum. It was a good one, down and just below the knees, and I took it somehow. I remember thinking, *Oh, I'm locked in. I'm seeing him well.* He threw me a sinker, and I lined out to center fielder Nyjer Morgan.

In the seventh, I came up after Marcum walked Miguel Tejada to load the bases. The Brewers had a mound visit, and I told myself he was going to try and get ahead since he had just walked a guy. I was ready for something over the plate that I could drive deep enough to at least get the runner in from third, and on the first pitch, he threw me a curveball, which I had seen earlier in the game. I put a good swing on it, and obviously the rest is history.

I did a little clap going around first, which I don't think I had ever done up to that point, and I don't know if I've done it since. I probably blacked out a little bit, which was also rare. When I hit the grand slam in the Wild Card Game in Pittsburgh, I specifically remember feeling like I was floating around the bases. I remember rounding those bases pretty clearly, but I don't remember the one in Milwaukee as well.

I found out during postgame interviews that I was the only player other than Bobby Bonds to hit a grand slam in my first game for the Giants—and then I probably watched it about a hundred times that night. It was a great call by Kruk and Kuip.

Kuip had his signature home run call with maybe a little extra excitement because of the situation, and it was a cool reaction by Kruk—"Hooooly smokes!"—that showed how special it was. Growing up watching the Giants and listening to Kruk, Kuip, and Jon Miller, it made that moment even more special. It's pretty cool being able to hear that call every time.

Bochy named me the Opening Day starter the next year, and my first ground ball of the season was a hard-hit ball by Aaron Hill. On Arizona's infield it was like someone hit the turbo button, and it took off once it hit the dirt, hit me on the wrist, and rolled up my arm. It was an error, but we got out of the inning, and when I got back to the dugout, Ryan Theriot was waiting. What he said is funny now, although it may not have been at the time: "At least you don't have to worry about the Gold Glove," he said. "The pressure is off."

Seven months later, the Giants won the World Series again, and two years after that we won another one. Jalynne was pregnant during the 2012 parade, and I just remember us thinking how cool it was that we were on a cable car. I hadn't really known what my season was going to look like, and then I became the Opening Day starter and went through the grind of a season. In the playoffs we were down 0–2 to the Reds and down again to the Cardinals, but we ended up winning the World Series. It really was against all odds that we were in that parade.

It was so cool that it all ended up that way. It was a long season, but there we were in the parade! And it felt like the whole city of San Francisco was there, which made it all even more special.

—Brandon Crawford

PART 1

THE EVEN YEARS

1
The Comeback Kids

For the first few innings of a game, before "El Mechón" would test the limits of the ballpark's speakers and he would spin sliders past hitters (who were looking specifically for his slider), Sergio Romo could be found watching the action from the dugout steps. That's where Miguel Cabrera spotted him early in Game 1 of the 2012 World Series.

A foul ball had been hit between the third base coach's box and the dugout, and the American League MVP slowly walked over to pick it up. He faked a toss to Romo and then rolled the ball into the dugout.

"Your slider," he said. "I'll be ready for it."

George Kontos, sitting alongside Romo, couldn't believe what he had just witnessed. He angrily turned to his fellow reliever and asked, "Did he really just say that?" But Romo couldn't help but smile.

Whoa, he thought. *This dude knows who I am.*

From there, the two seemed destined to face off in a big moment at some point in the series, but Cabrera had to wait longer than he anticipated. The Giants ran away with Game 1 and Romo left Cabrera in the on-deck circle the next night. He was once again looming if the ninth inning of Game 3 got hairy, but Romo went 1-2-3.

In Game 4, it finally happened, and the spot couldn't have been any bigger. The Giants were three outs from a title as Romo was handed a one-run lead in the 10th inning, and he struck out the first two to finally set up the showdown. Romo watched as Cabrera strutted to the plate. He looked in at Buster Posey and saw his catcher put three fingers down. He shook, but Posey again put three fingers down, so Romo threw his slider, freezing Cabrera for strike one. After Cabrera watched one spin outside, Romo again shook Posey, something he did often. He used his slider as others used their fastballs, so sometimes he would shake multiple times to make a hitter think something else might be coming. And then, of course, he would deliver a perfect slider, like the one Cabrera swung through for a second strike.

As Romo stepped off the mound to receive the ball, he smacked his glove. He thought he could throw a fastball past Cabrera with his fourth pitch, but he also knew he would get only one chance to try it. Another slider missed wide, evening the count. The fifth pitch of the battle brought another double-shake and another slider, which was fouled off.

On the mound, Romo realized it was time. He would go away from his best pitch, the one that everyone in the baseball world expected him to keep throwing. He had learned the no-dot slider from his grandfather, but it wasn't until 2007 that he realized he truly held something special in his fingers. His previous season had ended with a broken pitching hand, an injury that permanently wiped out his fifth knuckle. For some reason, the absence of that small joint unlocked the magic of the slider, which he could throw three different ways. He noticed new reactions from hitters right away, and within 15 months he was in the big leagues, throwing his slider past the best in the world. In the biggest moment of his career, however, he was ready to change it up. Posey put down one finger at the exact time Romo was thinking it was time to attack with a fastball. For all of the intensity of that moment, he felt as calm as he ever had on a big-league mound. As he formed a sinker grip in his glove, he blinked at Cabrera.

Oh my gosh, Romo thought. *Just hit the glove. Hit the glove and it's over.*

The pitch was 89 mph and right down the middle. It was perfect.

The Giants had a sweep and a second title, and Romo—who had been given the ninth only after the first option got hurt and the second flamed out—cemented his spot in Giants history. As beer and champagne covered the visiting clubhouse, Cabrera admitted the obvious in a quiet room down the hall. The bat had never left his shoulder. "I was looking slider," he said.

With a massive storm brewing on the East Coast, the Tigers hoped to extend the series and bring their aces back into play. But there would be no comeback. In 2012 that path belonged only to the Giants. They made history in the first two rounds on the backs of players who at one point couldn't have imagined being there, and in the tightest moments, Romo led a group of relievers that altered the course of a franchise.

The Core Four was so vital that the Giants changed their Wall of Fame qualifications so Romo, Jeremy Affeldt, Santiago Casilla, and Javier Lopez could be enshrined together in 2024. They combined for 1,789 regular-season appearances in orange and black, but it was in October that they really put themselves on that wall. During the 2010, 2012, and 2014 postseasons, Bruce Bochy had an additional ace in his back pocket every night. No other manager could match his options in the late innings, and it was particularly unfair en route to the first title, when the Core Four carried leads to All-Star closer Brian Wilson.

During those three title runs, Affeldt, Casilla, Lopez, and Romo combined for 78⅔ innings and a microscopic 1.14 ERA. Opposing batters hit just .164 off them. The Core Four faced 296 total batters and allowed just two home runs—an impossibility in the postseason, when series are won and lost on big swings.

They were a cheat code, the perfect combination of left and right, hard and soft, moxie and tranquility. "No matter where you were in the lineup, you could kind of place those guys where you needed to," Posey explained.

The Core Four filled in the gaps for a dynasty. If you looked at their individual stories, they were unlikely choices to one day end up on the wall outside the ballpark, but that was a theme throughout the championship years. It was never more prevalent than in 2012, when the Giants counted heavily on players who never could have imagined it turning out that way just a couple seasons earlier.

On the final day of the worst spring of his life, Barry Zito threw pitches off a bullpen mound at Scottsdale Stadium as Dave Righetti and Mark Gardner watched in dress clothes. The rest of the team was flying home, but Zito—the team's highest-paid player—was lost, so out of sorts that the front office started having conversations about releasing him. When the Giants flew back to San Francisco, Zito was left in Arizona to pitch in a minor league camp game, the only place the staff could be guaranteed that he wouldn't be knocked out before getting his pitch count up.

Righetti stayed with him, and not just because he felt it was a duty that came with the title of pitching coach. He took Zito's struggles personally, and he couldn't figure out why he wasn't able to help him the way he had others. The once-dominant repertoire was no longer working. Hitters had stopped offering at the gorgeous curveball, and the change-up wasn't getting easy outs. The four-seam velocity had dipped so dramatically that Zito was afraid to throw the pitch over the plate, and he wasn't biomechanically built to sink his fastball in search of groundballs. The Giants added a cutter to more easily get him through at-bats, but it wasn't going well.

Had the Giants had other options, they likely would have taken them. Left-handed prospect Erik Surkamp looked promising, but his elbow started barking in the spring, leading to Tommy John surgery and eliminating a potential off-ramp for the front office. As rumors swirled, Zito did his best to ignore the possibility that his career might be nearing an end. After facing teenagers at the club's minor league facility, he preached optimism. Something had clicked, he insisted.

The 2012 season started with a sweep at the hands of the Diamondbacks, who hammered Tim Lincecum, Madison Bumgarner, and Matt Cain in succession. But on a sunny Monday afternoon in Denver, Zito came through with one of the best performances of his life. He had not won a game on a big-league mound in nine months, but in his season debut, he became the first Giant to throw a shutout at Coors Field. As the clubhouse celebrated a surprising first win of the season, Bochy turned to a staffer and asked if the media was ready to enter or if everyone in the press box had passed out from shock.

Righetti was thrilled. He was also stunned. "For me, that's the most out-of-the-blue thing I've ever seen," he said.

Zito rode that momentum the rest of the season, and on a staff that got 160 of 162 starts from five pitchers, he became a stopper. The Giants won his final 11 starts en route to a division title, a run that emboldened them when they entered Game 5 of the NLCS facing a 3–1 deficit. With #RallyZito trending on Twitter, the left-hander gave them 7⅔ shutout innings in St. Louis and contributed an RBI with the first bunt single of his career. Five nights later, Zito faced off against Justin Verlander and threw 5⅔ innings in an easy win, setting the Giants on a course to a ring that would carry considerably more weight for the left-hander than his first one.

October 2010 was one of the most magical months in franchise history, but it was a difficult one for Zito. He called his father after being left off the postseason roster and told him he was thinking of quitting baseball. He also admitted in his autobiography that he rooted against the Giants that fall: "[If] they lost, it proved they couldn't win without me," he wrote in *Curveball.*

Then–Giants GM Brian Sabean once told Zito he might as well get the contract figures tattooed on his forehead. The biggest deal in franchise history was an anchor, particularly when he pitched poorly, but in the end, Sabean viewed it differently. When the oft-tumultuous seven years were over, Sabean insisted he would make the same deal all over again. "Quite frankly, when we needed him the most, he helped us win the World Series," he said. "I find great satisfaction and solace in that."

Zito's performance in the World Series ignited a sweep that allowed the Giants to finally exhale. In the NLDS, they became the first team in MLB history to wipe out a two-game deficit in a five-game series by winning three straight on the road. A round later, they became the first to win six elimination games on the way to the World Series. When the sweep of the Tigers was complete, the Giants had won seven straight after falling behind in the NLCS, outscoring opponents 36–7, a steamrolling that was up there with any in baseball history. "It's hard to comprehend," Posey said during the celebration.

But perhaps it shouldn't have been. Nobody had ever come back as many times as the 2012 Giants, but then that's what they had been built for. Zito was far from the only one who clawed his way back from the depths of baseball hell. He hadn't even taken the most difficult journey.

Ryan Vogelsong stepped off the back of the mound and took a deep breath. "You have to do something different with your life," he told himself. "You can't keep doing the same thing and thinking everything is going to change."

The epiphany came in Caracas, of all places. Vogelsong was 33 years old and half a decade removed from his last big-league win, and as he looked around Estadio Universitario, a cozy multipurpose stadium in Venezuela's capital, he realized it was time to mix it up. Vogelsong was pitching well, but Leones del Caracas, one of the Venezuelan Winter League's best teams, was threatening with no outs in the fifth inning of a scoreless game. The only hard contact through four innings had been a double from infielder Marwin Gonzalez, and when he stepped up again with the bases loaded, Vogelsong quickly went 2–0. He stepped off the mound to gather his thoughts.

For Vogelsong's entire career, the easy call there had been a sinker to get back in the count. But where had that gotten him? Traded by the Giants. Bounced around by the Pirates. Sent to the minor leagues in Japan. Released midseason by the

Phillies. It was time to take a different approach, and when the best 2–0 curveball of his life landed for a strike, he could see in Gonzalez's eyes that perhaps he had found something. The look conveyed a clear message: *Holy shit. Where did that come from?*

Vogelsong threw another one and got the same reaction. A fastball at the letters ended the at-bat, and he struck out the next two to leave the bases loaded. As Vogelsong walked back to Tiburones de la Guaira's dugout, he thought about how a simple tip from a Triple A pitching coach had fixed his shoulder rotation a few months earlier. In winter ball, he had made an adjustment with his hips, thanks to that team's pitching coach. Everything was starting to sync up, and in the middle of a game in Caracas, it had all fallen into place. "That was the at-bat. That was the delivery and the feeling that I had wanted to have," Vogelsong said years later. "Everything clicked."

He had waited years for that moment, and done so on three continents and through multiple seasons that would have led just about anyone else to quit. Of all the comeback stories during the 2012 season, Vogelsong's was the most remarkable. He allowed just three runs over 24⅔ postseason innings, and the Giants won all four of his starts. It was exactly the type of dominance they had hoped for when they took him in the fifth round of the 1998 draft out of Kutztown University in Pennsylvania, but the path to postseason stardom was more circuitous than anyone expected.

Vogelsong reached the big leagues at 23, but he was traded to Pittsburgh the next summer. It was a homecoming for a man who had broken just about every record at Kutztown, but injuries and ineffectiveness kept him from sticking. By 2007 he found himself devouring *You Gotta Have Wa*, a book about the cultural shock that American players faced when they signed in Japan. It didn't take long for Vogelsong to realize that much of what was written would apply to him too. He pitched well at first but eventually found himself in the Japanese minor leagues.

"You're standing there going, 'Man, what am I doing?'" he said. "'I'm a year removed from the big leagues and this is where I am?' But those are the defining moments of your life, right? You can go one way or the other. 'Am I going to be done because this sucks right now, or am I going to find a way to get through this because this sucks right now?'"

It should come as no surprise that Vogelsong's best years in the big leagues were dotted with starts where it was grind, grind, grind, and never give in. That's the mentality he had in Japan for three seasons, then back in Triple A, and in the Venezuelan Winter League as a 33-year-old. There were plenty of times when he was ready to quit, but that never outweighed his love of pitching or his desire to compete. And one simple thought was always omnipresent: "Man, I just wanted to be good," he said. "At the end of the day, that's all there was."

Four years after his debut in Japan and nearly 12 months to the day after he was released by the Lehigh Valley IronPigs, the Triple A affiliate of the Phillies, Vogelsong stood on the line at Chase Field and got introduced as a National League All-Star. He had never stopped believing he could be a good big-league pitcher, and eventually that's exactly what he became.

That night in Caracas was one of many that winter when he dominated. Giants hitting coach Hensley Meulens was managing a rival team and alerted his bosses. The Giants started talking to Vogelsong about a reunion, but they had some competition. "The Dodgers called about a minor league deal," Vogelsong said. "I did not want to be a Dodger, obviously."

When the Giants tweaked their offer, Vogelsong was back where it had all started, and he found a crucial ally in Posey. Vogelsong was a non-roster invitee and a long shot to make an impact, but when he threw to Posey for the first time, the young catcher called the game like they were in the middle of a pennant race. When he went home that night, it hit Vogelsong that Posey had grasped the magnitude of what that moment meant to him. A non-roster invitee, especially a journeyman approaching his mid-thirties, might get just one chance to impress. Posey made sure it counted.

A good spring led to a shot in April, and this time Vogelsong didn't waste it. He posted a 2.71 ERA in 2011, and when the Giants made the postseason the next year, Vogelsong was ready for his star turn. He also realized he was uniquely built for October.

Everything slows down in the playoffs. Everything is more intense. Every pitch feels like the most important one you have ever thrown. It was the perfect environment for a guy who was unapproachable in the clubhouse even the day before his starts. Whether it was spring training, the middle of May, or Game 3 of the World Series, Vogelsong treated every appearance the same after he got his second chance. He had learned that it was the way he had to be. "I played little games with myself. I would stare across the field at the other team's starter, and if he was having a good time and joking around, [in my head] I would be like, *You're going to lose tomorrow; you're not ready*," he said. "And that included guys like Clayton Kershaw. I looked across the field at Kershaw a couple of times and he was joking around. It was like, *He's not ready*. That's how I had to prepare myself."

It was unorthodox, but it worked. Vogelsong had made 33 starts in the big leagues before going overseas. When he returned at an age when most had long since retired, he made 146 starts and won two titles. After all those years, he became the perfect fit for a 2012 team that constantly needed to throw punches with its back up against the wall.

It was Vogelsong who got the ball in a must-win Game 3 in the NLDS and allowed just one run. In the next round, it was two runs over 14 innings in two starts. Giants fans embraced #RallyZito and then moved on to #RallyVogey. When the team reached the World Series, Vogelsong pitched 5⅔ shutout innings to win Game 3.

At times when it seemed he should quit, Vogelsong always pushed back. He wanted to prove that he was a good pitcher, but when the lights were brightest, he showed that *good* was not nearly a strong enough adjective.

When the cameras were on and reporters' notebooks were out, Bochy would never play favorites. One of his defining traits was that he always supported his players, from the superstars to the last man on the bench, and it was rare that he would even utter a negative word about any of them. When the going got tough, Bochy would criticize the team as a whole or himself, not say anything that could strip one of his 25 players of even an ounce of confidence.

There were certainly some who meant more, though, and there was no hiding the special bond that formed early on between Bochy and popular third baseman Pablo Sandoval. "He was like my dad," Sandoval explained. "He taught me a lot in my career, and he was also tough and let me know when I was doing things right or doing things wrong."

Signed out of Venezuela as a teenager, Sandoval had one of the more fascinating careers in franchise history. It spanned two decades, with Sandoval bitterly departing as a free agent and then twice returning to the organization later in his career. The initial breakup might have been avoided with a bit more structure.

For much of his prime, Sandoval dealt with questions about his weight, which ballooned to nearly 300 pounds in the darkest days. He was such a tremendous athlete—not just a switch-hitter but also an ambidextrous thrower—that he often was able to get away with it, but at times it was a losing battle that became too much for the coaching staff. The most glaring example came in 2010, just a year after Sandoval hit .330 with 25 homers in his first full season.

The Panda played with a joy that lit up the ballpark, and he appeared to be a foundational star. But as the Giants chased their first title, he couldn't keep up. His production plummeted as he packed on the pounds, and he got just three at-bats in the 2010 World Series. He watched the entire clincher from the bench, although when Wilson recorded the final out, a screaming Sandoval was one of the first to reach the mound.

That passion was one of the things that Bochy appreciated most about his third baseman. Sandoval loved to play the game, showing up with a smile every day, ready and eager for just about anything. He was born left-handed, but he wanted to play shortstop and catch in Little League so he could be in the middle of the action. That required throwing right-handed, so his grandfather Luis, taught him to use his right hand, motivating him by demanding laps around the field if Pablo failed to hit him in the chest. He ran a lot of laps, but he was so naturally gifted that before long he was a right-hander, one good enough to hit 88 mph and snap off five curveballs with elite spin rates when Bochy threw him on the mound late in his career.

Sandoval was born with tremendous eye-hand coordination, and whenever he got his weight under control, it made him the team's most frustrating hitter to face. He was equally adept at digging a pitch out of the dirt or driving one that was at eye level. He was so quick at third base that on more than one occasion, Bumgarner stormed into Bochy's office and told him he wouldn't be pitching if Sandoval were not behind him.

Sandoval was a popular teammate, and at times that made it more difficult to walk a disciplined path. Players and coaches would laugh as they told stories that shouldn't have been funny but were. Sandoval arrived sick to a game early in his career, and the staff sent him home to rest—only to later hear someone had seen him walking out of a nearby Amici's with an armful of pizza boxes. On road trips, staff would instruct hotels not to deliver room service to Sandoval, but he got around that by putting his brother in the adjoining room. One year, the Giants planted their strength coach in the seat behind Sandoval on flights to try and limit his in-flight snacking.

After 2010, though, Sandoval took Bochy's stern message to heart. He lost 40 pounds and made back-to-back All-Star teams, and when the Giants reached the postseason, he was ready for the spotlight. He hit a two-run homer to put Game 4 of the NLDS out of reach and had nine hits in the NLCS. It was all a warm-up act for one of the greatest individual performances in postseason history.

Verlander was the reigning Cy Young Award winner and American League MVP, and he was well rested ahead of the first game of the World Series. But when he tried to blow Sandoval away with a fastball at the letters, the 95 mph pitch was scorched into the first row of seats in center field. In the third, Verlander again tried to get 95 mph past Sandoval. This time he found the seats in left. As the ballpark shook, Verlander turned toward the bleachers, put his hand on his hip, and scrunched his face in confusion. "Wow," he muttered before turning to his dugout and shaking his head.

When the ballpark opened on April 11, 2000, Los Angeles's Kevin Elster hit three home runs, an out-of-nowhere performance that had the Giants players and the media briefly wondering if the dimensions were actually friendly to hitters. It didn't take long for those thoughts to be washed away, and nobody else hit three homers in a game at Third and King until the World Series in 2012. Sandoval's third came on a hanging breaking ball in the fifth inning.

The performance earned Sandoval Series MVP honors two years after he had been left in the shadows. He became just the fourth player to homer three times in a World Series game, joining Hall of Famers Babe Ruth and Reggie Jackson and future inductee Albert Pujols. In a way, he would be there with them. Sandoval's bat from Game 1 was sent to Cooperstown.

The graphic was probably made by a producer at the Fox Sports headquarters in Los Angeles. It's likely nobody at Ford had a hand in the "Ford Keys to the Series" and that color commentator Tim McCarver didn't create the list he talked about before Game 1 of the 2012 Word Series. Nobody stopped and thought about how insulting the graphic might be to the Giants, who had built an organization and one previous title run around starting pitching.

But Vogelsong did.

"Oh, yeah," he said a decade later. "Two. Two checks."

The graphic had a Tigers logo on one side, the Giants logo on the other, and five categories listed: starting pitching, bullpen, defense, base running, and power. The broadcast team put checks underneath the Giants for bullpen, defense, and base running and gave the Tigers the nod for power. In the column for starting pitching, there were *two checks* underneath the Tigers.

The Tigers had a tremendous staff led by two future Hall of Famers, but the Giants had Cain, Bumgarner, Vogelsong, and a resurgent Zito. Lincecum was in the bullpen after a season that ended up being the start of his decline, but he was still Tim Lincecum. Maybe it was fair to say the Tigers had better starting pitching, but two checks? An overwhelming edge? If that were reserved for any group, it should have been the Giants bullpen.

As the teams warmed up for Game 1, Vogelsong caught the graphic on a TV behind the home dugout. He asked Bumgarner if he had seen it, and the young left-hander nodded. The Giants didn't need extra motivation at that point. In the run-up to the World Series, just about everyone was picking the Tigers to win, and do so quickly, but from the first inning, it was clear that wouldn't be the case.

Sandoval and Zito were the stars of the opener, but the Giants also got two hits, two runs, and two RBIs from Marco Scutaro, who was on an all-time hot streak. The Giants picked up the 36-year-old second baseman in a minor deal with the Rockies, and soon teammates started calling him Blockbuster. Scutaro hit .362 after the trade.

Scutaro was nearly knocked out of the NLCS by a hard slide from Matt Holliday that sent him for X-rays and an MRI, but he toughed it out, winning MVP honors after tying a League Championship Series record with 14 hits. There were four more singles in the World Series, the final one proving to be the Series-winning hit. It set the stage for Sergio Romo, the closer at that point for one of the best bullpen quartets the game has ever seen.

The other right-hander was Casilla, a man of faith and a filthy repertoire. Later in his career, he threw the first immaculate inning by a Giant in more than two decades. It was an appropriate bit of history for the pitcher who had the best stuff of the Core Four but often embraced ninth-inning "torture," as Duane Kuiper so famously put it. "Santi was the calm and the storm at the same time," Romo explained.

Lopez just provided calm. Or perhaps it was cool. Aside from a brief flirtation with Digital Underground's "The Humpty Dance," the left-hander would jog to the mound to "Coastin'" by Zion I. For all of the memorable walk-up and entrance songs those championship teams had, you can argue that nobody found a more suitable fit than Lopez. Teammates marveled at how easy he made everything look, and not just when he was called in to face a tough left-handed hitter.

Before games, Lopez would effortlessly rob teammates of batting practice homers as he tried to relive his days as a college outfielder. He once grabbed the microphone at a karaoke bar in the Marina and dropped jaws with a perfect rendition of Dr. Dre's "Nuthin' but a 'G' Thang." He was the rare big leaguer to finish his degree, completing his work as a psychology student at the University of Virginia while he was in the minors.

For seven seasons and nearly 500 appearances in San Francisco, Lopez always appeared to be coastin,' which was ironic, because few had a rockier path to becoming a key part of those title teams. Three years after he was drafted, Lopez was a struggling Double A reliever with an ERA that started with a seven. The writing was on the wall, and it was written in bold letters. "I was the long reliever in Double A, which usually means a pink slip is coming," he said.

Before his last appearance of the year, he told his pitching coach that when a left-hander stepped into the box, he was going to try something new. He was a traditional overhand pitcher, but he had played first base in college and was used to whipping throws across the dirt from a lower arm angle. He wanted to try it on the mound. At that point, he had nothing to lose, and the coach replied that he could do whatever he wanted as long as he did it quickly. Lopez thought that day might be his last as a professional, so he decided to empty the tank on the way out and throw as hard as he could, even if he got hurt. What did it matter at that point?

The outing ended up changing his career. The sidearm delivery lit up the radar gun at 94 mph and added movement to his pitches. He thought he would spend the off-season looking for a nine-to-five. Instead he was told to keep working on the new delivery.

Within a year, Lopez was in the big leagues, riding the ups and downs. He was released by the Rockies and Diamondbacks but also won a title in Boston. That was followed by a trip back to Triple A as a 31-year-old, but the down times taught him to embrace the grind. When the Giants traded for him at the deadline in 2010, he was fully formed. He was ready for what Bochy was about to ask of him.

Lopez had a 2.47 ERA as a Giant, and despite not joining the organization until he was 33, he retired eighth in franchise history in appearances. Thanks to Bochy's game planning, many of those lasted just one out. The man who became a sidewinder on a whim ended up being a matchup nightmare for the game's best left-handed hitters, but he wasn't the only one.

Affeldt had always wanted to be on a big stage, and he finished his Giants career with 22 consecutive scoreless postseason games, the second-longest streak in MLB history behind only Hall of Fame closer Mariano Rivera. The final one was the strangest.

In Game 7 of the 2014 World Series, Affeldt was the bridge from Tim Hudson to Bumgarner. But in the biggest game of his life, Affeldt couldn't see straight. He took the mound and realized he was seeing two Poseys, the result of a water bubble on his eye caused by a combination of pain medication and stress. He convinced Posey not to tell Bochy and coaxed enough ground balls to get seven outs and hand the lead to Bumgarner. On the flight back to San Francisco, Affeldt finally came clean. "Well," Bochy replied slowly, "you throw more strikes when you can't see than when you can."

The injury was par for the course for a pitcher who was known for being equally comfortable against lefties and righties, an ability to pitch multiple innings—and a litany of incredible injuries. Affeldt hurt one knee while picking up his four-year-old son and the other while getting off an inflatable toy at a lake. The most famous injury came when he put a blade through his right hand while trying to separate frozen hamburgers.

Affeldt was the type to have a sense of humor about all of that, but it was a lot easier to laugh at himself when he seemingly never gave up a run in a big game, and that was true for every member of the Core Four. Their reliability made them a very popular part of the title runs, although Romo's backstory and stature certainly elevated him with the fans a bit.

Affeldt was a third-round draft pick in 1997, and Lopez's name was called in the fourth round a year later, but Romo's experience was quite different. The Giants took him out of Colorado Mesa University—his fourth college stop—with their 28th-round pick in 2005. He immediately called his father, Frank, and his grandfather, Evaristo, a former semipro player. Evaristo started running through his favorite life lessons, eager to embolden his grandson, who'd had to sit and watch 851 players get selected ahead of him.

"Your foot is in the door," he told Sergio. "Now you can show who you are. You can show them what you've got." Evaristo hung up and immediately called back. "Hey," he said. "You forgot to tell me what team drafted you."

His grandson paused and searched for the right words.

"Anybody but the Giants," Evaristo said, before rattling off a list of teams he would rather support.

"Well, my foot is in the door," Sergio replied, echoing his grandfather. "It's a great opportunity—I can show what I've got."

The day that changed his life was a bittersweet one for three generations who loved the game. Evaristo was a die-hard Dodgers fan, a passion he passed down to his son and grandson, who attended his first game at Dodger Stadium as a nine-year-old when fellow Brawley, California, native Rudy Seanez left the Romo family tickets near the left-field pole. The Giants were the last organization the Romos hoped would come calling, but you don't turn down an opportunity based on rooting interests, and you certainly don't do it when you're already facing the longest of odds.

Sergio ended up saving 137 games over 15 big-league seasons. He was such a star in San Francisco that the Giants brought him back 18 years after the draft, allowing him to say goodbye in an exhibition game. When he was a kid, Romo used to climb into strangers' backyards in Mexicali so he could be in position to catch his dad's prodigious home runs. Occasionally he had to tell his father he couldn't retrieve a ball because a dog had been let loose to chase him away. Now, at 40, he was back along the outfield wall, trading stories and laughs with kids who were thinking that one day it would be pretty cool if they could grow up to be like him. Whenever a young Giants fan asked him to sign their cap, he would first ask them to sign his. During his final inning on an MLB mound, he wore that hat, covered with dozens of signatures.

It was one final emotional moment for a player who wore his heart on his sleeve. Two rounds before that final World Series pitch, Romo won an epic 12-pitch battle with Cincinnati's Jay Bruce to close out the NLDS. Afterward, he wiped tears from his eyes as he crouched behind the plastic sheeting that was protecting lockers from champagne. A few feet away was a sign with a message that players had walked past before the game: EVERYTHING YOU'VE GOT FOR THE MAN BESIDE YOU.

Romo epitomized that attitude, and in Detroit, he threw the shocking pitch that cemented a title. A few years later, he got the text he had long been waiting for: His father, Frank, had put in his retirement papers. His son's right arm had given him the freedom to walk away when the time was right. Three generations of Romos had fallen in love with the game, and it was giving back—sometimes in unexpected ways.

When the Giants won their first title in 2010, Sergio presented his World Series jersey to his grandfather for Christmas. Evaristo passed away in 2016, and the lifelong Dodgers fan asked to be buried in the jersey and a Giants hat. Over time, "anybody but the Giants" had taken on a very different meaning. For Sergio Romo, it couldn't have been anybody but the Giants.

"In between the lines, it's the only time I didn't feel small," he said. "I thought it was cool that I ended up playing for the Giants and had my best days with them. That's the biggest I've ever felt."

2

The Bumgarner Show

On the surface, the ceremony to commemorate the 2014 championship was absolutely perfect. With 42,019 fans roaring before the 2015 home opener, Bruce Bochy held a championship flag in the air with both hands and handed it to World Series MVP Madison Bumgarner, who deftly mounted a police horse named Fritz that had the team logo painted on his side. With the Marshall Tucker Band's "Fire on the Mountain" blasting, Bumgarner grabbed the reins with his pitching hand and started making his way down the warning track, occasionally lifting the flag above his head and saluting fans in the bleachers. When he reached the track, Bumgarner handed the flag to Matt Cain, who joined others from all three title teams in walking it to the flagpole as a rendition of Queen's "We Are the Champions" played.

The moment was creative and heartwarming, and it provided the levity and slight swagger you might expect from a group that had become pretty used to those types of days. It was perfect. But it almost didn't go off that way.

For weeks leading up to the event, Bumgarner tried to change the organization's plans. He wasn't worried about Fritz getting spooked by a big crowd—riding horses was as natural to him as throwing cutters—but he didn't love the idea of being the star of the ceremony, even if he had been by far the biggest reason the Giants were celebrating. "I don't like being the center of attention," he said.

Finally, Bumgarner gave in, and he was immediately glad he did. The ride was a memorable one, and after the game, he joked that he had been tempted to take a few laps around the field but thought his outfielders might not appreciate what that would do to the warning track.

Regardless of how it happened, there was no way for the Giants to go through that day other than to make Bumgarner the focus. The afternoon started with Bochy, Tim Lincecum, and Buster Posey carrying three trophies onto the field, but it was Bumgarner who received the loudest cheers, twice tipping his cap to a crowd that wouldn't stop screaming. For years, Lincecum had been the organization's rock star, but Bumgarner stepped to the front of the line in October 2014.

His postseason performance was historic and looks more preposterous the more time passes and the more the sport changes. Bumgarner threw a record 52⅔ innings with a 1.03 ERA. He went at least seven innings in all six of his starts, and the Giants won five of them. To cap it all off, he threw five two-hit innings in Game 7 of the World Series, picking up the only save of his career.

At that moment, it seemed Bumgarner was doing something the sport might never see again. Now, that's pretty much a guarantee. The following decade all but eliminated the 200-inning workhorse, with teams using more bullpen games and becoming hyperaware of the penalties a starter faces the third time through the order. When Bochy returned to the World Series in 2023, his Rangers faced an opener in Game 4.

But that month in 2014 turned Bumgarner into a national star. He might not have loved the spotlight, but for a few months at least, he tried it on. He appeared on *The Tonight Show Starring Jimmy Fallon*, shocking teammates by handing Jimmy Fallon a pair of black jockeys that had MAD BUM printed on the back. He donned a suit and tie—a rarity—to accept *Sports Illustrated*'s Sportsman of the Year honor. He showed up in Instagram posts with *Game of Thrones* star Jason Momoa and chopped down a tree in a Carhartt commercial. A few days into spring training in 2015, he dressed like Paul Bunyan and walked out to the parking lot at Scottsdale Stadium, posing with an ax and a massive ox for a *Giants Magazine* photo shoot.

Teammates were surprised and amused, but nobody could blame Bumgarner for milking the moment, especially since he was working on one of the most team-friendly contracts in the sport. Early in his career, the Giants locked Bumgarner into a contract that guaranteed the then-22-year-old $35 million over four years and came with two option years that became steals for the organization. After 2014 the Giants still had him under control for five more seasons, and they didn't feel the need to tear up the existing deal. They—correctly, it turned out—saw an iceberg on the horizon for the entire organization, and they decided to exercise a bit more caution with extensions.

Bumgarner never publicly complained, but it gnawed at him at times. After Clayton Kershaw signed a three-year, $93 million deal a year before Bumgarner would hit free agency, he privately wondered why he wasn't in line for something similar given all he had done for the Giants. When Farhan Zaidi took over as president of baseball operations before the final season of the contract, a potential extension loomed as his biggest initial question. That spring, the Cardinals and Miles Mikolas agreed to a four-year, $68 million deal that the Giants tried to use as a template for an extension for their ace.

At the annual Play Ball Lunch a few days before the start of the 2019 season, Mike Krukow and Duane Kuiper introduced Bumgarner and ran down his list of heroics during the 2014 postseason. As the event ended, Bumgarner walked past Zaidi's table. He never broke stride as he delivered a message: "Miles Mikolas never did that," he said.

Nobody had. The 2014 title was about Bumgarner at the time and will forever be remembered for one player willing his team to victory. But there were others who came through in big moments along the way, most notably a pair of left-handed-hitting first basemen who at one point looked like long shots to even be part of the conversation in October.

Throughout his career, Bumgarner carried himself with the confidence of someone whose father once told the *New York Times* that his son "would try to steal a steak off the devil's plate." But there was one other Giant who could match that bravado, albeit in a much different way.

Long before Brandon Belt stepped onto the dirt at Wrigley Field with an electrical-tape *C* on his chest and became the Captain, he was telling anyone and everyone who would listen that *he* was the team leader, the best player, the standard not only at baseball but everything else he tried.

Belt often bragged about being undefeated in races at the Nacogdoches, Texas, community pool, a claim that would at least lead to a second or two of thought given that he did have size 15 flippers on his feet. In the minors, he once decided to go swimming in a filthy dugout that had been flooded during a rainout. "I got in trouble. They said I was going to get malaria," he said later. "I was fine, though."

Belt would sometimes joke that he was the best soccer player from a town that also happened to produce US National Team star Clint Dempsey. He needed very little prodding to talk about his speed, especially after a triple. When he had a flurry of outfield assists one season, he told reporters that during a game he had been standing in the outfield grass thinking, *I'm quickly becoming one of the best outfielders in the game.* On seemingly dozens of occasions, he told Bochy, coaches, teammates, and reporters that the Giants should let him take the mound. And, of course, he predicted he would pitch a perfect inning. He said that as a teenager, he had ranked above Clayton Kershaw on a list of Texas's best left-handed pitching prospects—and that one might actually have been true.

"He's claiming it for himself, huh?" Kershaw said, laughing. "He really was, though. We played on a couple of Team USA teams, and he really was. I think he was the best left-handed pitcher in our state. He was really good."

The swagger peaked down the stretch in 2021, when Belt proclaimed on a flight to Chicago that he was the team captain. That surprised no one, although there was quite a bit of shock and laughter when he doubled down the next day. Evan Longoria taped a *C* to his jersey, and Belt wore it in the game, reaching base four times and hitting a homer. As he approached the dugout after the blast, he patted the *C* on his chest. "You know, somebody has got to step up," he said after the game. "And when you're the alpha male on the team, it's got to be you."

True to form, he complained that the captain's mark nearly flew off during the game because he was running too fast. He said his teammates had known to follow his lead, and that he had insisted on getting off the team plane first since he was the captain. "And they did," Belt quipped. "When people know that you're the guy, they don't say anything; they just do it."

For most of his 12 seasons in San Francisco, Belt was happy to fill reporters' notebooks and keep teammates laughing, showing off the kind of comedic timing that made one wonder if he had missed his true calling. The straight face melted just once in all those years, when Belt crushed the 69th Splash Hit at Oracle Park. For years, he openly talked about how he wanted to be the one to do it. As he walked up to his locker with his arms raised and saw a large collection of microphones and TV cameras, he turned to a couple of the team's beat writers and whispered, "I let some shaft out on that swing." He couldn't help but smile throughout the interview.

The jokes were always appreciated over a long season, but they served an important purpose too. Others were tasked with keeping the train on the tracks, but Belt contributed in his own way, bringing lightheartedness to the room at times when players were in danger of gripping their bats too tightly or getting in their own heads. The Captain was born on an undefeated road trip through Denver and Chicago that helped the Giants capture the NL West in 2021—one that started with Posey addressing his teammates in the cage at Coors Field and reminding them not to let up after an emotional series win over the Dodgers. Belt also spoke up. "Listen, down the stretch, you all are going to have to play better than you ever have," he said. "For me, I'm just going to have to be me."

The fascinating thing about the whole Captain turn, which included Belt riding into Oracle Park on a boat before the 2022 home opener, was that with three small pieces of electrical tape, he won over some segments of the fan base that had held out for a decade. The Belt Wars raged pretty much from the moment the lanky first baseman made the Opening Day roster in 2011, but the discourse was quietest during that stretch in 2021, when there was no doubt that Belt was the best hitter on the team and others were following his lead to a shocking result in the NL West.

For a moment at least, it seemed Belt had finally ascended to the level that fellow homegrown infielders Posey and Brandon Crawford had reached years earlier. Perhaps that feeling would have been permanent had he stayed healthy and helped the Giants upset the Dodgers in the postseason.

A couple of years later, Belt paused when asked if he ever felt that he fully won over the fan base. He started to answer and then paused again. Finally, he laughed and shook his head. "It's tough to say. I don't know if I was ever fully accepted," he said. "I had a different game. I just had a different game than most other guys. I think my game when I first came up was probably built more for today. I liked to walk. I wanted to drive the ball, and that led to some success, and it led to some failures too. But for the most part, I felt like I probably came into my own—I don't know—maybe in 2017–18 when the game started switching a little bit. It was more of an OPS-type of ball game."

Belt's two best seasons by OPS came nearly a decade after he tore through the minors, and that always seemed to be part of the perception problem. The Giants took Belt in the fifth round of the 2009 draft, and he dominated three levels, posting a .456 on-base percentage in his first professional season with 23 homers, 10 triples, 43 doubles, and 112 RBIs in 136 games.

He entered the next spring as a consensus top 25 prospect and a potential godsend for an organization that had consistently failed to develop position players. After he won a job in camp, an endearing moment was caught by cameras that were following the team for a TV series. As Belt wiped tears from his eyes and tried to digest the news, Bochy told him to take his time. "If you need a beer, grab a beer," he said.

What followed was perhaps the strangest great career in franchise history. Only six men have played more games for the San Francisco Giants than Belt, and the list is a who's who of franchise stars and fan favorites: Mays, McCovey, Bonds, Crawford, Davenport, and Posey. Belt's name is all over the franchise's leaderboards, and while he made just one All-Star team, he finished his Giants career with an adjusted OPS that put him 23 percent above league average as a hitter over 1,310 games. He never won a Gold Glove Award, but there was little doubt he was one of the league's better defensive first basemen in his prime. His scoops and wingspan encouraged Crawford to be more aggressive with his throws, and his ability to play impossibly far off the line and still make it back to the bag allowed the Giants to set their shifts.

For years, Belt listened as detractors grumbled about his body language and "slumpy shoulders" after strikeouts. It was one complaint he could never wrap his head around. "I've thought about doing jumping jacks all the way back to the dugout," he said one day. "Maybe that would please people?"

The truth is there was perhaps nothing he could have done to change his fate. Late in his career, his body, particularly a knee that required surgery three times, started to fail him. He played 150 games just three times over a dozen seasons in San Francisco, but much of that was due to unimaginably bad luck when he was in his twenties. Throughout his career, Belt insisted he wasn't injury-prone. "I would be fine if people would stop throwing baseballs at me," he would say.

That magical run at the plate in 2021 ended when Belt was hit by a pitch that fractured his left thumb. A decade earlier, his rookie season had been halted by a fracture on a similar pitch. The same thing happened in 2014, and just two weeks after he returned from a fracture, Belt got drilled in the head by an errant Marco Scutaro throw during batting practice. He tried to come back from the concussion a few weeks later, but it quickly became clear that something was off. An avid cinephile who often took in bad movies by himself on off days, Belt knew he was in trouble when he couldn't shake a headache and had to walk out of *Teenage Mutant Ninja Turtles*. That time, he was sidelined for six weeks, but he got healthy just in time to provide the most important homer of his career.

Because the minor league season was over by the time he was cleared, Belt had no other option but to wear out a pitching machine at Oracle Park in a bid to find his timing in late September. The machine could be turned up to 94 mph, and with Belt's bat feeling slow, hitting coach Hensley Meulens would have him stand just 30 feet away as he cranked it all the way up. Belt returned in time for the postseason and was part of a futile effort for the first eight innings of Game 2 of the National League Division Series at Nationals Park.

The Giants had taken Game 1, but they managed just three hits over the first eight innings the next night against Washington Nationals ace Jordan Zimmermann, who retired 20 straight in the late innings before Joe Panik drew a walk with two outs in the ninth. Zimmermann was at just 100 pitches, but manager Matt Williams went to his closer, Drew Storen, stunning the home crowd and delighting the visiting dugout. "They could have brought Sandy Koufax in and we probably would have had smiles on our faces," Giants starter Tim Hudson said much, much later that night.

Within minutes, the game was tied. Storen had not allowed a run since August, but Posey lined his first pitch into center. When Pablo Sandoval smoked a fastball into the left-field corner, the game was headed for extra innings. Unbeknownst to them, the Giants and Nationals were only halfway through one of the great marathons in MLB history.

The filibuster went on for 6 hours and 23 minutes, at the time an MLB record, with the Zimmerman show giving way to the best night of Yusmeiro Petit's career. Petit had gone from being a journeyman to one of the most reliable long relievers in the game, and during the regular season he had set an MLB record by retiring 46 straight batters over eight appearances. A year earlier, he had been a strike away from throwing a perfect game.

Bochy had never known Petit to be nervous, but he started to worry as the right-hander struggled through the top of the 12th. He didn't look like himself, but when he got back to the dugout, Petit told everyone to relax. It had been so cold in the bullpen that he lost feeling in some of his fingers, but he warmed up in the dugout and proceeded to allow one hit over six relief innings.

Frame after frame, Petit sat down a deep lineup that had posted the best record in the NL. The 29-year-old threw 80 pitches, knowing that one mistake could end the game and tie the series. He never wavered, and as midnight approached, Belt saw he was due up again and reached for a sugar-free Red Bull, his favorite drink.

Belt had watched Posey, Bryce Harper, and Anthony Rendon launch balls that got knocked down by a wind that was so chilly that reporters up in the elevated press box turned on a hot-dog roller just to keep their hands warm enough to update their stories. When Tanner Roark grooved a fastball in the top of the 18th, Belt was ready, blasting a go-ahead homer into the second deck and dramatically tossing his bat aside.

Belt had missed nearly 100 games because of injuries, but he worked his back in time to contribute, and he had inadvertently prepared himself perfectly for the biggest moment of his career. As he rounded the bases, the scoreboard's radar gun lit up. Roark's pitch had come in at 94 mph.

Even with Belt and Angel Pagan missing so much time, and a star-filled rotation not quite living up to expectations, the 2014 Giants spent 96 days in first place over the first four months. Their lead in the division swelled to 10 games on the first weekend of June, and after a big win, Lincecum said he couldn't remember a time when the Giants had consistently played such dominant baseball. Bochy agreed. "There's nothing I can complain about," he said.

A June swoon soon changed all of that. The lineup's injuries finally became too much, and the Dodgers took over the NL West for good with a sweep in late July. With the trade deadline approaching, the Giants scored six total runs during a six-game losing streak. A desperate front office tried prospects, journeymen, and even Dan Uggla in a bid to inject life into the lineup, but nothing seemed to be working. On July 29 the Giants made a final swap, adding outfielder Juan Perez and first baseman Travis Ishikawa from Triple A.

While Ishikawa had played nearly 300 games for the Giants earlier in his career, the move was a surprising one. When he returned to the organization in late April after getting cut loose by the Pirates, team officials were open about the fact that there wasn't a real path to big-league playing time. When the call did come, nobody was more surprised than the 30-year-old, who had contemplated quitting the game he loved just a few weeks earlier.

Ishikawa had spent just a couple of weeks with his family during the entire 2013 season, spending most of it in Triple A on the East Coast. When the Pirates released him early the next season, he flew back to the Bay Area and spent a few hours going over Triple A rosters to try and find a new home. He realized the Fresno Grizzlies were short on first-base depth and called his agent. It turned out the Giants were seeing the same thing.

Brian Sabean and Bobby Evans loved a reunion and had never forgotten the power that flashed in spring training, the minors, and occasionally the big leagues. Ishikawa found himself back with the Giants' Triple A affiliate, but for a couple of months it looked like Fresno would just provide him with a chance to finish his career where it started. As the big-league team went into a slump, so did Ishikawa. He tried to stay optimistic, but after a difficult game one night, he broke down on a call with one of his closest friends. Ishikawa didn't know what to do, but he knew he didn't want his kids to see him hit a rough patch and quit. He committed to playing out the season, but beyond that there was uncertainty about whether he would look for another minor league deal. He was tired of being away from home.

Everything changed in July, when he found his old swing and discovered he was having fun playing baseball again. He was waiting for a connecting flight from Phoenix to Fresno one day when he got the call back to the big leagues, and he immediately called his wife, Rochelle, and told her he wasn't going back to Fresno. "I'm so sorry you got released," she said. Ishikawa laughed and said he had gotten called up. All he heard on the other end was a loud scream.

"It was a complete shock getting called up," he said. "I didn't expect that, let alone the fact that two months later I would be the outfielder in the postseason."

The position has always been a fascinating one for the Giants, who once built their organization around the best left fielder the game has ever seen—Barry Bonds—but have not had a player make two consecutive Opening Day starts in left since Bonds's final season. In October 2014 it was Ishikawa's turn, and 12 days after Belt's heroics, Ishikawa one-upped him.

After taking down the Nationals, the Giants had jumped out to a 3–1 lead against the St. Louis Cardinals in the NLCS. In Game 5 the Cardinals handed a one-run lead to sidewinding righty Pat Neshek, who had made the All-Star team because of the way he devoured right-handed hitters. Bochy had a surprising antidote.

He called on Michael Morse to pinch-hit. Morse was a lovable goofball who used the 1980s hit "Take On Me" as his walk-up song but was deadly serious about his craft. The size of a defensive end, he spent off-seasons working out with 49ers running back Frank Gore and other football players. His bats were shuttled from city to city in a portable humidor gifted to him by Ichiro Suzuki. They measured 34.5 inches and weighed 34 ounces, making them the largest bats on the team.

It all added up to a whole lot of power, and as Morse watched Neshek warm up, Posey called him back to the dugout. He told him to remember how strong he was and to focus on making contact. "Just touch it," he insisted.

"Look at him," Posey said later. "He's 6-foot-6 and built like a house."

Morse hammered a solo shot to left and floated around the bases as the ballpark shook. An inning later, the first two runners reached ahead of Ishikawa, who felt a sense of calm as he dug in to the box. After taking two fastballs from Michael Wacha, he looked down the third-base line and made eye contact with Tim Flannery. The third-base coach signaled for him to let it rip, and Ishikawa prepared for another fastball, knowing Wacha wouldn't want to risk loading the bases with a walk.

"I knew I hit it well, but it came off low, and every time I've ever hit a ball like that at Oracle, the right fielder makes the catch," Ishikawa recalled later. "But I saw his back turn, and he never turned back around. It was like a movie where everything was in slow motion. I saw it go out and I hit first base, and that's when I kind of blacked out."

Ishikawa wasn't the only one to lose his senses. As he approached third base, he was stunned to be confronted by Jake Peavy, another one of that season's unlikely saviors. Peavy had such poor vision that Posey would often wear neon stickers on his fingers so the right-hander could see his signs, and he was still foggy from laughing gas administered during an emergency dental operation on two teeth that chipped when he used them to try and open a pack of gum. Not realizing Ishikawa's liner had cleared the wall, Peavy rushed to meet him on the infield dirt and tell him how proud he was. "Move!" Ishikawa screamed at him. "I hit it out."

He eventually made it home, and later he sat on his couch and watched the replay get shown over and over again on postgame shows. It was an odd sensation because he couldn't remember running the bases. It felt like he was watching somebody else.

That doesn't happen to guys like me, he thought. *That happens to the superstars of the league*. But it had happened, and the biggest hit of his life sent the Giants back to the World Series, where once again their superstar was ready to take control.

With the Giants leading 8–0 in the ninth inning of the Wild Card Game, Hunter Strickland started to get loose. Bumgarner was already north of 100 pitches, and as he worked his way through the ninth, he looked back at the bullpen and caught a glimpse of Strickland. He held his left arm up and signaled for the reliever to sit down.

When the shutout was secured, Bumgarner walked into the middle of the celebration in the visiting clubhouse at PNC Park and cracked open two beer cans and two bottles. He held them above his head and drank from all four at once, the beer soaking his jersey as teammates laughed and cheered. Six days later, a fifth beer was added, and when Ishikawa's homer sent the Giants to the World Series, Bumgarner grabbed three Budweiser bottles in each massive hand and doused himself again.

After every viral beer chug, Bumgarner would retreat to back rooms, content to celebrate quietly with family members. He loved talking about the game of baseball, and if a trusted reporter found him standing around before batting practice, he could easily spend half an hour discussing the state of the league. But when it came to building the myth during his best postseason, the job was left to teammates who were all too happy to do it. Trainer Dave Groeschner joked that Bumgarner might be part horse. Ryan Vogelsong said it seemed Bumgarner had the cheat code to life. Hudson might have summed it up best: "He's got a set of brass balls on him like I've never seen," he said, laughing.

Much of that 2014 roster was built the same way, and Bochy squeezed every ounce out of an aging group that wasn't afraid of big moments. Ishikawa and Belt had the most memorable blasts, but the title run also included a postseason-record 26 hits from Sandoval. Posey caught every inning but two in the postseason. Panik and Crawford teamed up for a memorable double play in Game 7 of the World Series, and Crawford's strong arm kept Alex Gordon from testing his luck with a championship on the line. The grand slam in Pittsburgh at the start of it all was Crawford's most important hit as a Giant.

While the power was there in big moments, the Giants were also happy scraping it together. After Gregor Blanco's bunt was whipped into the outfield to end an NLCS game, Flannery gleefully talked about his famous RTIs—runs thrown in. "Rocks and slingshots, man," he said, laughing. "We can score runs without hits."

The rotation felt taped together at times. After Matt Cain had elbow surgery, the team acquired Peavy. He had been 1–9 in Boston but posted a 2.17 ERA the rest of the way. The Giants went 3–0 with Vogelsong on the mound in the postseason. Hudson was an All-Star in the first half before tailing off. Still, he was ready for Game 7, and he was the man Bumgarner, a close friend after just a few months as teammates, wanted on the mound at the start of the game. He considered it fate that Hudson would start a potential clincher as he chased a title in his 16th season, and he knew how much it meant to him. A few days earlier, Hudson had annoyed his three children by repeatedly asking, "Do you realize we're in the World Series?"

As Hudson prepared in the trainer's room, Bumgarner and Peavy stood in left field during batting practice and talked about a meeting Bochy had held to remind all 25 players that it was "all hands on deck." Bumgarner finally delivered the message Peavy had been waiting for. "Once I get in this game," he said, "I'm not coming out."

Sixty-eight pitches later, Bumgarner had his third ring and a secure spot in the game's history books. His 52⅔ innings may stand the test of time. In the decade after his remarkable run, nobody got within even 15 innings of that record. "I could never say never," Bumgarner said at the reunion 10 years later. "But I would say it's a pretty safe bet that it's not going to happen in the near future."

Kershaw will go down as the best pitcher of his generation, but there's little doubt Bumgarner was the one every manager would want on the mound in a big game. The two lefties formed a friendship over the years, always meeting hours before rivalry games for long conversations in the outfield. Bumgarner was the first pitcher to homer off Kershaw and later did it a second time, but Kershaw didn't hold a grudge. When Bumgarner pinch-hit against the Dodgers in his final appearance as a Giant, Kershaw threw him seven straight fastballs. He wanted to go head-to-head one last time, and he figured that if Bumgarner homered, well, good for him.

Bumgarner would often sit in the video room when he wasn't starting, getting a different view of the game and talking baseball with anyone who would wander in. He paid particularly close attention when Kershaw was facing the Giants, eager to learn as much as he could. Kershaw was one of the few who could understand the weight that was on Bumgarner's shoulders that October. He tried several times to come out of the bullpen or pitch on short rest in the postseason, but nobody in the modern game has ever done it quite like Bumgarner.

"The competition part of that is what I really appreciate about him," Kershaw said. "He'll forever be a legend for that. I've done it a few times and pitched on short rest, and you have to say 'Screw it.' You just go get people out. You don't worry about routines; you just pitch. He was really good at that."

For 29 days Bumgarner pretended conventional wisdom didn't exist. Bochy joked before the World Series that he didn't want to insult his ace by asking how he was holding up.

Bumgarner had always felt pitch counts were overrated, so he set his hypothetical limit for Game 7 at "maybe 200." Privately, Dave Righetti told Bochy the left-hander had somewhere between 50 and 70 pitches in him.

It wasn't until Sandoval secured the final out that Bumgarner finally let his guard down. His 702nd pitch of the month was an elevated fastball that Salvador Perez popped up, and as Sandoval circled under it and the rest of the Giants prepared to rush the field, Bumgarner walked slowly off the mound. Posey approached with a smile on his face, but Bumgarner watched the flight of the ball, the intensity still flashing from his eyes, just in case there was somehow more work to be done. When the final out was recorded, he finally let the emotion pour out. There would be no beer chug this time, though.

A half dozen photographers stood around the beer trough in the clubhouse waiting for one last shot, but Bumgarner never showed. Finally, team photographer Andy Kuno was sent to see what was going on, and he found a spent Bumgarner sitting in a quiet clubhouse kitchen with his wife, Ali. There would be no seven-beer salute. The historic performance had won him MVP honors, which came with extra interviews. During one of them, Bumgarner finally came clean. "You know what? I can't lie to you anymore," he said. "I'm a little tired now."

3

Building a Dynasty

Brian Sabean had no idea what was waiting for him. The architect of the first championship team in San Francisco Giants history was sitting with family members in a staging area for the parade when managing general partner Bill Neukom, his boss, approached. Neukom had just finished a dry run of the parade route, which would take cable cars down Market Street and through downtown. He had seen the fans who had camped out overnight and the hundreds of thousands who had started to line up early in the morning. He noticed the crowds getting deeper with each passing moment.

Neukom told Sabean he wouldn't believe the turnout for the World Series champions, but it wasn't until Sabean's car turned down Montgomery Street that he fully grasped what his team had accomplished. He knew the parade was 52 years in the making for a city that had been poised to celebrate in 1962, 1989, and 2002, but in that moment, the magnitude of it all fully set in. One by one, Giants executives, coaches, and players experienced the same sensation.

"You realized that this was a long time coming and it was a life experience for not only our fans but the Bay Area and all of Northern California," Sabean said later. "It was an emotional time. To see the turnout, it was validation for all of the great teams in years past. The Mays, McCovey, and Marichal teams that couldn't quite do it. We were the chosen ones. It was an amazing thing to see."

They were an unlikely group to be chosen. Five decades earlier, in 1958, the Giants left New York and the Polo Grounds for a brighter future in San Francisco. Within four years, a team with five future Hall of Famers on the roster made the World Series but fell short. The 1989 run was halted by an earthquake and then a fearsome pitching staff from the other side of the Bay. In 2002 it was an infamous ball flip and one of the worst collapses in playoff history. In between came the 1993 team, about as talented as the city has ever seen. That group still believes the parade would have happened 17 years earlier had the Wild Card spot existed.

In a way, the 2010 championship had its roots in 1993. The Giants have never been able to stomach a rebuild since Peter Magowan and a new ownership group saved the franchise before that 1993 season, preventing a move to Tampa Bay. They have always believed it's something they cannot afford to do. At first it was because the team needed to stay competitive as support was drummed up for a desperately needed new ballpark. When that park opened and the sellouts started to pile up, the motivation shifted: it became to keep fans coming back.

There has been no bottoming out, no tanking. When the Giants picked second overall in the 2018 draft, it was by accident. The 2017 team was never supposed to lose 98 games or come anywhere close, but the roster got old in a hurry. Ownership and the front office saw the warning signs but ignored them. Another losing season led to the end of the line for a front office that had started to be put in place in 1993, when the new owners hired Bob Quinn away from the Reds. Quinn had one condition for Magowan and Larry Baer: "I'll come, but you have to give me the okay to get Brian Sabean to come run our player development."

Sabean was a rising star, a former coach at the University of Tampa who had quickly proven to be one of the industry's sharpest scouts. He was instrumental in the drafting of Derek Jeter, Andy Pettitte, and Jorge Posada, among others, and was the Yankees' vice president of player development and scouting when the Giants called. Their timing turned out to be perfect, a theme in the construction of their first San Francisco championship. The Yankees would go on to win four World Series titles with many of the players Sabean drafted, but at the time when Quinn was looking for a No. 2, they were an organization in chaos. Owner George Steinbrenner had been suspended, and Sabean was ready for a change. A few years later, so were the Giants, and Quinn stepped down as GM.

Sabean was promoted to general manager at a low point for the franchise, which hadn't been able to build on the 103-win campaign in 1993. The Giants went 55–60 in a strike-shortened 1994 season and finished 10 games under in 1995. Despite having Barry Bonds and Matt Williams in the heart of their lineup, they went 68–94 in 1996, failing pretty much across the board. On the field, the club was hit hard by injuries, which led to Bonds, in a sign of what was to come, setting an NL record for walks. On the other side of the ball, the Giants set a franchise record for homers allowed. The poor play combined with the lingering effects from the strike led to the organization losing more than $30 million over two seasons.

A day after he was given a four-year deal to succeed Quinn as general manager, Sabean told reporters he would try to walk parallel paths, noting that the Giants would get younger while also attempting to quickly catch the Dodgers and Padres. His first big move was meant to push them toward both goals, and it was a stunner.

The Giants had too much payroll committed to just two players—Bonds and Williams—so Sabean made the difficult decision to send his third baseman to Cleveland for a package headlined by second baseman Jeff Kent. The reaction was so one-sided that he met with reporters a few weeks later to defend himself. "All of a sudden I went from being the guy who was going to help the club to being an idiot," he said. "Well, I'm not an idiot." Four years later, Kent was named the National League's Most Valuable Player.

Bonds and Kent never quite got to the finish line as teammates, but they helped build momentum as the Giants opened their new ballpark. They had a run of eight consecutive seasons finishing first or second in the NL West, but they were walking a tightrope. Bonds became the greatest show the game has ever seen, which meant no stepping back, not even for a moment. The Giants surrounded him with aging veterans year after year, eager to ride the wave. There seemed to be no off-ramp. "We opened the ballpark in the right fashion, but we could never sync up an exit strategy with Barry," Sabean said. "And more so, figure out how to build a team for the future [with] him still being in the ballpark."

As the lucrative and wildly entertaining Bonds era was coming to an end, the Giants pivoted. It was time to build around pitching, and they eventually put together a staff that would lead them further than they had ever been before. It took more than a decade, but Sabean and a front office filled with trusted and tenured voices found the right formula.

Dick Tidrow commanded a group that drafted Tim Lincecum, Matt Cain, Madison Bumgarner, and Jonathan Sanchez. The bullpen was led by Brian Wilson and the eclectic Core Four. In the big leagues, they all worked with Dave Righetti and Mark Gardner and found themselves in the right spots thanks to Bruce Bochy, whom Sabean had aggressively pursued after finding out the Padres would let him out of his deal. One key ingredient was initially missing, but in May 2010 Buster Posey arrived for good. The puzzle was complete.

On October 7, 2010, the Giants returned to the postseason with a new look. They would do it with homegrown pitching this time, and right away they found validation. Lincecum opened the postseason run with a 14-strikeout masterpiece against the Braves. "It set the tone," Posey said. "We knew we had really strong starting pitching, but it was like, this is the biggest stage now, this is our guy on the mound, and to come out and dominate a really good Braves team like that, it just kind of buoyed everybody else into believing."

The Giants rolled through the Braves and then knocked down the Phillies. When they took a decisive lead into Game 5 of the World Series, it once again was Lincecum's turn. Sabean sat with his four oldest sons in Bochy's office at the Ballpark in Arlington and watched as Lincecum took control. When Wilson recorded the final out, he dropped his head into his hands and started sobbing.

It had been an unexpectedly long road for the entire organization and fan base, but few had felt the weight of history more than Sabean. The eighth general manager in franchise history had finally brought the trophy back to San Francisco, but it had not been easy. The endless calls for his firing were the tip of the iceberg, but Sabean understood. This was what he had signed up for. The Giants could never rebuild, especially after coming so close in 2002.

As he sat in Bochy's office and waited for players to come racing in to grab bottles of champagne and buckets of cheap beer, Sabean thought about that team that had been six outs away. He has never gotten over the 2002 loss, in large part because there were so many players and staff members on that team who didn't get to experience the euphoria a few years later. When the Giants finally won it all, the first emotion was simply relief. This time, they had gotten past the finish line. They knew they would have to find a different path there, and eventually they did. Homegrown pitching, Sabean would say, was the organization's "gold standard." "Fortunately it did click," he said. "And we opened a window that was historic."

The coaches called it "getting Sabed" and they would go to great lengths to avoid it. They would sneak out of back doors, duck down as they passed doorways, even crawl on their hands and knees, but sometimes there was nothing they could do.

During their years running the franchise, Bochy and Sabean lived in a high-rise apartment building across the street from Oracle Park. They would walk home after games, although not right away. It wasn't uncommon for the two to emerge out of the back gate of the ballpark and see that the sun was starting to rise.

What began with an unlikely recruitment turned into a partnership that changed a franchise and a city. There was a lot of champagne in October, but for the rest of the year, wine flowed in Bochy's office on a nightly basis. Sabean's office was right behind his, and the two would sit for hours after games, dissecting what had just happened and what was to come, but also simply telling stories. "We would talk about the players and the team, but we also had a lot of laughs during those late-night discussions," Bochy said.

Over the years, a routine began to build—one started by Felipe Alou. In Bochy's early years, Alou would occasionally stop by after a loss and joke that it was no time to waste good wine. Bourbon would pour after the losses and wine after the wins, and it was the best Napa had to offer, a nice perk of managing in a ballpark that was a couple of hours from the world's best wineries. Eventually, Bochy's coaches discovered the stash. They would sneak in and grab a bottle or two as he was addressing the media and then scurry back to the coaches' locker room. They had to be quick too.

"When Sabes came by, that's when they would run for the hills," Bochy said. "Sabes would see them and go, 'Hey!' They would have to come in there and three, four, five hours later, there they still are. They would hide the next week."

This became the routine for two men who lived and died with the game. It was so ingrained that some of the coaches moved; living closer to the ballpark made for an easier trip home late at night, but being farther away provided a convenient excuse for ducking out. Bochy would get back after the 27th out and find text messages waiting from Sabean, who would then walk over to revisit everything that had just happened. They talked about lineups and pitching decisions and impending call-ups, anything and everything that could lead to more wins. But there was a line Sabean would not cross. It was part of the reason the working relationship worked out so beautifully. "I'll tell you what, he never questioned anything I did," Bochy said. "He had suggestions and things we could do a little bit differently, of course, but no, he never questioned me. Sabes has such an edge to him and a great edge, and that's what made him so good, but when it came down to me, he was behind me 100 percent."

Sabean believed in putting good people in vital spots and trusting them to succeed. The two most important draft picks of that era—Lincecum and Posey—were made because he trusted his top lieutenants to follow their guts. He had a tight-knit front office that included Bobby Evans, who would succeed him, and longtime Giants executives Jeremy Shelley and Yeshayah Goldfarb. He had an inner circle of scouts who often would accompany him around the ballpark in spring training, all of them wearing some variation of black. It could be intimidating, and perhaps that was the point.

While there was a fair amount of distance from Sabean's office to the areas where coaches and players got dressed, they could still hear him slamming doors and cursing up a storm after bad losses. Back when dugout phones were more regularly used, Sabean would occasionally call down during games to ask why something had just happened. One time, he called and asked bench coach Ron Wotus if the outfield had been in a no-doubles alignment. Wotus said they were playing straight up. "It should have been no-doubles," Sabean snapped before hanging up.

That was part of his famous drive, which proved to be the right approach for an ownership group intent on never losing momentum. There were times, though, when it felt that all involved would have been better off backing away from the table instead of splashing more chips on the pile. As Bonds's career was ending, Sabean pleased the veterans in the clubhouse by bringing in Barry Zito and Aaron Rowand on huge deals that proved to be mistakes. After Posey's season-ending injury in 2011, he kept pushing for a repeat, trading top pitching prospect Zack Wheeler for Carlos Beltran.

But two years later, that approach paid huge dividends. The industry expected the Giants to sell Hunter Pence, Javier Lopez, and Lincecum at the 2013 deadline, and Evans took calls from rival execs who were in disbelief that the Giants were holding on. After a quiet deadline, Sabean said the offers for his players were "almost embarrassing." He insisted the Giants would keep all three and compete in 2014. "In reality, Brian didn't want to ever not go for it every year," Evans said. "That was part of the culture of the organization, that we need[ed] to win and do everything we [could] to win all the time. I think when we didn't have the team that could do it, that was a pretty big letdown for Brian."

In the years after the crushing 2002 defeat, there were a few Giants teams that proved to be disappointments. But Magowan stuck with his front office, and when Neukom took over, one of his first acts was giving a show of support behind closed doors for an embattled baseball operations leader who would become the longest-tenured general manager in baseball. Sabean returned the favor with his coaches. He was fiercely loyal to them, especially during some lean times following the Bonds years. After one of them, he met with the staff. "I want you to know you guys are doing everything you can, and it's not your fault," he told them. "We just don't have the horses, and that's on me."

That was slowly changing, though. As the Giants finished their first decade in a new ballpark, Sabean could see a light at the end of the tunnel. His players could too.

When a team finally breaks through and wins a title, the first inclination is to try and figure out when everything shifted. Maybe it was when Sabean aired out his star-studded starting staff late in the 2010 season. Maybe it was when Bengie

Molina was traded to the Rangers, finally opening the door for Posey. Maybe it was the Pat Burrell signing in late May or the somewhat accidental Cody Ross waiver claim in August.

There were dozens of checkpoints along the way to Wilson's strikeout of Nelson Cruz that set off the greatest celebration the city has ever seen, but the seeds had quietly been growing for years before the 2010 team rushed the mound.

The 2008 group lost 90 games and shuffled through rookies, and while many of them wouldn't stick, that was the debut year for Pablo Sandoval and Sergio Romo. Wilson became an All-Star closer and Lincecum won the Cy Young Award, teaming with Cain to give Bochy two aces who were younger than 25.

The 2009 team leapt to 88 wins but finished third in the division. A new cast of characters was settling in, though. That was the first season in San Francisco for Jeremy Affeldt, Juan Uribe, and Edgar Renteria. Sanchez, signed five years earlier out of Ohio Dominican University for $2,500, started to harness his electric left arm. Posey and Bumgarner got a cup of coffee in September.

The build was slow and methodical, and for the first time, the front office really got to follow its vision. Sabean and Tidrow had been adamant that the only way at Oracle Park was to build around pitching and defense, although sometimes that led to setbacks. When Tidrow pushed for a new ace and Magowan pushed for a new face of the franchise, the compromise was Zito. There were a lot of moves that didn't work out, but sometimes the moves you don't make become even more important.

Four straight losing seasons in the middle of the decade gave the Giants multiple shots at the top of the draft, and they couldn't have done any better. Starting in 2006, they went Lincecum, Bumgarner, Posey, and Wheeler with their four top-10 picks. The first step is getting the draft right. The second step is developing the top prospects. The third step is making sure you don't make the wrong trade as you try to fill gaps elsewhere.

The Giants ultimately did flip Wheeler to the Mets in an ill-fated attempt to repeat, but his injuries kept that from stinging too much. As the trio of Lincecum, Bumgarner, and Cain formed, they resisted overtures from rival executives, even as it became clear they didn't yet have enough hitting to compete. The juiciest rumor involved a swap of Lincecum for Blue Jays outfielder Alex Rios, a 26-year-old power-hitting All-Star. "It wasn't a rumor. They had repeatedly approached us," Sabean said "But Timmy was on a meteoric rise."

Sabean hoarded his best young pitchers, which was a notable shift for those who watched what the organization did in 2003. At the height of Bonds's powers, the Giants signed 32-year-old outfielder Michael Tucker hours before a deadline for teams to offer arbitration, a move that purposely cost them their first-round pick and allowed them to shift that draft money over to a veteran free agent. The move shocked even most of Sabean's lieutenants, but he was under constant pressure from ownership to win with a strict budget.

The patience with pitching paid off when 2010 rolled around. The Giants had put together the best young rotation in baseball, and their bullpen was starting to become just as dominant, especially once the front office added minor league free agent Santiago Casilla and veteran lefty Javier Lopez to Wilson, Romo, and Affeldt. There was just one problem: the lineup, as has just about always been the case at Oracle Park, was often falling short.

The first big domino to fall was Posey. He called Evans one night in the spring and asked if he was going to make the team, and when he was informed he was headed to Triple A, he asked if it was because of his struggles in the Arizona Fall League the previous October. Posey had batted just .225, but there was a valid reason. He played in the minors a few weeks after signing in 2008 and then caught in winter ball in Hawaii. From there it was back to spring training, and then A ball, Triple A, a September call-up that consisted mostly of riding the bench, and then the Fall League. There had never been a chance to really rest his body, but Posey took the organization's decision in stride, hit .349 in his return to Triple A, and forced the issue. Molina was a popular veteran, but trading him on July 1 was the only way to begin the next era of Giants baseball. "The moment we traded Molina to give Buster the starting job, I felt like we had a new face," Evans said. "The turning point that season was that trade."

Posey's roster spot in Triple A went to Burrell, a veteran outfielder and San Jose native who had been released by the Rays after a brutal first month. Bochy loved nothing more than a three-run homer, and he was willing to look past shaky defense if it came in left field. Burrell joined the big-league roster a week after Posey and hit 18 homers the rest of the way. That took care of left field and the Giants already had a breakthrough in center field thanks to the speedy and energetic Andres Torres. Their solution in right field would come with some luck.

When the Marlins waived outfielder Ross, the Giants put in a claim partly because they liked the player but mostly to block a Padres club that also needed him and was their main competition in the NL West race. The Marlins initially made unreasonable trade requests, and the Giants backed off, figuring the Marlins would just pull Ross back. But their front office finally gave in and let Ross go to San Francisco for free as just a waiver claim. The Giants figured they had stumbled into a nice piece who was under team control for an additional year; they never could have pictured him winning NLCS MVP honors.

After years of building, the group was finally fully formed. "I watched Lincecum pitch and watched Cain pitch, and it was like, 'Guys, we have what we need here. We just have to come together as a lineup and get four runs a game,'" Burrell said. "I just kept pushing that narrative: 'Listen, we have enough.' Everybody that came, to the credit of the front office, played a massive part. It was just a perfect storm, really. I think everybody in the building knew that this pitching group was a special group and this was the time we had to capitalize on it."

Sabean felt there were two waves coming—first the pitchers and then homegrown hitters such as Posey, the Brandons, and Joe Panik. They would help with the final title, but during that 2010 parade, it was Lincecum, Cain, and Bumgarner who tried to make sense of the massive crowds. One of the cars in the parade belonged to Willie Mays, who would have delivered that first title to San Francisco 48 years earlier had Willie McCovey's line drive been just a little bit higher. As the Giants moved their celebration from Market Street to the steps of City Hall, Sabean took his family over to Mays and snapped several photos. He could tell Mays understood the role he had played in the title, even if he never swung a bat or chased down a deep fly ball that season. It was all connected, from Mays to Bonds to a team that finally won in a new ballpark others had taken from dream to reality.

"In his own way, he had been a big part of it," Sabean said. "It was just special to see him so happy, and so relieved."

PART 2

THE PILLARS

4

Willie Mays

Known simply as the Catch, it is the greatest defensive play in Major League Baseball history. But to the man who made it—the only man who could have made it—it perhaps should have been known as the Throw.

Willie Mays was an estimated 450 feet from the plate when he robbed Vic Wertz of at least a go-ahead double in the eighth inning of Game 1 of the 1954 World Series. The Giants went on to win the game in extra innings and sweep the series, giving Mays, then just 23 years old and in his first season back from military service, his first and only World Series ring.

The degree of difficulty came from the depth of center field. The Polo Grounds wall measured 483 feet at its deepest point, and Mays just about reached a section that jutted out as he made an over-the-shoulder grab. Historians have tried to figure out the exact distance of the blast and have come up with varied numbers. What has never been up for debate is that

Mays made it look remarkably easy, his mind already churning as he approached the wall and peered back over his head.

Mays always played shallow because he knew he could reach anything hit behind him. He had no doubt he would get to the ball, but he also knew Larry Doby, the runner on second, might tag and score given how deep the ball was hit. Mays's reasoning was simple, and you can imagine him announcing it in his truth—alternately brash and humble. He easily would have scored on a play like that one, so why wouldn't Doby try? Mays quickly spun and fired a strong throw back to the infield, his New York Giants hat flying off as he hit the ground and watched the rest of the play unfold.

In his biography, *24: Life Stories and Lessons from the Say Hey Kid,* Mays explains how he threw a strike to second base to limit the damage. Doby tagged and reached third, but the runner on first couldn't advance. When the inning ended a few minutes later, Doby was still standing on third. "I think the throw was the key to the play, and I think the play was the key to the whole World Series, because if that ball gets past me, Cleveland has two runs in and Vic on third," Mays wrote. "Maybe we don't catch up."

The whole sequence lasted just a few seconds, but it summed up Mays's brilliance, the physical gifts that were matched by one of the greatest minds the game has ever seen. For generations, scouts have graded players on baseball's five tools. There has never been anyone with a better collection than Mays, who played in 24 All-Star Games, was Rookie of the Year, and twice was named National League MVP—in his second full season and again when he was 34. From the time he broke into the big leagues, Mays checked every box. Even a rival could admit that. "Without a doubt," Dodgers broadcaster Vin Scully said, "the greatest player I ever saw was Willie Mays."

Two of the five tools cover hitting, one for average and one for power. Over nearly 11,000 at-bats, Mays had a .301 average. He hit .300 in 10 seasons, peaking at .347 in 1958, his first season on a new coast. Mays is the only Giant in the 3,000-hit club and ranks 13th in MLB history with 3,293. Nobody has ever hit more homers or doubles in a Giants jersey than Mays, who put up those numbers despite missing nearly two full seasons early in his career to serve his country.

The power numbers are particularly impressive given that Mays started his career in the massive Polo Grounds and spent most of it at unforgiving Candlestick Park, an environment that bothered even the most accomplished hitters. Mays found a unique way to gain a home-field advantage. When future Giants manager Bob Melvin met Mays in 1986, he asked how he hit so many home runs when the wind was blowing in from left field. "When the wind blew in from left, I hit it out to right," Mays explained. That was that.

Mays altered his swing to take advantage of the ballpark and hit 203 home runs at Candlestick. He led the majors in home runs on three separate occasions and reached 50 twice. On April 30, 1961, he set a franchise record by hitting four home runs at Milwaukee County Stadium. For decades he was third all-time with 660 home runs, although his godson, Barry Bonds, passed him en route to the all-time record, and Albert Pujols and Alex Rodriguez have since bumped him down to sixth.

Even the best pitchers of the era couldn't slow Mays, who batted .286 with 56 home runs against the 14 men he faced who would end up in the Hall of Fame. He went up against Don Drysdale and Warren Spahn more than anyone else, hitting .330 with 13 homers against the former and .305 with 18 homers against the latter. Mays even dominated the All-Star Game. His 23 career hits are a record, and he scored 20 runs in 24 appearances. "They invented the All-Star Game for Willie Mays," Ted Williams once said.

Mays's ability at the plate was matched by his speed, which led to 339 stolen bases, including 20 in 23 attempts as a 40-year-old in his final full season with the Giants. The otherworldly blend allowed Mays to become the only player in MLB history to have both a 50-homer season and a 20-triple season, and in 1956 he became just the second player at the time to hit at least 30 homers and steal at least 30 bases in a season, something he did again the next year.

It was in center field, however, where Mays showed off his greatest gifts. When he joined the Birmingham Black Barons at the age of 17, he told his corner outfielders to cover anything from where they stood all the way to the lines. Everything in the center of the field belonged to him. Mays had not even graduated high school yet, but he already knew nobody could get to a ball faster than he could. He holds the all-time record for putouts by an outfielder and won 12 consecutive Gold Glove Awards. He would have more, but the award wasn't introduced until his sixth season.

In totality, it was the greatest collection of skills the game had ever seen, but Mays was about much more than what you could measure. He had a sixth tool, an intellect between the lines that was unmatched. He was a savant on the diamond, so far ahead of others that even in his late eighties, when he would visit the clubhouse, he was dispensing pearls that longtime players and coaches had never heard of or even considered.

Mays could score from second on any single, but sometimes he would subtly slow down to draw a throw to the plate, allowing his teammate to reach second as he slid in safely in a pile of dust. Opposing catchers swore he swung wildly at breaking balls early in games just to guarantee the pitcher would try that pitch again later but in a bigger situation. Mays would even manage games from center field, calling pitches by touching his head for a fastball, his chest for a breaking ball, or his knees for a change-up. When Alvin Dark became manager, he named Mays the captain, an announcement teammates found unnecessary. "I said to myself, 'The captain of the team? He has been the captain," Felipe Alou said at a celebration of Mays in 2024. "Willie Mays should be named general."

His intellect was a powerful match for his physical gifts, but Mays also might have possessed a seventh tool, one that could not be seen on paper. Nobody ever had a better time playing the game of baseball, and that joy carried Mays through more than 3,000 games in the big leagues.

It showed not just in the transcendent smile and the stickball games with local kids in New York but also the desire to simply be at the ballpark as long as possible. When the Giants moved to San Francisco, Mays would stay at Seals Stadium for hours after the final pitch, playing games with the batboys and swinging left-handed to try and make things fair. The love of the game also meant great disgust for missing a game, and on multiple occasions in his career, Mays played so hard and for so many consecutive days that he was hospitalized with exhaustion. When he returned from his service in the military, he played at least 150 games in 13 consecutive seasons, a feat unmatched by even Cal Ripken Jr. and Lou Gehrig, the game's iron men. The streak took him through his 35th birthday.

As a 40-year-old, Mays got more than 500 plate appearances and led the league in on-base percentage, but that was his final year in orange and black. Mets owner Joan Payson had always wanted to bring him back to New York, and in 1972 he was traded to his first big-league city, where he would hit his 660th and final homer on August 17, 1973. A few weeks later, the

Mets hosted Willie Mays Night at Shea Stadium. "The game of baseball has been great to me. I have just about everything I need," Mays said during his speech. "The only thing that I'm looking for out of baseball now is that I can teach other kids to be as good an athlete as I was in my day."

It was an impossible bar to reach, but Mays promised that day that he would help anyone he could, and until his passing in 2024, he made good on that vow. For decades, Mays was a fixture not just in clubhouse manager Mike Murphy's office at the ballpark but also in the spring training clubhouse at Scottsdale Stadium. He would sit at a big round table, and Murphy would bring him a plate of food that sometimes went cold because Mays was too busy telling stories, giving advice, or showing superstars how he held a bat or rested the glove in his left hand.

Mays played golf with one president and rode on Air Force One with another, but in retirement, that table was where he was most at ease. Without realizing it, he allowed generations of fellow Giants to make memories that would last a lifetime. Nobody has ever forgotten a meeting with Willie Mays. Whether you were the team's best player or a behind-the-scenes employee, you came away with a story to tell.

WILLIE REMEMBERED

Brandon Crawford

Two of the longest-tenured players in franchise history met long before Crawford became the Giants shortstop. His family saw Mays eating at Don & Charlie's during a trip to Scottsdale, and young Brandon got an autograph in the homemade assignment book his mom would make him fill out every spring. Years later, Crawford was blown away when Mays mentioned something specific about his game. It was then that it became apparent to the childhood Giants fan that the greatest Giant was paying attention to what he was doing every night.

"He signed five or six different things out of my locker. He told me to keep bringing more stuff. He signed a ball, bat, one of my brand-new gloves. During a question-and-answer session, someone asked him what [he did] when [he got] in a slump. It was classic Willie. He said, 'I don't remember ever being in a slump.'"

Juan Marichal

The Dominican Dandy first saw Mays in 1957, when the center fielder brought the Willie Mays All-Stars to his country while barnstorming through Mexico, Puerto Rico, and the Dominican Republic. Three years later, Marichal shook Mays's hand when he walked into spring training in Phoenix for the first time. They were teammates for a dozen years, and from the start, Mays took Marichal under his wing.

"Willie used to take not only me but a big group of players to the clothing store, the shoe store, a place to get golf clubs—everything. Willie used to get everything free, and he would take all of us with him. Willie was a very good teammate."

Dave Flemming

It took Flemming nearly three minutes to finally get the words out. About an hour before the Giants announced Mays had passed away on June 18, 2024, Larry Baer walked into the broadcast booth at Wrigley

Field to inform Flemming, who thought he would have plenty of time to process his own emotions before he was cleared to give the news to the public. In the bottom of the fourth, it was finally time, but Flemming just couldn't do it. Finally, after the third out, he announced that the greatest Giant had passed away.

The moment was more personal than Flemming ever would have imagined. He could never quite grasp that he was in a position to actually call Mays his friend. To him, Mays was an icon and hero, but for Mays, Flemming was pretty important too. As Mays's health deteriorated, KNBR's broadcasts became his greatest connection to the action on the field. It was common for the broadcasters to hear from Mays's assistant, Rene Anderson.

"He just loved the Giants. He loved baseball unlike probably anybody who ever lived. He would talk all the time about, 'What'd you mean by that?' He would ask about a certain play. He was watching and listening all the time. Especially as his eyesight got worse and worse, he relied on the radio broadcast a lot. How cool is that? If it was his birthday or the anniversary of an event and we said, 'Hey, today is the anniversary of his four-home-run day in 1961 in Milwaukee,' we would get a text from Rene—like, 'Oh, Willie is watching; he just smiled. He says to say hi.' We knew he was always watching. Talk about a thrill of this job—to know that Willie Mays is watching and listening, it's awesome."

LaTroy Hawkins

Of the right-hander's 1,042 appearances over 21 years, only 45 came in orange and black, but he spent enough time in San Francisco to build some incredible memories with Mays. Hawkins was traded from the Cubs in 2005 and quickly found he could talk to Mays about anything and everything. He particularly loved when Mays told stories about "the old days," which reminded him of the times he spent listening to his grandfather tell similar tales.

"Willie was my grandfather's favorite player," Hawkins said. "One day I told him that, and he was like, 'Call your grandfather.' I did, and they had a chance to talk, and it was cool to be able to be that [conduit] between my grandfather and his favorite player. My grandfather was about six years older than Willie, but he saw him play during his time traveling around the country, and he was super excited about talking. The only other time I've seen him that excited was when I called him with B. B. King on the phone. That's the only other time."

Joe Panik

Three months after the Giants won the 2014 title, Mays and the trophy flew to New York City to accompany Panik—who had grown up in nearby Hopewell Junction—on a visit to Harlem. They spoke to students at the Arthur Tappan School, located on the site of the old Polo Grounds. Years after playing there, Mays quietly donated to the school's music and arts programs. Before an assembly in the auditorium, Panik, a rookie second baseman, sat with Mays and listened to stories about his days in New York. What struck him most was Mays's love for the Giants, but when they took the stage, Panik saw that helping children held just as big a place in his heart.

"I didn't get many questions, as you can imagine," Panik said. "He was so gracious and was talking to everyone, and doing it person-to-person. The way he was talking to the kids and opening up was special. He didn't have to do any of that. He could do whatever he wanted with his life, but here he was traveling to New York and speaking to elementary school kids, signing autographs for these kids, giving his time. It sticks with you. I was like, *This is how it should be done.* You just watched him and saw the grace that he carried himself with."

Logan Webb

Mays was the first "face of the franchise" in San Francisco, a title Webb inherited early in his career. Webb's jaw dropped at his first big-league camp when young Giants were put in a big room with Mays, Marichal, Willie McCovey, Gaylord Perry, Orlando Cepeda, and Dave Dravecky.

"It was surreal," Webb said. "It was awesome just to be in the presence of those guys, especially Willie. He kind of lit up the room and talked for probably 30 to 45 minutes, and every year he would come and do that, and every year it got better and better. He just kept going with awesome stories, and I do remember him talking about something that I've talked about a lot, which is having more fun while you're out there. He was big on that. He played like he was having fun every single time he went out there."

Bruce Bochy

When at the ballpark, Mays was almost always in Murphy's office, which was right across the hall from the manager's. He already had an existing relationship with Dusty Baker when he got hired. During his playing days, Baker got introduced to Mays by Bobby Bonds and casually mentioned that he liked Mays's kangaroo glove. He was stunned when Mays handed it to him. When Bochy took over a few years after Baker departed, Mays greeted him right away.

"My first day of spring training, he walks in with a dozen baseballs signed, and he goes, 'You're probably going to need these,'" Bochy said. "That was such a great gesture, because the last thing you want to do is go ask him for baseballs. We had our Hall of Fame spring training talks with him and McCovey and Gaylord and Orlando—and Willie, he dominated the conversation. He was great too. He would get on these guys about not playing enough in spring training. With his little office—so to speak—across from my office, we had a lot of daily chats, and I loved talking baseball with him."

LaMonte Wade Jr.

Mays visited the ballpark for the final time on his 92nd birthday, greeting family members, friends, and Giants as he sat in a room across from the clubhouse. Wade was among those who stopped by, getting a photo with Mays and Bonds. When Wade walked into the room, Mays asked about an at-bat he had the night before and told him to wait for his pitch in big spots.

"Everyone said to shake his hand, and he had a real strong grip," Wade said. "I did it, and he said mine wasn't strong enough. His hand strength was incredible. He started talking about how he would listen to games and brought up situations. Someone came in after me, and he asked if he was playing, and the guy said no, there was a lefty on the mound.

Willie said, 'It doesn't matter if it's a lefty or righty. You should be in there every day.'"

Michael Morse

At 6'5" and 245 pounds, Morse was one of the most imposing players ever to set foot in the Scottsdale Stadium clubhouse. But Mays wasn't awed. He stood up the first time Morse approached his table and grabbed his hand. Morse squeezed back, and he could tell Mays was impressed by his grip strength. Mays then grabbed Morse's forearm. "You need to work on those forearms, son," he said, flexing his own massive right arm. "Feel mine." Morse did as he was told and immediately started laughing. "They were harder than concrete," he said later.

Morse decided at that moment that he was going to become friends with the greatest living ballplayer, and the two would talk often during his time in San Francisco. One night, Morse asked Mays how he could beat pitchers who were jamming him with sinkers on his hands. Mays took out a piece of paper, drew home plate, and started scribbling on it. He explained how he would change his feet depending on where the pitch was, and he gave Morse an impromptu lesson, one that Morse had a hard time focusing on. The whole time, he was transfixed by the piece of paper. "I've got to get that," he told himself. "Willie Mays is writing on this piece of paper and explaining how to hit. I've got to get this." When Mays was done speaking, he crumpled the paper, wiped his forehead, and threw it in the garbage.

Morse was disappointed, but he soon learned Mays had a much grander gift in mind. "One day I had a bad game, and I was sitting in my locker, and one of the clubbies came and said, 'Hey, Willie is in Murph's office and wants to talk to you.' I said, 'Just tell him not today.' But as he was walking away, I thought I should at least go and say hi. I went over, and Willie goes, 'I heard you have a daughter on the way. Is that true?' I told him it was, and he goes, 'I've got something for you. This is going to put her through college.' He gave me his jersey, and it was signed. There was an authenticator in the room, and he asked if I wanted him to authenticate it. Willie Mays gave me his wool jersey and signed it, and I have it framed in my house."

Ryan Vogelsong

Like most Giants who got to sit with Mays, Vogelsong wasn't sure how closely he was watching every game. But one day, he realized Mays did, in fact, know him pretty well. When Vogelsong sat down at Mays's table, Mays chuckled and said, "Boy, you really like to pitch inside, don't you?" Years earlier, in his second big-league camp, Vogelsong had gotten the thrill of a lifetime.

"Part of the reason I wore No. 32 was because my dad grew up a huge Sandy Koufax fan," he said. "I came off the field one game and walked into the old clubhouse, and sitting at the table were Willie, Orlando Cepeda, and Sandy Koufax. I was like, *This is unbelievable*. They started talking to me like I had played against them for 20 years, and Willie looked at Koufax and goes, 'Hey, show Vogey how you used to throw your curveball.' It was a day I'll never forget. I got Sandy to sign a ball, and I took it to my dad."

Erwin Higueros

Erwin Higueros joined the Giants in 1998 and became their full-time Spanish-language broadcaster in 2007. He wears as many hats as anyone in the organization, working as a member of the media-relations department and serving as the clubhouse's interpreter. But back when he was still finding his way, it took some time to get to the point where he felt comfortable introducing himself to Mays.

Higueros had an easy connection, because he did radio broadcasts with former Giants infielder Tito Fuentes, who played with Mays in the 1960s and '70s. He would watch from the door of the clubhouse at Scottsdale Stadium as Mays traded stories with current and former players. One day, he decided it was time to shake the legend's hand, and he learned right away that he should have done it much sooner. Mays was as famous as it got, but most of the time, he simply wanted to talk with other people in baseball.

"I built up the courage to go up and introduce myself to him," Higueros said, "and I said, 'Hey, Willie, nice to meet you. My name is Erwin.' He said, 'Who?' I said it again: 'Erwin.' And he went, 'Who in their fucking right mind would name their kid Erwin?' I laughed and told him my mom did it, and he asked me what I did with the Giants, so I told him that I worked with Tito on the radio. He went, 'Does he let you talk? Man, he wouldn't shut up when he was a player with me. I had to tell him to tone it down.' After that, every year I would go over there and say hi to him, and he loved to talk baseball; he had the best stories. I would always say, 'It's good to see you again; it's Erwin,' and he would say the same thing every time: 'Who would name their kid Erwin?'"

Buster Posey

Aside from his godson, there's nobody in franchise history who could more closely relate to Mays than Posey. Both were Rookies of the Year who won the MVP Award early in their careers. Like Mays, Posey had a long run as the franchise's best and most important player, and his number will soon join 24 on the wall at Oracle Park. He'll one day join Mays in the Hall of Fame too, but in 2019 they teamed up in a different kind of way. For a Toyota commercial, Posey drove a truck through muddy hills to find Mays and ask him for the secret to the game of baseball. The shoot allowed them to spend some quality time together.

"I just remember thinking to myself how cool and lucky I was that the greatest player of all time would take time out of his day to do this, and it would be somewhat memorialized in a commercial," Posey said. "He had a replica ring from the 1954 team, and at the end of it, he gave it to me and said, 'Here, give this to your kids.' It's a replica ring, but still, it's a ring Willie Mays wore, and it'll be special for our family for a long time."

5

Willie McCovey

At the start of the last home series of every season, the Giants give out their most prestigious award: the Willie Mac Award. It is voted on by players, coaches, support staff, and fans, and honors the most inspirational player on the team.

The award is a snapshot of that season in Giants history, each name accompanied by a story. Dave Dravecky won in 1989 after recovering from cancer. Andres Torres was the choice in 2010, when he was an unlikely 32-year-old spark plug for a team that would win a title a month after the ceremony. Mike Yastrzemski's perseverance was rewarded in 2020. The list includes stars such as Buster Posey, Madison Bumgarner, Brandon Crawford, and Jeff Kent but also players who moved on within a season or two. The only two-time winners are Mike Krukow, J. T. Snow, and Bengie Molina.

This award is named after Willie McCovey, and it's a big part of the legacy of a gentle giant who played alongside the best player in franchise history—one who shared the same name—and still managed to carve out his own Hall of Fame career. McCovey's power was matched by his dignity and warmth, and while Willie Mays was the better player, many will tell you McCovey is the most popular man ever to represent the San Francisco Giants.

He certainly made an impact on Bob Lurie, whose purchase of the team in 1976 prevented its move to Canada. As he put together the financing to buy the Giants, Lurie talked often about how much it bothered him that McCovey was across the bay with the Oakland A's. Lurie vowed to bring McCovey home, which he did in 1977, and when Stretch called it a career in 1980, the Giants created the Willie Mac Award. "Bob wanted to do something to cement Willie's legacy in San Francisco," explained Corey Busch, Lurie's longtime vice president. "An annual award lives forever, as will Willie McCovey in Giants lore."

Mays was the greatest Giant, but McCovey was their most feared hitter. Of the five Giants in the Hall of Fame, he's the one who might be most fascinating in today's game. His prodigious home runs were measured by stories, not Statcast, and he was leading the league in exit velocity decades before anybody knew that was a thing. Legendary Yankees manager Casey Stengel put it best. "We have to decide where to play Mr. McCovey—in the upper deck or the lower deck," he once told Roger Craig.

There's no way to know exactly how far or how hard McCovey was truly hitting the baseball, but there is one measure of the fear he instilled in pitchers: He was intentionally walked 45 times in 1969, shattering the previous record of 33 held by Ted Williams. The mark stood until 2002, when Barry Bonds was challenging home run records, and opposing pitchers responded with so many free passes that the Giants started selling rubber chickens. To this day, McCovey has the fourth-highest single-season total, trailing three Bonds seasons. The two Giants sluggers are the only players in history with multiple seasons of 40 or more intentional walks.

Not even Candlestick Park could slow McCovey. He slugged .538 at home and holds the notorious ballpark's records with 236 homers and 690 RBIs. A lot of that production came in 1969, which was McCovey at his absolute best. When pitchers did let him swing the bat that season, he hit 45 homers and drove in 126 runs. His 1.108 OPS stood as the franchise record until Bonds arrived in 1993. A few years later, Marichal tried to explain to Bonds that while he idolized Mays, he was perhaps more similar to McCovey. "If he played today, they would do the same thing they did to Barry Bonds," Marichal said. "They would walk him with nobody on, walk him with the bases loaded, all of that."

Jon Miller grew up watching McCovey at Candlestick, and when he became a broadcaster and started traveling the country, he heard a story he was eager to dig into. "They say that in every park the Giants went to, there was a place that local people would point out and say, 'See that spot? That's the longest home run ever hit here, and that was Willie McCovey,'" Miller said.

When the Giants visited Busch Stadium in St. Louis one summer, Miller told that story to Cardinals broadcaster Mike Shannon. The former big leaguer immediately pointed to a spot way out in the right-field seats. "Oh yeah, right there," Shannon told Miller. "I've never seen anybody come close to that."

Born and raised in Mobile, Alabama, McCovey got his start with the Giants at what was perhaps the greatest tryout in MLB history. Legendary scout Alex Pompez invited him to a camp in Melbourne, Florida, where the skinny 17-year-old joined Orlando Cepeda and Jose Pagan, among others. The Giants would end up with both first basemen, and at times that created problems.

McCovey reached the big leagues a year after Cepeda, and the Giants weren't quite sure what to do with two players best suited for first. Nicknamed Stretch because of his defense, McCovey seemed the likely choice, but he was moved to the outfield, and at times early in his career, he was platooned. When the Giants won the pennant in 1962, manager Alvin Dark started McCovey just once against a left-handed pitcher. He still managed to hit 20 homers in just 229 at-bats. That type of production had become the norm for him. He was Rookie of the Year in 1959 despite playing just 52 games, and he did so much damage before his promotion that he led the Pacific Coast League in homers despite playing just half a season.

While McCovey didn't have a great reputation in left field, Mays always insisted he was better than people thought. Mays loved to tell the story of Marichal's no-hitter. After a one-out walk in the seventh, Marichal gave up a deep drive to left-center, the only scare of the game. McCovey reached up at the wall and saved the bid with a running catch. "He made a great catch," Marichal recalled. "The only way he could catch that ball was because of his height. He didn't know much about how to play the position, so he played real close to the fence, and he just reached his arm up and caught the ball."

The Giants eventually moved McCovey back to first, where he made four straight All-Star teams after Cepeda was traded. He retired with 521 home runs and a .515 slugging percentage, making it somewhat ironic that the most memorable moment of his playing career is a ball that wasn't hit far enough.

McCovey made the final out of the 1962 World Series, hitting a line drive right at second baseman Bobby Richardson with the winning run on second. For a while, he said there was not much else he could have done, although later in life he admitted the moment had stuck with him. Asked once how he would like to be remembered, McCovey said, "As the guy who hit the line drive one foot over Bobby Richardson's head."

There was no World Series title in San Francisco in 1962, and when McCovey returned in the late 1970s, it was to an organization that hardly resembled the one he had come up with. But he enjoyed those final years, and in 1986 he went into the Hall of Fame as a Giant, joining his friend and former partner in the outfield, Mays.

Mays always said McCovey hit the ball farther than anybody he ever played with, and at times that impacted the way he played the game. When opposing managers started intentionally walking McCovey, Mays would occasionally stop at first on a sure double to guarantee McCovey would get pitches to hit. He would sometimes stay put on a wild pitch to guarantee the same result, but McCovey felt he returned the favor. "I was there to protect Mays," he would say of his job.

The Willies formed as imposing a duo as the game has ever seen, and as Hall of Famers, they were reunited in a wonderful way. Lurie wasn't the only Giants owner who had an affinity for the first baseman with a personality that did not at all match the ferocity of his swing.

When the Giants built Oracle Park, Mays's statue went out front. The back of the ballpark is surrounded by water, and *San Jose Mercury News* columnist Mark Purdy came up with the idea of naming the area after another Giants legend: McCovey Cove had a flow to it, but it also just made perfect sense.

McCovey was given a suite on the broadcast level, and he attended by far the most games of any of the franchise's five Hall of Famers. Just about every night, he would take the elevator up to the third floor and watch left-handed hitters take aim at a body of water he knew he would have hit with ease.

6
Juan Marichal

In the 14th inning, Alvin Dark had finally seen enough. He could sense he was watching something special unfold, but Juan Marichal wasn't going to be part of it anymore. Dark waited for the right-hander as he came off the field and told him his night was over. Marichal pointed out to the mound, where Milwaukee Braves lefty Warren Spahn was preparing to throw warm-up pitches.

"Mr. Dark, do you see that man on the mound? he asked.

"Yes," Dark replied. "What about him?"

"Well, that man is 42 years old. I'm only 25," Marichal said. "If that man is still on the mound, nobody is going to take me out of the game."

It was hard to argue with that logic.

Marichal ended up going 16 innings on that night in 1963, and Spahn did the same in what is considered the greatest pitchers' duel in baseball history. Spahn finally gave up a run in the bottom of the 16th, making a winner of Marichal, who put up a pitching line that looks like a mistake: 16 innings, 0 runs, 8 hits, 4 walks, 10 strikeouts. Only when the marathon was finally over did Marichal realize quite how deep he had to dig. He was shocked to find out he had thrown 227 pitches. "I didn't know I threw that many, but I felt good," he recalled 60 years later. "I felt like I could go all night."

Marichal paused and grinned as he remembered details from the historic night. "Hank Aaron went 0-for-6," he said. "I must have been throwing good, right?"

The game's most powerful hitter could do nothing to slow Marichal. On the other side, a lineup that included Willie Mays, Willie McCovey, and Orlando Cepeda needed 16 innings to finally get to Spahn, who took perhaps the toughest loss in MLB history. The future Hall of Famer went 15⅓ innings and scattered nine hits and a walk. The one run he gave up was all it took, and for hours two teams struggled to get there.

Dark approached his starter for the first time after the ninth, but catcher Ed Bailey encouraged Marichal to keep going, and the righty gave Dark a pitch that was as good as any he threw at the Braves. He told him the weather was good and he felt strong, and he asked for just a couple more innings. They met up again in the 14th, and this time Marichal pointed at Spahn and made his case. The manager was upset, but he relented, turning around and marching back into the dugout without saying a word.

After getting two pop-ups and a fly ball to right in a quick 15th inning, Marichal finally stopped petitioning his manager. He told Dark he could get a reliever up and tucked his glove and cap into a small locker in the dugout. But as Dark called down to the bullpen, Spahn cruised through the bottom of the inning. "I grabbed my hat and put it on, and grabbed my glove and put it on, and I ran to the mound," Marichal said. "I had already told him I was done, so thank God I had another quick inning."

When the top of the 16th was over, Marichal waited for Mays to jog in from center field. Mays was essentially an on-field manager, and he had always looked out for Marichal, who told him he probably had to stop pitching since Dark's anger was building. Mays patted Marichal on the back. "Don't worry," he said. "I'm going to win this game for you."

Spahn retired two years later as the winningest left-hander in baseball history. He had been a professional for 21 years by the time he went toe-to-toe with Marichal, and he was so good for so long he was already one of the game's best when he squared off against a young Mays in 1951. Mays went hitless in his first 12 big-league at-bats before homering off Spahn. A dozen years later, he hit the first pitch out to left with one out in the bottom of the 16th. At 12:31 in the morning, the Giants had a 1–0 win.

"With all of the arguments that I got in with Alvin, if we [had] lost that game, I could have been in trouble," Marichal recalled, laughing. "When Willie homered, I felt like I was in heaven."

The marathon at Candlestick was, incredibly, not the first time Marichal and Spahn had gone into extra innings. In his third big-league start, Marichal allowed just 2 runs over 10 innings to edge Spahn, who had a similar line going until Joey Amalfitano doubled in the bottom of the 10th and scored on Felipe Alou's single. It was the third straight win for the 22-year-old, who already was showing signs that he one day would give a speech in Cooperstown.

The Giants had signed Marichal without ever getting much of a look at him. The word of trusted scout Horacio Martinez was enough, and the 18-year-old without much experience on a mound received $500 to start his professional career. It was a dream come true for Marichal, who had known from an early age that he would be a baseball player, although not necessarily on the mound.

He had a habit of skipping school to play with other six-year-olds on the fields in Laguna Verde, Dominican Republic, and he often would come home and find that his teacher had visited his mother, who would lecture him about being prepared for his future. Young Juan Marichal had the same answer every time: "Mother, I'm going to be a baseball player." He didn't quite know what it would take to get there. At the time there had never been a Dominican in Major League Baseball, but that was the dream, and it was nudged along by his brother-in-law, who took him to watch the country's best amateur teams.

When Marichal was eight, he found himself transfixed by a sidearming right-hander named Bombo Ramos, who played for the country's best amateur team. He decided he was going to be a pitcher and imitate Ramos. He kept working on the delivery during 14 months in the Dominican Air Force, but when the Giants signed him and sent him to a minor league camp in Florida, they started thinking about making a change.

In 1959 Marichal's manager, Andy Gilbert, asked why he threw with a sidearm delivery. Marichal didn't want to explain that Ramos had been his inspiration, so he simply answered that it was the way he had learned. Gilbert kept pressing and asked if his arm had ever been injured, so Marichal finally told him about his childhood idol. Gilbert asked if he wanted to learn how to throw overhand and explained that it would be more effective against left-handed hitters, and soon the two were walking down to the bullpen with a catcher and two baseballs. Marichal was eager to keep getting better, but he had never tried throwing over the top. Right away, he realized there was only one way for it to feel comfortable. "It seemed to be impossible to do it without kicking my legs," he said. "That's how the high leg kick started."

One of the most iconic deliveries in history was born out of convenience. Marichal found it comfortable to lean all the way back, kicking his left foot over his head, and the Giants soon discovered that hitters found it to be a nightmare. Opposing managers occasionally complained that it was illegal, and some players wondered publicly if Marichal would just get bunted to death, but they learned it was hard to even try. It was impossible to pick up the ball, and even though it looked like Marichal might tip over with the slightest gust of wind, his trademark command didn't suffer. He could dot the corners with a fastball that seemed to rise as it reached the zone, a curveball, a slider, a change-up, and even a screwball. Marichal hadn't been pitching for long, but he proved to be remarkably adept at changing speeds and arm angles, turning a five-pitch arsenal into so much more. "Most rookie pitchers have to learn control the hard way," Giants farm director Carl Hubbell told the *Sporting News*. "But Juan had it, impeccably, from the start."

In his first minor league season, Marichal struck out 246 batters in 245 innings and walked only 50. Two years later he was in the big leagues, and on the first day of his career, he very nearly became the first Giant since Hubbell in 1929 to throw a no-hitter. Marichal retired the first 19 hitters he faced before an error ruined his perfect game. He took a no-hitter into the eighth and recorded the first two outs, but Clay Dalrymple bounced a single up the middle. Marichal had been told during a mound meeting not to throw a fastball to the pinch-hitter, who was known as a good fastball hitter. He threw a first-pitch curveball and watched as Dalrymple ended the bid for what would have been the first no-hitter of his life.

The first three appearances of Marichal's career were complete games, setting the tone for a 16-year run defined by durability as much as by dominance. Nobody else in the Giants' San Francisco years is within even 1,000 innings of Marichal's 3,443⅔. His 446 starts and 52 shutouts are second only to Christy Mathewson in franchise history, and he holds San Francisco–era records for career wins and strikeouts. He's the only pitcher to have a 25-win season since the team moved west, and he did it three times. He twice led the majors in innings pitched, setting a career high with 325⅔ in 1968, when he posted a 2.48 ERA and made the 7th of his 10 All-Star appearances. When Marichal retired in 1975, he had 244 complete games and 243 wins. He had gone the distance in more than half of his appearances.

The Giants knew exactly what they were getting every time their star right-hander took the mound, but on occasion he turned it up a notch. Two years after the close call in his debut, he completed a no-hitter against the Houston Colt .45s on just 89 pitches. It was one of 191 wins for Marichal in the 1960s, the most in baseball, but midway through the decade, he dealt with a low point that threatened to permanently stain his legacy.

A matchup between Marichal and Sandy Koufax drew a sold-out crowd to Candlestick Park on August 22, 1965, and early on the rivals exchanged brushbacks and glares. When Marichal walked up to the plate in the bottom of the third, he figured another inside pitch might be coming. He took a strike from Koufax and then a ball, low and away. Dodgers catcher John Roseboro already had a bad reputation with the Giants after a collision with Orlando Cepeda a few years earlier had left the Giants star with a right knee injury. Roseboro dropped the second pitch to Marichal and then whipped it back to Koufax. Marichal felt it nick his ear and turned to confront Roseboro, who took his mask off. Marichal later claimed he thought Roseboro was about to hit him, so he swung his bat, hitting Roseboro in the head and setting off a 14-minute fight that was one of the ugliest incidents in MLB history.

Roseboro was left with a two-inch gash on his head and Marichal was suspended for eight games and fined $1,750, a punishment that infuriated the Dodgers. Outfielder Ron Fairly told reporters the suspension should have been for 1,750 days and eight dollars, and the Dodgers hired extra police officers to prepare for riots when the Giants visited a few weeks later. The rivals were in a tight pennant race at the time, and National League president Warren Giles admitted that impacted the punishment, saying he didn't want to severely penalize the other 24 players on the roster. The Giants ended up losing the division by two games.

Roseboro sued Marichal for $110,000, although they ended up settling for a much smaller sum. Years later, after Marichal spent a season with the Dodgers, the two became friends. Marichal was an honorary pallbearer at Roseboro's funeral, and when Marichal missed out in his first two tries at making the Hall of Fame, Roseboro pledged his support.

In 1983 Marichal became the first player from the Dominican Republic to be voted into the Hall. He was enshrined exactly 10 years after Spahn, his partner in painting a masterpiece that would become known as the greatest game ever pitched.

Marichal first met Mays in spring training a couple years after he signed, but he first laid eyes on him in 1957, when Mays was part of a team that played exhibition games in the Dominican

Republic. The teenager watched in amazement as Mays hit a home run, and immediately he had a new player to idolize.

Six years later, on July 2, 1963, Mays made sure the young right-hander wouldn't have to keep testing the limits of what was physically possible, although a couple hours earlier, Mays had helped ensure the two pitchers would make history. A walk and a single in the fourth gave the Braves their best threat, and when Del Crandall hit a single to center, it appeared Marichal had fallen behind. But Mays, as he always did, charged the ball like a shortstop, picking it up on one hop and making a strong throw to the plate to nail the runner and end the inning.

Spahn himself nearly broke up the dueling shutouts in the seventh when he doubled off the wall in right. Two innings later, Willie McCovey hit a soaring fly ball down the right-field line that the Giants thought was a game-winning homer. First-base umpire Chris Pelekoudas disagreed, signaling that it had curled foul, prompting Dark to run out to protest. The Giants loaded the bases in the 14th, but Bailey, who caught all 227 pitches, lined out.

Spahn needed 200 pitches to get through the night, and the final one was a mistake. Mays hit a solo shot to left, setting off a celebration among those who had lasted the entire 4 hours and 10 minutes at Candlestick. In the visiting clubhouse, Spahn told the *San Francisco Chronicle* that the pitch was a screwball. "But it didn't break worth a damn," he added.

Marichal went back to the home clubhouse and wrapped his arm and shoulder in towels. He tried ice just once in his career after reading about Koufax doing it, but he didn't like the way his arm felt afterward. He preferred warm water and towels, and it always worked, although that early in his career, nobody could quite be sure Marichal would be okay. Dark told *Sport* magazine that the night had been a difficult one to manage. “I kept telling myself to take Marichal out of there. It killed me to see him going that long, but whenever I’d look into his face to see if he was tiring, all I could see was a pitcher feeling no pressure and simply enjoying himself,” he said. “You had the conviction he was bound to beat Spahn.”

Marichal’s back was a little sore the next day, but the arm was fine, and it would remain that way. The only concession the Giants made was to give him an extra day of rest before his next start, but he went seven innings that night and then threw 10 complete games over his final 20 appearances. After the battle, Hubbell had told reporters Spahn should donate his body to science. The same could certainly be said of Marichal. He had back surgery later in life but never dealt with arm trouble. His body let him live out those dreams that he had as he ran away from school decades earlier. “Thank god I became a baseball player and played for the Giants with Willie Mays behind me,” he said in 2024, his eyes lighting up. “That was a dream. Who could ask for more than that?”

7

Orlando Cepeda and Gaylord Perry

The final game of Willie Mays's career, No. 3,005 in the big leagues, came in a New York Mets jersey. After 446 starts with the Giants, Juan Marichal's last year was with the rival Los Angeles Dodgers, a stunning visual for anyone who watched his most infamous moment in the big leagues. Will Clark's final season was spent in St. Louis. Tim Lincecum went out with nine starts for the Los Angeles Angels, and longtime teammate Madison Bumgarner finished as an Arizona Diamondback. Even Brandon Crawford, a childhood Giants fan who lived out his dream for 13 seasons, ended his career elsewhere a year after Brandon Belt had to deal with the same reality; Belt was a Blue Jay and Crawford became a Cardinal.

There are two truths when it comes to the final years of a player's career. These are men who get to play a child's game for a living, and you can't blame them for holding on as long as they can, even if that means continuing to live the dream in strange colors. At the same time, they are reminded constantly that this is a business. There are very few who have full control of their fate once they're on the wrong side of 30. Buster Posey and Matt Cain are the exceptions, not the rule.

Giants fans have repeatedly learned this lesson the hard way, and players have too. The business side caught up to many of the Giants' most popular players over the last three decades. Clark and Matt Williams were traded because of the financial crunch brought on after a new ownership group made Barry Bonds the highest-paid player in history. Bumgarner signed an extension early in his career, then learned that ownership and the front office were in no mood to renegotiate after his World Series heroics. Crawford wanted his five children to experience one more summer at the ballpark, but the Giants were ready to go younger at the position.

The vast majority of the Giants who finished elsewhere did so while hardly resembling the players they were in their best years in San Francisco. But there were two who got away and then went on to reach their greatest heights in the big leagues, and they happen to have statues about 10 yards apart on the corner of 2nd and King.

The Giants traded Gaylord Perry to Cleveland in 1971, never imagining the 33-year-old had more than 3,000 innings left in his arm. In theory, Perry should have been exiting his prime, but there was no such excuse with Orlando Cepeda, who was only 28 when he was sent to the Cardinals.

The Giants happened to be in St. Louis as trade rumors swirled, and Cepeda went 2-for-4 with two RBIs in the third game of the series, continuing to show that his old form was returning after an injury-marred 1965 season. As players walked back to the clubhouse to celebrate the win, Marichal draped his arm around Cepeda's shoulder. "I said, 'No way they're going to trade you,'" Marichal recalled years later. "We were walking and got to the clubhouse, and when we walked in, there was a group of writers, and they announced the trade."

The Baby Bull got his nickname from his father. Pedro "Perucho" Cepeda was a star shortstop, one of the best players in Puerto Rico's history, such a force at the plate and on the bases that he was compared to Babe Ruth and Ty Cobb. He was a tremendous hitter who won batting titles in his home country and the Dominican Republic, and that gene was passed down to his son.

By the time he was 17, Orlando Cepeda already had the powerful build that would lead to 379 homers in the big leagues. He joined a group of fellow teenagers at a tryout camp in Florida and showed enough that the Giants signed him for $500 and sent him to Salem, Virginia, and then Kokomo, Indiana. While there was a culture shock, he was right at home in the batter's box.

Cepeda hit 22 home runs in 1955 and followed that with 26 and 25 the following two seasons, showing even as a teenager that he was the one you wanted at the plate with runners in scoring position. He drove in 100 runs in every one of his minor league seasons, and when he hit .309 and drove in 108 runs in Triple A, the Giants brought him to camp. Cepeda wasn't supposed to make the initial roster in 1958, but there was no way to hold him back. A plaque at Oracle Park recounts a conversation that spring between manager Bill Rigney and first baseman Whitey Lockman.

"He's a few years away," Lockman said during Cepeda's first spring training.

"No! He's ready now!" Rigney countered.

"A few years away," Lockman said. "From the Hall of Fame."

The 21-year-old didn't waste any time winning over the fan base in San Francisco, which initially had been a bit cold to some of the stars who had come over from New York. On April 15, 1958, the Giants hosted the Dodgers in the first game on the West Coast for both franchises. Cepeda started at first base, and in the third at-bat of his big-league career, he hit a homer to right.

Cepeda hit 25 homers, led the National League with 38 doubles, and drove in 96 runs that season. He batted .312 as a rookie, the first of nine seasons above .300 for a man who finished his career at .297. At the end of that first season, Cepeda was a unanimous Rookie of the Year. When Willie McCovey won the award a year later, the Giants had the heart of one of the most feared lineups the game has ever seen. It almost seemed like fate. Cepeda and McCovey had been discovered in the same tryout, but Mays had first noticed Cepeda when he played winter ball in Santurce, San Juan, Puerto Rico, in 1954.

As Cepeda became ill late in life, Mays penned a letter that he planned to read for a memorial service. He recalled his first time seeing Cepeda, then a teenage batboy in Puerto Rico. "There was this big kid hanging around. They called him the Baby Bull, after his father, Pedro Cepeda, the Bull," Mays wrote. "Sometimes the kid caught balls [Roberto] Clemente and I would throw in from the outfield. You could just feel how much he loved the game. Four years later, he'd be my Giants teammate."

That wasn't just limited to Candlestick Park. Cepeda joined Mays on the All-Star team for six consecutive seasons, although not everything about his career was going smoothly. McCovey's arrival left Rigney with two players best suited to play first base, and both at times reluctantly became left fielders. Cepeda also dealt with persistent right knee problems, and in 1965 he was limited to just 34 at-bats because of soreness that ultimately required surgery.

Cepeda returned to left field the next year, and to his old form. He was hitting .286 with three homers and 15 RBIs over his first 19 games, but the Giants needed starting pitching depth and were enamored by Ray Sadecki, which in retrospect looks odd. Sadecki had a 5.21 ERA in 1965, but a year earlier he had won 20 games—back then that was the most important accomplishment for a starting pitcher. So a trade was executed. "We were both crying," Marichal said of the trade. "[Cepeda] took it hard. He didn't want to leave the Giants. He was a true Giant, but baseball is like that."

The trade proved to be one of the most infamous swaps in baseball history. The Cardinals moved Cepeda back to first base full-time and put him in the cleanup spot. He was still in his prime, and with a healthy knee and a return to his desired position, Cepeda hit 25 homers and drove in 111 runs the following season. A year and a half after the trade, he was named the league's Most Valuable Player, becoming the first to win that award and the Rookie of the Year unanimously. The Cardinals won the World Series.

Cepeda went on to star for the Atlanta Braves, and while his body failed him late in his career, he became the first designated hitter for the Boston Red Sox as a 35-year-old and turned back time with 20 homers and 86 RBIs. In 1999 Cepeda became the second player from Puerto Rico to get inducted into the Hall of Fame. The Giants retired his No. 30 and later built him a statue outside the left-field corner of their new ballpark.

Sadecki went 3–7 with a 5.40 ERA after the trade, and while he was much better the next two seasons, he made just 96 starts in San Francisco before getting sent to the New York

Mets in 1969. The Giants missed Cepeda on the field but also in the clubhouse. He was a mentor to the waves of young Latin American players who were starting to fill the roster—a man who enjoyed the simple things in life but did so to the ultimate degree. He fell in love with the city of San Francisco right away, and fans returned the sentiment.

In retirement, the Giants leaned on Cepeda in their charitable efforts, and he spent 33 years visiting schools and senior facilities as a community ambassador. His passion for a good local meal led to the organization building Orlando's Caribbean BBQ beyond the center-field wall at Oracle Park, with the Hall of Famer occasionally getting behind the counter to serve the signature Cha Cha Bowls to fans, who always found one of the franchise's greatest hitters waiting with a smile on his face.

"Orlando was a wonderful human being," Marichal said. "He loved music, he loved to eat good food at fancy restaurants, he loved to laugh. He was so nice to everybody."

Marichal considered Cepeda not just a teammate but a brother. Mays felt the same way, and the two remained close until the end of their lives. In 2024 Cepeda passed away just 10 days after Mays.

The Giants held a celebration of life for Cepeda on Roberto Clemente Day a few months later, a perfect choice not just because of their similar roots but because they had been close friends. When Cepeda attended that first showcase for the Giants, it was a 20-year-old Clemente who chaperoned him to Melbourne, Florida. At the ceremony, Mike Krukow read the letter from Mays. "He made his own way, but he will always be my little brother," Mays wrote. "You always look after your little brother, even after they grow. So long, kid."

In his later years, Perry would often laugh off questions about the spitball. He would point out that you don't win 300 games with just one pitch and state that he had a great forkball, a legal pitch with similar action. During a TV interview in the 1980s, Perry smiled and admitted hitters didn't believe he threw a forkball. "Let them think what they may," he said.

Even in his Hall of Fame speech in 1981, Perry was coy. Despite his résumé, the writers made Perry wait until his third year on the ballot. As he stood behind the podium, he noted that he knew all of the umpires by their first names since they made so many visits to the mound. He also listed off some of his catchers in the big leagues. They, he pointed out with a smile, were the ones who called all of those pitches. The first one Perry listed was Tom Haller, who played seven seasons for the Giants in the 1960s. Perry credited Haller with setting him on the path to all of that success after an uneven start to his career.

Perry was born in Williamston, North Carolina, a small town about 90 miles from the coast. He was the son of farmers and the brother of Jim Perry, a right-hander who was three years older and had nearly as accomplished a career. Over 17 years in the big leagues, the elder Perry won 215 games.

The Perry boys grew up on 25 acres used to grow tobacco, corn, and peanuts, and they started working the land at a young age. But that hard work didn't keep them from picking up baseball, as their father, Evan, intended. Evan Perry had been a good player himself, and he played baseball in a cow pasture with his sons during lunch breaks. "I remember our neighbors saying, 'All those Perry boys want to do is play baseball,'" Gaylord recalled during his induction speech. "And their dad is even worse."

Gaylord was a three-sport star in high school who was promising enough on the hardwood to receive college basketball offers, but baseball had always been his true passion. He won a state title with Jim at Williamston High and signed with the Giants, using his bonus to pay off his parents' debts.

Gaylord Perry reached the big leagues four years later, and he arrived in San Francisco early in a season that ended with a pennant. But 1962 was a rough year for the 23-year-old, who got knocked out in the third inning of his big-league debut and spent much of that summer back in the Pacific Coast League. Perry made seven starts and six relief appearances as a rookie, but he was left off the World Series roster for the only pennant-winning team he played for in more than two decades in the majors. A year later, he went 1–6 with a 4.03 ERA, pitching primarily out of the bullpen for Alvin Dark.

Perry was still a reliever in 1964, but that allowed him to break through in late May with a startling performance in the second game of a doubleheader at Shea Stadium. Jesus Alou and Willie Mays helped the Giants jump out to a 6–1 lead, but the Mets stormed back in the middle innings. After a four-run third inning, the Giants went scoreless for 19 consecutive frames, a seemingly impossible outcome for a lineup that had Mays and Cepeda in the heart of it.

In the middle of that run of futility, Dark turned to Perry, his last available reliever. An exhausted Haller came out to the mound. "Kid," he said, "it's time to put something on the ball."

Perry had learned the spitter from Bob Shaw, who often found himself getting checked by umpires, and for good reason. They had worked on the new pitch all spring, and Perry watched Shaw's starts to learn more about the craft. Soon, the student became the master. Perry threw 10 shutout innings against the Mets that night, and the Giants won with a rally in the top of the 23rd.

Perry ended up pitching 206 innings with a 2.75 ERA that year, and two seasons later he was an All-Star for the first time. The Giants had come out of the 1950s with a lineup led by Hall of Fame hitters, and in the ensuing decade, they would ride Marichal and Perry, two of the greatest workhorses the game has ever seen. Marichal led the league in innings in 1968, and Perry did it the next two seasons, throwing 654 frames over two seasons as he entered his thirties, and doing so with a 2.85 ERA. The Perry brothers made history in 1970, becoming the first brothers to each win at least 20 games in the same season. Jim went 24–12 with the Minnesota Twins and won the Cy Young Award.

Throughout that time, Gaylord Perry found umpires eager to check his face, neck, belt, or cap. They would call for balls and then throw them out in suspicion. The league was cracking down on long-running forms of cheating, but the constant checks became such an issue that Giants general manager Chub Feeney finally called the league to complain.

Perry had another strong year in 1971, but team owner Horace Stoneham was starting to realize his star-studded roster would have to be broken up. The aging right-hander was the first to go, getting shipped to the Indians along with Frank Duffy, with pitcher Sam McDowell coming back to the Giants. The left-handed McDowell was four years younger than Perry and a six-time All-Star, making it a strong deal on paper. But he lasted just two seasons in San Francisco, going 11–10 with a 4.36 ERA. The switch to the American League brought out the best in Perry, who had the lowest ERA of his career (1.92) and led his new league in wins and complete games. He edged Chicago's Wilbur Wood to win his first Cy Young Award.

Gaylord Perry spent 10 years with the Giants, but his time there somehow represented less than half of his big-league life. After the trade, he pitched for an additional 12 seasons, reaching 314 career wins and retiring with a 3.11 ERA. He ranks sixth all-time with 5,350 innings, throwing at least 200 in 17 different seasons. The Giants might have lost that trade, but they weren't the only one to mistakenly think they were getting out of the Perry business at the right time. He was traded four more times over the next decade and pitched for eight different franchises.

Speculation about the spitter followed Perry at every spot, and he leaned into it. He would touch his eyebrows, belt, cap, or hairline before throwing pitches, doing it all so quickly that even trained observers couldn't keep up. Confusion could be just as effective as the actual spitter, although Perry didn't really try very hard to hide what he was doing. In 1974 he wrote a book titled *Me and the Spitter: An Autobiographical Confession*. In it, he claimed to be a reformed citizen, although that was about as hard to believe as his earlier claims.

Years later, he ran into Marichal, his old teammate. "I said, 'Gay, you made me a liar,'" Marichal recalled, laughing. "Writers asked me about you throwing a spitball, and I said "'No, he doesn't do that.' And then later, you came out with a book!"

Perry's was an unusual and controversial career, but in 1991 he was elected to the Hall of Fame, and when it came time to create a plaque, the trade was long forgotten. Like Cepeda, Perry went into Cooperstown as a Giant.

PART 3

THE ACQUISITIONS

8

Barry Bonds

As the annual Winter Meetings approached in 1992, the Giants found themselves in a remarkable position. They had a new ownership group, one that had saved the team from leaving San Francisco. For the first time in years, they had hope. What they did not have was a general manager. Or a manager. But for Peter Magowan, Larry Baer, and the rest of the newcomers, those two major decisions could take a back seat. They had to.

As free agency has evolved, the best available players are often willing to wait deep into the winter to find the right deal. When the Giants pursued Bryce Harper, they didn't even meet with him until February, but the bidding had a much different tone when they sought an MVP outfielder in 1992. The best players back then would usually find new homes in November, and as the new ownership group prepared to make a splash, they knew they couldn't wait until the agreement to take over for Bob Lurie closed in January 1993. It would be far too late by then to land the one player who could lead them into a future that needed to include enough momentum that they could finally build a downtown ballpark. And really, there was only one player who could do that. "Barry was just so perfect," Baer said. "He was family."

Barry Bonds was also the best baseball player in the world. He was a two-time MVP by that point and coming off a season in which he hit 34 home runs, stole 39 bases, and led the majors in runs, on-base percentage, and slugging. He had also won a third consecutive Gold Glove Award in left field.

It was a true five-tool package, the type you might expect from a man whose father played 14 seasons in the big leagues and whose godfather was the greatest player of all time, Willie Mays. Bonds wasn't just family because he had grown up in the Bay Area and starred at Serra High School in San Mateo. He had learned the game on the field the Giants still called home.

There has never been a more perfect fit for a marquee free agent, and the Giants' urgency to bring Bonds home was amplified by their need to grab a real foothold in the Bay Area sporting scene as they figured out all of the next steps. As the off-season began, the new ownership group got in touch with Dennis Gilbert, Bonds's agent at Beverly Hills Sports Council. Gilbert told them to call back when they owned the team, but they couldn't wait that long and insisted on a call with Bonds as soon as possible.

Once on the line, Magowan and Baer immediately knew they had a shot. Bonds grew emotional as he realized the team of his father and godfather had real interest in bringing him home. He was surprised by the interest, because he had never heard of the Giants as a potential suitor as he finished the final year of his contract with the Pittsburgh Pirates, but he could tell even over the phone that Magowan's passion was legitimate. He told Magowan that all he wanted to do was be a Giant. "I wanted to go home," Bonds said in the documentary *Say Hey, Willie Mays!* "This is what I've always wanted my whole entire life, and that was really, really important to me. The most important thing in the world."

Bonds flew to San Francisco to meet Magowan and Baer at the airport Hilton. They had convinced Gilbert that they were soon going to be in control of the team, but now it was the agent's turn to do the selling. Chicago Cubs second baseman Ryne Sandberg was the game's highest-paid player at $7.1 million, an average annual salary that Bonds's suitors had to top. The Giants and Bonds finally agreed to terms on a record six-year, $43.75 million contract, but there was one more significant hurdle to clear.

Many around the game were livid that Bonds had signed with an ownership group that technically did not own a baseball team, so the Magowan group found a workaround. A canceled press conference on the first day of the Winter Meetings in Louisville led to several days of intense and unique negotiations, and the Giants reached an agreement with the MLB Players Association stipulating that if their deal to buy the Giants fell apart, their ownership group would still make sure Bonds, who was also heavily courted by the New York Yankees at that time, ended up with his full guarantee. If he had to sign elsewhere for less, the Magowan group would make up the difference.

The new owners didn't yet have full control of the Giants when Bonds was introduced to the media and fans, but it was Magowan who stood at the podium and welcomed the newest star, a man who one day would inherit the title of greatest living ballplayer from his own godfather. Magowan admitted it was a big commitment, but he said it was one Giants fans deserved. "It's a lot of money," he said. "But there's only one Barry Bonds."

Bonds played 22 seasons in the big leagues, terrorizing opposing pitchers until he was 43 years old. When the Giants moved to what later would become Oracle Park, he shattered many of the game's most hallowed records and came a few outs from bringing San Francisco a first World Series title. But it was during that first season at Candlestick Park that he won his most games as a big leaguer.

The 1993 Giants went 103–59, and just about to a man, the members of that roster—some of whom went on to win titles elsewhere—say that was the best team they were a part of. The Giants followed the Bonds acquisition by hiring Dusty Baker as manager, and it didn't take long for him to realize he had taken over a juggernaut. "I had speed, I had power, and I had a bullpen. The game was six innings," Baker quipped.

On Opening Day, Baker slid Bonds in behind Will Clark and Matt Williams, who hit 38 homers and drove in 110 runs, repeatedly taking advantage of pitchers who didn't want to face Bonds with runners in scoring position. Second baseman Robby Thompson hit 19 homers, and center fielder Darren Lewis stole 46 bases. Thompson, Williams, and catcher Kirt Manwaring joined Bonds in winning Gold Gloves. For the new left fielder, it was the fourth of eight he would win in the 1990s. Baker still proudly displays a photo on his wall of the four Gold Glove winners. "I had gold everywhere," he said years later, shaking his head in amazement. "We were not going to lose on defense."

The Giants didn't lose a whole lot, period, and as the season went on, their confidence swelled. They were already sky-high leaving camp. Bonds's arrival in Scottsdale had changed the attitude of an entire organization. One day Bonds looked over at Lewis in center field as they shagged fly balls and asked why players weren't talking much. Lewis said he wasn't sure, but soon it wasn't just Bonds's bat that was filling the air with noise. "He brought a whole new energy," Lewis said. "As soon as he walked into the room, it was just a whole new vibe in the locker room."

Bonds led the charge, and he didn't waste any time in doing so. In his first at-bat at Candlestick as a Giant, he crushed a homer into the seats in right. As he rounded the bases, he slapped hands with his father, who was standing in the first-base box. Bonds hit 46 homers that year and drove in 123 runs en route to the third of a record seven MVP awards. He was a true five-tool threat every single night, and teammates found that he was energized by his return to the Bay Area. Many of them believe that the 1993 season was the best of his career, despite the more eye-popping numbers in later years.

"He was just so dynamic in every way," Williams said. "He'd get on base, he'd steal, he'd hit the ball over the fence. He hit for average and power that year, and he would do everything in the outfield. He was just a really dynamic player, and he was somebody we needed in the middle of that lineup."

Looking back years later, there are parts of Bonds's introduction in San Francisco that missed the mark. It was pointed out that day that Bonds would get to play for a team that employed his father as hitting coach, but Bobby Bonds was fired after the 1996 season, which led to his son's agents telling Henry Schulman of the *San Francisco Chronicle* that the star outfielder wanted a trade. Magowan noted in his speech that the Giants were putting Bonds in the heart of the lineup with Clark and Williams, describing the massive potential of three under-30 power hitters who had won Gold Gloves. But Clark was gone after one season together, and Williams was traded in

1996—both moves made because the Giants found it financially unsustainable to keep them along with Bonds.

But for 162 games that first year, just about everything went right. Bonds changed the culture of the organization and reinvigorated a fan base that showed tremendous support for an ownership group that had found a way to keep the team in San Francisco. The Giants saw an increase of 1.1 million fans year over year, and drew about 600,000 more fans than any other team in Candlestick Park's history. It was a godsend for an ownership group that was working feverishly behind closed doors to secure a new ballpark.

A year after they reluctantly started to pack their bags for Tampa Bay, the Giants had one of the game's deepest rosters and its most electric player. There was one thing Bonds could not control, however. It would be two more years before MLB realigned its divisions and moved to a Wild Card format, and as the 1993 Giants crossed the 100-win mark, they still found themselves on the outside of the playoff race.

At his introductory press conference, Bonds had been asked about what looked to be a difficult NL West race. He stated that dominant pitching wouldn't matter to hitters of the caliber of Bonds, Clark, Williams, or Thompson. "You've still got to bring it across the plate," he said, smiling. The question was asked because the Atlanta Braves had made their own splash, adding Greg Maddux to what would become one of the greatest rotations of all time. While Bonds was the MVP, Maddux won the Cy Young Award in his first season in his new home, and the Braves and Giants entered the final weekend tied at 101 wins.

While the Giants hosted the rival Los Angeles Dodgers, the Braves faced an expansion Colorado Rockies club they had beaten in all 10 previous meetings. The Giants went into the final series assuming the Braves would sweep the Rockies one more time, and that proved correct. If there was one flaw to that Giants roster, it was a slight lack of starting pitching depth, and on the final day of the regular season, they turned to rookie Salomon Torres. He wouldn't make it out of the fourth inning.

In Bonds's first season in San Francisco, the Giants posted their highest win total since 1962, a season led by his godfather. But they came up one win short, and for the first time since 1989, Bonds would watch the postseason from home. He had given the Giants and their fans every reason, however, to feel that much brighter days were ahead.

The home runs are his legacy, but the true measure of Bonds's greatness in his Giants years is the fear that filled the opposing dugout.

Bonds actually only ended up leading baseball in home runs twice, but he shattered walk records. He led the majors in walks 12 different times and also in intentional walks 12 times. He's the only player in history ever to walk more than 170 times in a season, peaking at 232 in 2004, when he got a free pass in 38 percent of his plate appearances. Nobody had come anywhere close to Willie McCovey's record 45 intentional walks for three decades, but Bonds broke the mark with 68 in 2002, and then two years later, he obliterated it with 120. During that season, the 39-year-old became the only player in history to reach base 60 percent of the time and set a modern record with a 1.422 OPS. It's the most dominant a hitter has ever been. Bonds won the batting title in 2004 with a .362 average and posted a .609 on-base percentage. He didn't get many chances to swing for the fences, but when he did, he delivered. He hit a homer once every 8.28 at-bats.

"He made everything look easy," Baker said. "When Michael Jordan has the ball, everybody in the gym knows he's going to get the last shot and he's going to sink it. Everybody at the ballpark knew about Barry, and he still hit it out."

It was so automatic that managers resorted to unprecedented lengths to avoid getting beat by Bonds. In 1998 the Arizona Diamondbacks intentionally walked him with the bases loaded and two outs in the ninth inning of a game they led by two runs.

Bonds had always had power and a quick swing, but as a Giant, the complete package came together. You would expect a tremendously high baseball IQ from someone who was the son of a star outfielder and learned the game from the greatest ever to play it, but it took a few years for everything to click. When Bonds signed with the Giants, he told Magowan he was fully formed. "I already went and got my master's degree. I went through the training of school and through Pittsburgh, so to me, I'm the Harvard professor in my sport, and I went through the classes and courses, and by the time I was in San Francisco, I was already the instructor," he told Renel Brooks-Moon during an interview for Giants Productions. "I remember Peter Magowan said, 'How good are you?' I said, 'Peter, if I fail you, I'll give you a million dollars back to whatever charity you want.' That's how confident I was and how happy I was to go home."

Perhaps the greatest perk of Jon Miller's job came in the years when Mays was still a regular at the ballpark. Miller would walk into Mike Murphy's office and find several Hall of Famers sitting around a table, telling stories and giving advice to any young player brave enough to walk through the door. One day, Miller stood in the room and laughed as Bonds and Mays bantered about the younger outfielder's climb up the all-time home run chart. Bonds had just hit his 500th homer.

"Barry said, 'I don't care that much about 500. For me, it's 660; that's what I'm after," Miller recounted. "And Willie said, 'You'd better get busy, brother! That's a long way to go.' You don't hear many people who are able to kid around with Barry and get under his skin, but Willie Mays, he was the guy that could do it."

Bonds, it turned out, was ready to work quickly. He joined the 500 Home Run Club in April 2001, pulling a breaking ball from the Dodgers' Terry Adams into McCovey Cove. It was one of 35 Splash Hits by Bonds, who was the first ever to put one in the water and had 23 of the first 25 overall.

Bonds reached 500 career home runs in his 16th big-league season. The 500th was one of a record 73 Bonds hit that year, which allowed him to reach 600 on August 8 of the following year. There were only three others in the club at the time, and all of them needed at least 1,120 at-bats to get from 500 to 600. It took Mays 1,981 at-bats to bridge the gap, but Bonds did it in just 710, the final blast coming when he crushed a fastball from Pittsburgh's Kip Wells over the wall in dead center. As Bonds stepped out of the dugout for a curtain call, fireworks went off behind the center-field scoreboard. "And he does it at Pac Bell Park," Duane Kuiper said on the broadcast. To Bonds, that was no coincidence.

Bonds always claimed he was so far ahead of the game that he purposely waited until he was in front of his own fans to reach major milestones. Given his track record—and his talent—it was hard to argue. The homer that tied Mark McGwire's single-season record of 70 came in Houston, but 71, 72, and 73 were hit against the Dodgers at home. He went deep in three straight games in Milwaukee early in the 2001 season to get to 499 career home runs, but it wasn't until the first day back at Pacific Bell Park that he reached 500. The 600th came in the middle of a home stand, and two years later, Bonds tied and passed Mays on back-to-back nights in San Francisco. The Associated Press alert from that night read, "Bonds' blast catches Mays, ends dry spell," and it certainly seems that last part was done on purpose. He took Roy Oswalt deep in Houston on Opening Day to get within one of Mays, but he didn't homer again on that weeklong season-opening trip.

In the home opener, Bonds's 660th homer sailed over the 24-foot-high wall in right and landed in the water. Mays walked out and took part in a literal passing of the torch, handing his godson a prop that was used during the 2002 Olympic relay and had been adorned with 25 tiny diamonds, for Bonds's number.

Had everything gone according to plan 11 years earlier, there would have been 24 diamonds: Bonds originally planned to honor his godfather by wearing his No. 24 in San Francisco, and he teared up at the Winter Meetings as he talked of how special it would be to live out his dream in Mays's number, which the Giants and Mays had agreed to unretire specifically for Bonds. But when he put his jersey on for the first time in San Francisco, Bonds wore the same number his father had played in, No. 25. There had been some public outcry originally, and Bonds said he didn't intend to be a "spoiled rotten brat."

"It's going to be a great, great honor for me to play left field and still see that sign up there, No. 24, because I can still be a little boy pretending I'm in the outfield with my godfather, Willie Mays," he said, smiling. "I'm going to wear the No. 25 in honor of my own father, who I love very, very much, and let a great, great athlete who deserves everything keep his number retired, because that's the only place it belongs."

The No. 24 badge was looking down at Bonds as he hit his 70th home run of the season. Bonds had just turned 40, and his body was starting to break down, particularly a right knee that would require surgery and keep him out for most of the 2005 season. Bonds was caught up in steroid rumors by that time, and the frustration showed in interviews and public appearances, but a year later, the chase for records was back on.

He passed Babe Ruth late in May 2006, again showing he could bend the schedule to his will. His 715th homer came the day before the Giants started a trip to the East Coast, and it left just one man to run down, Henry Aaron. Bonds did that on August 7, 2007, crushing a pitch from Washington's Mike Bacsik into the crowded bleachers in right-center. It was an appropriate landing spot for the record-breaker. Bonds was the only man who ever consistently made the ballpark look small, and the ball landed well beyond the wall in Triples Alley, a canyon that has for years left other left-handed sluggers shaking their heads.

Bonds finished at 762, leaving the game as both the single-season and all-time home run champion. It was an unparalleled résumé, but the steroid suspicions—and the ensuing grandstanding by many in the voting body of the Baseball Writers' Association of America—kept Bonds out of the Hall of Fame during his 10 years on the ballot. It was a snub that Bonds rarely talked about, and when he did so publicly, he was always defiant. But in quiet moments, Bonds sometimes let his guard down.

The Giants held an 80th birthday party for McCovey at the Gotham Club early in 2018. Bonds's eyes filled with tears and his voice cracked as he talked of his desire to be elected while Mays and McCovey were still around to accompany him to Cooperstown. It never happened, but later that year, the Giants put Bonds in their own inner circle. They broke with tradition and their own policy to retire only numbers of players in the Hall, putting No. 25 up on a wall a few feet away from No. 24.

Bonds was with his godfather, and in a house that he built, no less. It had been 25 years since that first season as a Giant, and Bonds had made good on just about every promise from that press conference, his first moment officially wearing orange and black. "This is the city that my father started in," Bonds said that day. "Hopefully it's going to be the city that I end in, with a beautiful beginning and a beautiful end."

9
Bruce Bochy

There is a mural at Oracle Park listing all of the franchise's award winners, and if you look long enough, you'll see what seems to be a jarring omission: The section for Manager of the Year goes directly from Dusty Baker (2000) to Gabe Kapler (2021). Bruce Bochy never won the award as a Giant, a lack of recognition that might make one wonder whether the award should be abolished, but if you go through the years of voting, you see Bochy was often a finalist. He has finished in the top three for the award seven times, including the 2006 season, which was his 12th in San Diego. It was also his last, a decision that still angers many in the city and completely changed the course of history in the National League West.

Bochy led the Padres to back-to-back division titles in 2005 and 2006, but the team got swept by the Cardinals in the NLDS in 2005 and a year later lost to them in four games. When they landed back in San Diego, Bochy had lunch with general manager Kevin Towers and CEO Sandy Alderson. Towers was one of his closest friends, but Alderson had different ideas about the way games should be run, and he left Bochy with the impression that he should talk to other clubs. Bochy had a year left on his deal. He didn't know others could inquire given his contract situation, but the Padres were ready to move on, and they weren't going to stand in the way if someone else wanted to hire their manager. In fact, they helped push the process along. "I was in Arizona having some meetings, and I got a call from Towers," Brian Sabean recalled. "He gave me a heads-up. He said, 'I can't guarantee that they give him permission to leave, but if there ever was a window, it's now.'"

The timing might have been a surprise to Bochy, but it was perfect for a Giants team he had been beating. The Giants parted with Felipe Alou after back-to-back third-place finishes, and in Bochy, Sabean saw someone who might be perfect for an organization that had a pipeline of pitching on the way. He had watched Bochy from the other side and felt he was getting more out of his roster than anybody could have expected.

The familiarity went both ways. Bochy and Sabean had not met often, but the manager had always been intrigued by what he heard about the Giants GM. He watched closely as Sabean continually pushed to contend at trade deadlines, a style that fit his own competitive nature. He loved the city too, and after brief conversations with the Cubs and Nationals, he flew up to San Francisco to drive around with Sabean and special assistant Pat Dobson, who knew Bochy well and helped make both men feel more comfortable. The group spent hours talking baseball, with Bochy and Sabean connecting on a mutual desire for the Giants to be more pitching-centric. Until he actually took the job, Bochy didn't realize quite how old his roster would be, but that didn't bother him. He always believed in his veterans.

Bochy hadn't planned to leave San Diego, but the Padres had no intention of offering him a contract extension. They left the door open for Sabean. "Brian called me and said, 'We'd love to have you up here,'" Bochy said. "He convinced me that that's where I should be."

Six years later, Sabean stood in the hallway outside of the visiting clubhouse in Detroit and smiled as players doused one another in champagne. When asked about his close friend, the man who had just led the Giants to a second title, he left no room for equivocation. "He's a Hall of Fame manager," Sabean said that night. "Enough said."

The second title put Bochy in position for Cooperstown. The third made it a lock, and he wasn't done. In his final month as Giants manager, he reached 2,000 career wins, 1,052 of which came in orange and black. He's the only manager in MLB history with 900 wins for two different franchises, and when he retires for good, he will get that call from the Hall. And when it happens, he likely will think back to his first day on the job in San Diego. The Padres got blown out in his debut, and on the ride home, Bochy made the mistake of turning on his radio. Fans were already turning on the new manager.

A dozen years later, fans sang a different tune, but his bosses wanted a new direction. They were so eager to move on that Alderson didn't even ask for compensation in return for Bochy joining a division rival. The players, however, knew what they were about to be missing. "We stay away from trades within the division so you don't get burned," closer Trevor Hoffman told the *San Diego Union-Tribune*. "This is obviously running the risk of getting burned."

Tim Flannery was walking his dog when he got the call. Bochy was on the other end, and as always, his timing was perfect. The hardnosed infielder had played five seasons with Bochy in San Diego in the 1980s and coached third base for him for seven years. Affable and endlessly energetic, Flannery is at home on the infield but just as comfortable with a microphone in his hand. He's an accomplished singer and songwriter and was doing radio for the Padres when Bochy called.

Bochy told his friend the Padres were making a change, which came as a shock. If either of them were going to get in trouble with the organization, it seemed it would be the brutally honest color commentator, not the manager. As Flannery tried to digest the news, Bochy circled around to his question. "You got one more ride in you?" he asked.

When Flannery finally made it back inside his house, his wife, Donna, knew what was coming.

"You're going again, aren't you?" she said.

"Yeah," he replied. "Boch says they're trying to win up there."

Bochy had his third-base coach and trusted lieutenant back by his side, and he soon found that much of the rest of the work was already done.

Coaches are often anonymous, but the continuity during the title years—along with all of the winning and some big personalities—turned Bochy's group into household names. The dynasty had Buster, Timmy, and Bum, but also Rags, Flan, and Wo. By the time the staff had a third ring, the longtime coaches were more recognizable in the Bay Area than most of the players.

Pitching coach Dave Righetti, a San Jose native who was an All-Star closer with the Yankees before coming home, spent 15 seasons with the organization. Mark Gardner was at his side just about the entire time. Bochy had four hitting coaches in San Francisco, but Hensley "Bam Bam" Meulens was in charge in the title years. In a sport where coaches often work nervously on two-year contracts, the stability was rare. But one man's record stood above the rest.

Ron Wotus spent nine seasons in the Giants' minor league system as a player, coach, and manager before spending a franchise-record 24 seasons on the big-league staff. With apologies to Barry Bonds, nobody has taken more walks at Oracle Park than the man who has been in the dugout for every one of the organization's managers over the past three decades.

One of the few perks of retiring as a player at 28 was the fact that Wotus no longer had to run sprints to keep in shape to play middle infield. He instead embraced walking the warning track every afternoon, and when he was named bench coach under Dusty Baker, it became a way to clear his mind early in the afternoon. He would wear down the grass along the track, thinking about that night's game, the moves that might be made, and how he could get the most out of infielders ranging from Rich Aurilia, Jeff Kent, and J. T. Snow to Brandon Crawford, Brandon Belt, and Joe Panik.

Alou kept him around, and Bochy did too. When Kapler took over, Wotus was the only holdover on a young and inexperienced staff. Even Bob Melvin couldn't resist. Wotus was a special assistant by the time Melvin was hired to succeed Kapler, but he couldn't stay away from the dirt, hitting grounders to the big leaguers when the Giants were home and visiting minor league affiliates when they were on the road. After months of prodding from Melvin and Matt Williams, he returned to the dugout for the final month of the 2024 season, adding his expertise from his familiar perch on the dugout railing.

The September cameo put Wotus back in a dugout 40 years after his last appearance as a big-league player. Before being taken in the 16th round of the 1979 draft by the Pirates, he was a three-sport star at Bacon Academy in Colchester, Connecticut.

He was the only baseball player ever drafted out of the school, but that might not have even been his best sport. Wotus averaged 30 points on the basketball court and scored 89 goals as a center-forward in soccer, setting a state record that stood for more than two decades. He was All-State in three sports and spent so much time practicing that some of his teachers expressed concern to his basketball coach. They wanted him to spend more time on homework. "He's not going to be in sports his whole life," they said. Well, about that . . .

Many of Wotus's years in a dugout have been spent right alongside the manager, and under different circumstances, he might have been the one in charge. Wotus interviewed for the job that ultimately went to Bochy, but the new manager didn't view that as being awkward. He wanted the best coaches, period, and he put together a staff that got the absolute most out of players.

Wotus was in charge of the infielders, and nobody hit more grounders to Crawford, who would always end their sessions with a behind-the-back or between-the-legs attempt as Wotus held his nose. When the four-time Gold Glove winner returned for his final game as a Giant on the last day of the 2023 season, it was Wotus who was called out to hit some balls with his trusted SSK fungo. He is never seen without it, and he rarely needs a replacement. Occasionally a thrown ball will hit the fungo as it leans against the cage, snapping it in half, but Wotus can go entire seasons without breaking his bat. "The key to fungo hitting is you've got to pitch yourself well," he once said, laughing. "You don't want to jam yourself."

Like the rest of Bochy's coaches, Wotus knew he mostly had autonomy—unless a mistake was made. "Boch is not the easiest manager to work for," Flannery said. "His military chain of command is his strength, and if you're a coach, it lets you do what you have to do. You're in charge, but if anything goes wrong in that department, he's going to make you feel it. But there was a benefit to that. I think if the players respect you enough as a coach and they see the pain that's caused if they screw up on the bases or something like that, they realize that they caused it and they take it a little more personally."

Bochy was the father figure hovering over it all, and he would snap when needed. But day-to-day, the discipline was up to the coaches, which was another reason the continuity was so important. It was easier to be hard on stars when the coaches had been there for them from the moment they were drafted. "We weren't yellers or screamers, but we took care of business," Righetti said. "I think Boch liked that, so he didn't have to. I didn't mind doing it, because it was all for a proper cause. It was for winning."

The Giants did a lot of it, and the stress in the coaches' room proved worth it. They worked hard, but they played hard. Bochy would organize staff dinners on road trips that Sabean would often join as the entire group paired good food with better wine. The stories might have been the most memorable part, though. Members of that coaching staff still crack up when they recall the time a dinner went so long that knives started being thrown against the wood paneling of a fancy restaurant. Wotus had to duck as Flannery held impromptu target practice with a section above his head.

The dinners were legendary but paled in comparison to three toasts held after postseason runs. In Arlington, Detroit, and Kansas City, the group retreated to the coaches' room at some point for cigars and champagne. The first one was a little rushed, but by 2012 and 2014, they had a well-worn routine of bringing in family members and making sure to take group photos. Wotus later turned them into videos with special soundtracks that he plays on his TV. "We got after it pretty good," he said, laughing. "You're riding such a high and you're all smiles, and nothing can get you down. We got pretty good at it, and we wanted to capture the moments. Those are memories I'll be watching 20 years from now, and it's going to bring a smile to my face."

As the Giants worked their way through the Braves and Phillies in October 2010, Jeremy Affeldt sat on ice. He had not appeared in the first round, and through the first five games of the NLCS, he faced just three batters. Affeldt had been the best setup man in baseball in 2009, and while the ensuing regular season included a lot more hard contact and some disappointing results, he had not lost his belief that he should be out there in big moments.

The Giants took a 3–2 series lead into Game 6 of the NLCS, but Affeldt wasn't happy with his manager. That afternoon, he walked out to the bullpen at Citizens Bank Park and saw that Righetti and Gardner were watching another pitcher throw his regular session. Affeldt grabbed a ball and announced that he was throwing a pen that day too. He tossed a few pitches as hard as he could and then walked off without saying a word. After the bullpen cleared, he walked back up the steps and sat by himself. Affeldt desperately wanted to pitch in a game that mattered. He wanted to feel like he was an important part of the run the Giants were on.

A few hours later, he found himself right in the middle of one of the most chaotic moments in the franchise's postseason history. When Jonathan Sanchez drilled Chase Utley in the back in the bottom of the third, both benches and bullpens cleared. The custom in those fights, if you can call them that, is for relievers to drop everything and sprint to the infield dirt. They know the drill. They'll charge in as if they're gladiators, but by the time they get to the other players and coaches, everything will have calmed down. It's a way to get some cardio while showing support for whichever teammate decided it was time to throw down.

Affeldt was getting loose when Sanchez and Utley started jawing. He was ready to play the part, but as he started to run off the bullpen mound, Gardner grabbed him and bullpen catcher Taira Uematsu and told them to stay put. Whenever the squabble cleared up, Affeldt was entering the game. Gardner alertly kept Affeldt from spiking his adrenaline and instead made sure he properly warmed up.

Affeldt jogged to the mound in front of 46,000 foaming Phillies fans and found Bochy waiting for him. The manager knew his stubborn left-hander wasn't happy with him, and as he handed the ball over, he held on for an extra beat, just long enough that Affeldt's attempt to dramatically rip it from him wasn't successful. "Listen, I know you and I aren't seeing eye-to-eye right now—" Bochy started.

Affeldt cut him off. They could talk through their disagreement later, he said, but Ryan Howard was waiting in the batter's box. He told Bochy to get off the mound. "Listen," Bochy said again. "If you get me out of this, we're going to go to the World Series."

It was a perfectly timed shot in the arm for Affeldt, who whiffed Howard for the first out of the inning and stranded both runners. When he got out of the jam, Bochy gave him a big hug. Sabean found him in the clubhouse later and planted a kiss on his forehead. It was a sequence Affeldt never forgot, and it emboldened him with confidence that carried him through the rest of his career. He made 23 more postseason appearances for the Giants after that night in Philadelphia and allowed just one run. The moment was also the perfect example of why Bochy will soon stand at a podium in Cooperstown.

Affeldt is the first to admit he wasn't easy to manage. He was confident, loud, and unafraid to make his opinion known. But Bochy—as he did so often, and with so many different types of players—found the right buttons to push. With Affeldt, he did it again four years later in the hours before Game 7, telling him to have his knee brace on from the start of the game. If Tim Hudson wobbled at all, Affeldt would get the ball to Madison Bumgarner. Why Bumgarner? Bochy had read in the newspaper that the Kansas City Royals didn't expect to see him again, so they were going to see him again.

It was perhaps the best example of a trait that defined Bochy's Hall of Fame career. He wanted his players to always feel comfortable, because that was the way to get the best out of them. He would put them in the right spots, even if they were unorthodox at times, and if something didn't look or feel right, he would pull the plug. Relievers get used to the concept of having to "wear it," staying out there without their best stuff, even if it means having four or five runs go on an ERA that can take months to get back to form when you pitch an inning at a time. But Bochy didn't believe in that. If he saw that a reliever wasn't himself, he would call for the next one. It was important to save his pitchers from themselves, because they would need to be confident the next time out. They would need to feel comfortable when he called their names.

At the same time, Bochy did everything in his power to make opposing managers uncomfortable. They could try and guess how he would deploy his pitching, but they could never keep up. Bochy treated just about every October inning like he was trying to get the last three outs of Game 7, which meant Affeldt had to be ready at all times. Javier Lopez might pitch in the sixth inning one night and the eighth the next. George Kontos, whose slider and durability made him a valuable middle-innings arm, appeared eight times in his first postseason under Bochy, with those outings spanning every inning from the third to the ninth and ranging from one out to six.

Bochy did what he had to do to get out of an inning, and then he figured out the next one. It seemed he had the best gut in the game, but that was a simplistic view. That gut was informed by hundreds of hours of conversations every season.

Pitching coach Righetti would meet with the previous night's starting pitcher every day during batting practice to feel him out and plan what was next, and he was pleasantly surprised in 2007 when Bochy started joining the tail end of those conversations. When Righetti was an All-Star pitcher in the big leagues, he would sometimes go weeks without hearing from his manager, but Bochy was hands-on. He wanted to check in with as many players as he could every day, and he went out of his way to attend bullpen sessions and get an understanding of the minor tweaks his pitchers were working on.

Soon after Bochy took over in San Francisco, Righetti told his wife that things were changing. He said, "[I told her], 'We're going to get better one way or another.' I just felt it. Him being a catcher, those guys are different. They're the ones that are supposed to think of the whole staff and how they can make each guy better. It's ingrained in those guys to deal with pitchers and understand how important it was, and he took it to heart."

The Giants couldn't have fully known it when they first met with Bochy, but they couldn't have made a more perfect choice for what was to come. Bochy's first year in San Francisco was dominated by Barry Bonds, but after that the organization built around pitching and an MVP catcher. It was the perfect roster to pair with a former big-league catcher who became so in tune with pitchers that he raised one who reached the big leagues.

Bochy's proudest moment came in September 2014 when he became the first manager in MLB history to hand a baseball to his son. Bruce had rarely gotten to watch Brett pitch live because he was managing for most of his son's life. In college, Brett would send videos to his father, and then the Giants offered an easier solution. They took the right-handed reliever in the 20th round of the 2010 draft, allowing his father to watch as he worked his way through the minors.

There had been seven previous father-son duos, but Brett was the first pitcher, so his father got to hand the ball over during pitching changes. That wasn't always a positive. The first time Bruce inserted Brett in a spring training game, the bases were loaded. When he made his MLB debut against the Dodgers a year and a half later, the bases were once again packed. Bruce would always watch games from the top step of the dugout, his eyes darting back and forth, taking everything in. But when Brett made his debut, his father paced nervously back and forth. "I was very, very proud," the manager said after the game. "It was kind of surreal, really."

Bochy would often joke that the bases-loaded entrances would upset his wife, Brett's mother, but the 2014 debut ended up being pretty meaningful for more than the initial history it made. When Bochy won his third World Series title, his son got a ring. When the Giants reached Game 7 of the World Series six weeks after Brett's debut, the father and son got to decompress with a lengthy breakfast in Kansas City. That was the end of another brilliant month for the manager.

Bochy trusted his gut before and during Game 7, but Bumgarner's performance had actually been set in motion after the Giants lost Game 3, falling behind 2–1 in the series. There were cries to start Bumgarner on short rest the next night, and Bochy did his homework, reaching out to former players of his who had started on short rest. As he met with the team's beat writers before Game 4, he smiled and asked what the group would do. But his decision had been made long before anyone else chimed in. "He's not a toy," he said, insisting the staff had to protect Bumgarner.

There was another reason to hold his ace back, though. Bochy knew Bumgarner would win whenever he made his next start, and Kansas City's best starter, James "Big Game" Shields, was lined up for Game 5. Rather than putting Bumgarner up against Jason Vargas in Game 4, Bochy saved him for the Royals' ace. The Giants won both games. It was the type of three-steps-ahead plan that was evident during regular-season games too.

Bochy was known for superb in-game management, but his touch was equally effective off the field. The manager's preference was to leave the clubhouse to the veterans, but occasionally he would step in, and he always seemed to have the right words when the lights got bright. Whether it was telling a biblical story about Gideon or instructing his players not to bring suitcases to the park before a huge game that would lead to a road trip if the Giants lost, Bochy always had a trick up his sleeve.

Sometimes there was just a message from the heart. The road team had lost a Game 7 of the World Series nine consecutive times before the Giants broke through in Kansas City. Minutes before the first pitch, Bochy gathered his group and ran through the list of big road games the team had already won that October. It was a reminder that they had "champion's blood," as he had told them all season.

Bochy had an innate feel for what would work and, more important, *when* it would work. During rough patches, Larry Baer would occasionally ask Bochy if he was going to talk to the group, but the manager liked to feel things out, taking the temperature with veterans before delivering one of his speeches. The message was always carefully crafted, although sometimes it didn't come across quite as he planned. In his first season with the Giants, Bochy grew weary of watching a struggling team lose focus, so one day he held a meeting and smacked a clubhouse TV with a baseball bat. He expected it to disintegrate, but the first blow just led to a loud thud. That angered Bochy even more, and he kept taking the bat to the TV until it was destroyed.

The connections that were forged through all of those moments were never more apparent than on September 29, 2019, when Bochy managed his final game in orange and black. The day drew dozens of Bochy's former players back to Oracle Park, including Tim Lincecum, an appearance that to this day is his only public one at the ballpark since his final game. Several players who later would skip championship reunions found their way back to celebrate their manager, who, seemingly for the first time, had a hard time keeping his emotions in check.

Bochy grabbed a microphone at the end of the day, and as always, he spoke without notes. He thanked everyone he needed to and recalled some of his more memorable moments as manager, such as Matt Cain's perfect game and Edgar Renteria's clutch homer in the 2010 World Series. He joked that some of his relievers were responsible for the stents in his heart but added that managing the group was "one of the greatest joys of [his] life." On his final day as a Giant, Bochy finished his speech by echoing the famous words of Lou Gehrig: "I consider myself the luckiest man on the face of this earth," he said. "Thank you. Thank you. Thank you."

It was a perfect goodbye. But Bochy, it turned out, wasn't quite done.

Chris Young turned and saw his manager walking out of the dugout. He knew right away that his first career playoff start was over. Young was in his first season with the Padres, but it had not taken him long to figure out that Bochy's mind was already several steps ahead by the time he took his first step out of the dugout. The Padres had lost the first two games of the 2006 NLDS at home, but Young was pitching well in a must-win Game 3. He was given a 3–0 lead in the top of the fourth, but two innings later, he allowed a single and then issued a one-out walk. As Albert Pujols walked to the plate, Young snuck a glance at the visiting dugout. Bochy was coming to take the ball.

The 6'10" right-hander stood on the mound and waited for that familiar slow saunter to bring his manager all the way out to him. But when he arrived, Bochy didn't stick his hand out. Instead, he looked at catcher Mike Piazza.

"How's his stuff?" he asked.

"It's still good, Boch," Piazza replied.

Bochy turned to Young. "C. Y., you helped get us here," he said. "This is your guy. Go get him."

Bochy turned and walked back to the dugout as Young watched.

"I'm a tall guy, but I felt 10 feet tall in that moment," he said years later. "I don't think he came to the mound one time that year and left me in the game. But in that moment, he knew, and he did it. It always stuck with me. He probably didn't know how much it meant to me, but it stuck with me. He got the best out of me."

Fourteen years later, Young—who, by the way, struck out Pujols and got out of the inning unscathed—returned to his hometown to become general manager of the Texas Rangers. They had just finished last in the AL West, and as they moved into a new $1.2 billion ballpark, they were looking for someone who could get them back to the postseason. The wall at Globe Life Field had 10 banners commemorating past teams when Young arrived, but none were for titles. The closest they had come was in 2010 and 2011, when they won back-to-back pennants. Bochy, of course, had a hand in making sure that was all they got.

In August of his second season in charge, Young fired manager Chris Woodward. The front office soon got together to chart out a new path, and team executives put together a list of ideal traits in their next manager. After signing All-Star infielders Corey Seager and Marcus Semien for a combined $500 million, the Rangers were ready to go all in. They wanted someone who fit their style and would bring instant credibility. They wanted a good in-game manager but also someone who could adequately manage people. They wanted a manager who would command a room.

As they debated which traits should take priority, someone finally spoke up. "This sounds exactly like Bruce Bochy," he said. There was just one problem: Bochy, then 67, was technically retired.

Bochy had multiple heart procedures in his final years with the Giants, and the downturn in 2017 and 2018 was hard on him. One night, in the middle of a rain delay, he went out to the dugout to argue that the teams should continue playing no matter how long it took. He came back to the clubhouse to find that many of his players were already dressed in street clothes, eager to get away from the ballpark during a season that was going nowhere. At the end of 2018, Bochy spoke to Baer and Sabean about the possibility of soon hanging it up. When the Giants hired Farhan Zaidi a few weeks later, he felt the new president of baseball operations should get to hire his own manager rather than deal with the awkwardness of trying to merge two philosophies. Bochy had always managed with his gut, and his gut was telling him it was time.

In his 13th speech to kick off Giants spring training, Bochy told his players that the upcoming season would be his last. He then announced the decision to the media, and as he watched his pitchers play catch on a cold and rainy morning in Scottsdale, his eyes welled up. He joked about coaching Little League and said he was excited for the Giants to try and surprise outsiders in his final season. When he was asked if he could say he would never manage again, he paused. "*Never* is a big word," he said slowly.

The Giants and their opponents spent a season celebrating Bochy, who took it all in reluctantly. After 2,106 games in San Francisco, Bochy rode off into the sunset and focused on his two sons and three grandchildren. He moved to Nashville with his wife, Kim, embracing golf and fishing in a pond behind his house. The Giants named him a special advisor, and he came back for ceremonies and visiting minor league affiliates. Bochy was born in Landes de Bussac, France, because his father was an army sergeant major who once was based there, and he returned in 2022 to manage Team France in the World Baseball Classic qualifier. As he stood in a dugout in Ravensburg, Germany, he realized that his competitive fire had never gone away.

The Rangers couldn't be sure of that, but they had their suspicions. Young called and received permission from the Giants to interview Bochy before flying to Nashville for a seven-hour meeting at his house. He returned with owner Ray Davis, assistant general managers Ross Fenstermaker and Josh Boyd, and former Rangers star Michael Young. They spent five hours discussing philosophies and a potential staff. There were still some doubts within the group about whether Bochy would come out of retirement, but it quickly became clear he had done his homework.

Bochy asked about top prospects and the upcoming first-round pick, and spoke passionately about how he thought there was much more in the tank for Seager and Semien—who would go on to finish second and third in MVP voting the next year. The conversations kept getting deeper, and Kim brought the group sandwiches, salads, and homemade chocolate chip cookies. At one point, Bochy laughed as he talked about his pond. "I think there's just one fish in there, and we got to know each other pretty well," he said. "I'm tired of seeing the same fish over and over again."

The message was clear: Bochy was ready for a new challenge, and a few days later, he was introduced in Arlington. It didn't take Bochy long to show it was a shrewd decision. Bruce Bochy, Texas Ranger, proved to be very much like the man who had walked away in 2019. He brought calm to the clubhouse, particularly when the Rangers lost 16 of 20 in the second half. The phrasing before and after games had not changed from his Giants days, and Bochy talked about how his group had to be "big boys" and accountable in tough times. He called meetings when necessary, although he didn't pull out motivational *Braveheart* clips as he had done in San Diego and San Francisco. Young suspected perhaps the 1995 movie had finally become too dated for big leaguers to relate to.

When the games got particularly tight, Bochy managed with the same sense of urgency that won him three titles in San Francisco. Everyone always wanted to know what his October secret was, but a big part of his success was actually pretty simple: There was never a tomorrow to worry about. Every postseason out was the biggest one of the season, and Bochy acted accordingly. He once brought in his closer to get the final out of Game 7 of an NLCS despite the fact that the Giants had a 9–0 lead and it was raining so hard that the game was moments from being suspended. In Bochy's first October in Arlington, the Rangers felt those same vibes, and by the end of the month, he had his fourth title.

The championship was bittersweet in San Francisco. There wasn't a person in the organization who wasn't happy for Bochy, but for many, it was hard to watch him win elsewhere. When he looks back on how it ended with the Giants, Bochy wishes he had done just one thing differently. He felt strongly that it was the right thing to do to walk away at the end of his contract, but he never realized that announcing it in spring training would lead to a retirement tour. It humbled him, but at times he felt embarrassed by all of the attention. He was showered with enough hard liquor and wine to fully stock the Mauna Loa, a local bar that became the new home of Bullwinkle, the gigantic stuffed elk that hung in Bochy's office for a decade. There was also a tile from the scoreboard at Wrigley Field, a chair from Fenway Park, and multiple all-expenses-paid fishing and hunting trips that he never got to take because a pandemic soon shut the world down.

As for the rest of it? Bochy wouldn't trade it for anything. Years after he left the Giants, he quickly shook his head when asked if he had any regrets about the way things ended. "Shoot, man, come on, that was an unbelievable run that we had, and they're memories that I'm lucky to be a part of," he said. "Not just with the players but with Brian, the front office, the scouts, everybody. There I was with a storied franchise that we made even more storied. I'm proud to be part of that."

10

Hunter Pence

After one of the best starts of a surprisingly rocky 2012 season, Tim Lincecum found himself talking about someone else. It was deadline day, and Lincecum took reporters through a laundry list of what made Hunter Pence, the newest Giant, such a challenge for pitchers. He talked about how unpredictable Pence was and how well he covered the plate when he choked up, and then in the middle of the answer, he trailed off and looked past the cameras. "Oh, there he is," he said, laughing. "Just talking trash about you, man."

Lincecum reached over and shook hands with Pence, who was looking through his new locker for workout gear. Pence would go on to be one of the most impactful additions in franchise history, but in that lighthearted moment, nobody could have predicted what was to come.

The Giants had just gotten swept by the Dodgers, falling into a tie atop the NL West after back-to-back shutouts. They led the division by 7½ games in late May, but their edge was all gone. It was time to be bold, and general manager Brian Sabean knew exactly who he wanted.

Before trading for Carlos Beltran the previous summer, the Giants had also chased Pence, an athletic young outfielder coming off three straight 25-homer seasons in Houston. That was pushed in part by manager Bruce Bochy, who watched Pence's physicality while managing him in the All-Star Game and came back insisting the Giants needed him. The Astros instead sent Pence to Philadelphia, where he looked like the perfect fit for a deep lineup that played into October every year. A year later, everything was crumbling for a banged-up team that was last in the NL East. "We didn't want to trade Pence, because in a lot of ways, he was perfect in Philadelphia," then–Phillies GM Ruben Amaro Jr. said. "He has that kind of energy, he loves to play, he's got that 'it' thing that I think was really important for our organization. We wanted to target winners, and we always felt that's what he was."

The Giants did too. In Pence, they saw an ideal addition, and in the Giants, the Phillies saw the ideal trade partner. They had a specific wish list, and at the top of it was adding an impact catcher. The Giants had Buster Posey, so they were happy to build a deal around 21-year-old Tommy Joseph, a powerful catcher who reminded team officials of Chicago White Sox star Paul Konerko. The cost didn't bother Sabean, who had taken the Dodgers sweep personally. "In some ways," he said of the trade. "This is a reaction."

Privately, the Giants had another reason to swing the deal. The off-season addition of Melky Cabrera had been wildly impactful, and the outfielder looked like an MVP front runner as he surged to an All-Star appearance and then won the game's MVP honors. But Cabrera's representatives had informed

Giants officials that he had tested positive for a PED. The testing program was still relatively new, and the Giants didn't know how it would play out, but they feared they might be losing their best outfield bat, and at the very least, there was enough uncertainty that they felt they needed an addition.

As Pence drove to the ballpark on deadline day, Amaro called with the news. The outfielder, who later would do things with such effort that Bochy nicknamed him Full Throttle, went into overdrive. He quickly packed and booked his own flight to San Francisco since it was faster than waiting for the teams' travel departments to sort things out. The Giants had a night game, and he intended to get to Oracle Park in time to play. His mentality was that he played every day, even on deadline day, but there's only so much you can control when flying across the country.

Pence landed in the eighth inning and got in a car that took him straight to the ballpark. In the span of a few hours, he had not only switched sides of the country but also gone from last place to a pennant race. Since he didn't get an at-bat, he instead headed to the weight room to lift.

Two weeks later, Cabrera was suspended 50 games for testing positive for testosterone. He left the ballpark without addressing teammates, in such a rush that he didn't even pack up the bats in his locker. He never played another game for the Giants.

Pence, on the other hand, planted roots that went deeper than he ever could have imagined. He met his wife in San Francisco, and they held their wedding in the city. The Texas native made San Francisco his home after he retired. He spent eight seasons with the Giants, and while he didn't make it to San Francisco in time to play on deadline day, he was in right field the next day, starting a streak of 383 consecutive appearances that was halted only when a wayward pitch fractured his forearm three years later.

In every way, on and off the field, Pence was exactly the player the Giants hoped they were getting as they finalized the deal with the Phillies.

The bromance between Pence and Michael Morse became one of the most endearing storylines of the 2014 title run. The two seemed inseparable, combining not just for 36 homers but also for several memorable memes. It seemed obvious to the rest of the Giants that they would make a quick connection, and on day one, they became catch partners. They shared inspirational quotes and were often spotted around town having lunch together on off days. When Morse returned to the Giants for a second stint late in his career, the agreement was hashed out with general manager Bobby Evans as they attended Pence's wedding.

If you didn't know better, you would think the outfielders had been best friends since Little League. But things weren't always so seamless. "I hated him at first," Morse recalled, laughing. "When I was playing against him, I always watched him, and I thought, *This guy doesn't hit right, he can't throw right, everything is the total opposite of what you learn in baseball [in terms of] what to do. And he gets away with it!* But the one thing he always did was he hustled. He worked hard and he hustled."

That part of Pence's game came from his grandfather, who told him to "work hard and don't complain" just before he passed. Pence's father contributed another part of the legacy. In Little League, Hunter was heartbroken when he found out the No. 7 jersey his older brother had worn was already taken, so his father came up with a quick solution. He told his son, a

Texas power-tumbling champion, that he should wear No. 8 because it was the same right side up and upside down and would rotate with him as he did flips. It ended up being kind of perfect for another reason. The symmetrical number followed one of the more asymmetrical stars the game has ever seen.

"The first time I saw him, back when he was with Houston, I said, 'You're kidding me,'" Bochy said, laughing. "I thought it was a joke."

Even Pence found himself bewildered by parts of his own game. He had baseball's most unique warm-up swing, a stilted hack that would bring the bat down below his knees and then seemingly cut itself off at a different point every time. It looked like Pence was trying to backspin a golf ball out of a sand trap—and he didn't even realize he was doing it until he saw himself on the scoreboard in a visiting ballpark one day. "It was disturbing," he admitted later. But like with the rest of his game, that was just the way he did things.

"I mean, how can you change me? I don't know how to do it normal, you know?" he once said. "The way I'm doing it is normal to me."

The warm-up swing became a fixture on TV broadcasts, but once in the box, everything somehow came together. Pence's normal swing was a little wild too, but his natural strength and hand-eye coordination led to plenty of production.

Pence's running style didn't look particularly fluid, but advanced metrics pegged him as one of the game's best base runners. He was naturally fast and cut corners well, but there was more to it. Third-base coach Tim Flannery felt that Pence was as good a base runner as he had ever had because he was the same all the time. The effort level never changed, and Pence's superior conditioning allowed it to stay that way even when he was playing 162 games a year. "He doesn't know or doesn't believe there's another way," Flannery said. "He's beautiful."

The throwing mechanics were perhaps most jarring, and teammates sometimes noted that it looked painful when he played catch. That's in part because at some point it had been. Pence hurt his shoulder when he was 12 and found it uncomfortable to throw over the top, so he adjusted and lowered his arm angle. When Pence signed a five-year extension after his second season in San Francisco, the Giants discovered during the physical that his thoracic spine flexibility was, as he put it, "off-the-charts horrible." It all led to an odd technique, but again, *different* did not mean *bad*. Pence twice led the league in outfield assists.

There was a theme throughout Pence's career. You wouldn't teach most of what he did, but he turned himself into a four-time All-Star who hit .279 with 244 homers, 942 RBIs, and 120 stolen bases. Pence played 1,700 games over 14 seasons, becoming one of the most recognizable and well-liked outfielders of his generation. Throughout it all, there were two things never missing: he kept his pants pulled up above his knees for maximum flexibility and he just about always had a smile on his face. He was a relentless optimist, and that led to a memorable moment a few months after the trade.

Pence had been sent to a team with plenty of superstars who could serve as the face of a franchise, but he quickly embraced another role. As the Giants chased their second and third titles, the energetic and upbeat outfielder became their voice. He became the Reverend.

Pence's most famous speech happened in the visiting clubhouse in Cincinnati in 2012. His most raucous speech was two years later, when he grabbed a microphone and channeled his inner

WWE wrestler. But his best speech came in between those two days, at the end of a season that would not include postseason baseball.

The Giants voted Pence their Willie Mac Award winner in 2013, an honor that comes with a pregame ceremony. In front of 40,000 fans, teammates, and coaches, Pence gave a thoughtful and poignant speech about his least favorite subject: himself. He did it without notes, preferring instead to go with what came to his heart in the moment. "God, you didn't bless me with grace and very much style," he said. "But thank you for giving me heart and a chance."

Pence then turned to the dugout and addressed his teammates. His eyes were filled with gratitude. "I love every minute with you guys, and I tell you that every day," he said. "Buster, I know you don't like it when I say I love you. You think it's soft, but I actually think it's the strongest thing you've got."

In a funny way, the message was actually similar to the famous one he had delivered one year earlier—although through a very different lens. With the Giants facing elimination in the 2012 NLDS, Bochy addressed the group. Then Pence stood up, his eyes flashing as he looked around the room. As his voice started to rise, Pence implored his teammates not to give in. They owed it to one another to keep pushing, he said. Pence yelled about wanting to see which outfit goofy infielder Ryan Theriot would wear the next day, and he touched hearts by adding that he wanted one more game in right field behind Ryan Vogelsong because the right-hander had never been to the postseason before. "I need one more day with you guys," he said. "Play for each other, not yourself. Win each moment. Win each inning. It's all we have left."

It was a delivery more commonly seen in a high school football locker room, which perhaps was appropriate given that it came from a Texan, and it touched the Giants in different ways. Some were ready to run through the clubhouse wall; some stifled grins. But all found inspiration. "It really touched home," Vogelsong said. "It wasn't what he said; it was the intensity of it, the truth of it."

When the Giants responded with a season-saving win, Reverend Pence was born. He gathered his teammates in the dugout before every game and repeated the process, with sunflower seed showers accompanying shouts and laughter. Two years later, Pence brought the passion to an entire fan base. When the Giants gathered on the field to address fans after the final game of the 2014 regular season, Pence was an easy choice to take the microphone. Stalking back and forth, he asked fans to share in the team's vision and join a journey. "Right now we're not guaranteed another game here at home," he said. "We've got to go earn that. It's a part of the journey. Do you guys want to see another game here at home?" On cue, 41,000 yelled, "Yes! Yes! Yes!"

The speech was so spine-tingling that Bochy waved the mic away after Pence was done. Originally the manager was supposed to address the crowd too, but he laughed and admitted, "I'm not following that." A few days later, WWE wrestler Daniel Bryan's eyes widened as he came across a clip of the speech. The "Yes! Yes! Yes!" chant was one he had started, and he marveled at how Pence, who always told himself to feel as if he were speaking to just one person, had captivated an entire stadium. *Oh my gosh*, Bryan thought. *He's a great public speaker*. It turned out that a player who looked unnatural in just about everything he did on the field was a complete natural when handed a microphone.

The speeches were a side of Pence that had not come out at previous stops, in part because he had not had the right opportunities, but also because he had not felt the right sense of comfort. Pence embraced San Francisco because San Francisco embraced him. The city not only allowed him to be a free spirit; it encouraged it. That's what made him such a fan favorite, and after he retired, he talked proudly of how he was always able to be himself as a Giant.

That was perhaps never more evident than on the night at the end of the 2013 season when Pence agreed to an extension that would keep him in San Francisco. He could have headed out into free agency to try and find a bigger contract, but on the final Friday night of the season, he negotiated with team officials until 2:00 AM. Because it was so late, Larry Baer offered to call a car to take Pence home, but he declined, hopping instead on his reliable scooter and heading down the Embarcadero. It had taken him a while to get there, but San Francisco had become his home.

11

The Ones That Got Away

At its high end, the TOTO toilet will run you a little more than $22,000. The TOTO automatically pre-mists the bowl before every use and flushes on its own. It has a powerful "tornado" flush system, temperature-controlled seat, and a warm air dryer with five variable settings. There is an ergonomic remote control, although because the smart toilet can memorize the settings for up to four users, it's not really needed. When you're done, the toilet automatically deodorizes the air. It even comes with a nightlight.

TOTO describes its top model as the "most beautiful intelligent toilet" and claims it can be the artistic focal point of any bathroom. The TOTO is the Cadillac of toilets, and as the Giants prepared to woo Shohei Ohtani in the winter of 2023, it was brought up on one of their Zoom calls.

The Giants had about 48 hours' notice that Ohtani would visit Oracle Park near the end of his free agency. Plans were drawn up to get him into the ballpark in secrecy, and they ordered bento boxes for lunch with team officials and Buster Posey. In the midst of the rushed planning, Abe Silvestri, the organization's director of team operations, spoke up. "By the way," he asked a small group. "What about the toilet?"

For the Giants, this was a question that went all the way back to 2017, when Ohtani was first available. There was a TOTO showroom across the street from Oracle Park at the time, and the owner came and made a presentation to Silvestri and clubhouse manager Brad Grems. Ohtani ended up holding those 2017 pitch meetings in a conference room at his agency in Orange County, but as the Giants prepared another run at him, Silvestri thought back to that presentation and the team's visits to Dodger Stadium during the 2023 season.

He had noticed that the rival club was already deep into the process of finding subtle ways to send hints. There were signs in the clubhouse that were for the first time written in English, Spanish, and Japanese. Team employees who likely would never cross paths with Ohtani had added Japanese signatures to their emails. Some of the baseballs in the visiting batting cage had been stamped in Japanese. As Silvestri looked around at the little messages the Dodgers were sending to a player who was still a Los Angeles Angel and would visit Dodger Stadium just once that year, he kept thinking back to 2017 and how Giants officials who had scouted players in Japan kept mentioning how common bidet-style toilets were overseas.

There is a recruiting aspect to every off-season, and over the past decade, the Giants have gone out of their way to include personal touches in their pitches. If the bidding is close, you never know what might swing the balance.

When Aaron Judge arrived a year before Ohtani, Larry Baer called Rich Aurilia, one of the outfielder's childhood heroes, and asked him to join Logan Webb and Brandon Crawford at Oracle Park for Judge's visit. Gus Judge, a tiny dachshund, got off the private jet from the East Coast and found he had a dog bed, treats, and a personalized dog bowl waiting in the back seat of a Range Rover that would take everyone to Lafayette for lunch. For years, free-agent pitching targets have received a personalized high-tech video from the Giants that has wowed multiple players who ultimately signed on the dotted line. When it seemed Bryce Harper might be arriving at Scottsdale Stadium in the spring of 2019, the clubhouse staff ordered him a care package from Blind Barber, his favorite hair product.

The details add an extra layer to every pursuit, but sometimes there's nothing you can do. The Dodgers had had their sights set on Ohtani since he was a teenager, and while their front office at one point grew wary of the surprising Blue Jays bid, they never felt threatened by the Giants. They had spent years quietly gathering intel and felt confident that Ohtani wasn't a huge fan of the city of San Francisco and had concerns about the organization's ability to get him to the playoffs right away.

The Giants knew they were a long shot, and on a Saturday afternoon in the middle of December, it became official when Ohtani posted a Dodgers logo on Instagram. His agent had brought the same surprising terms—$700 million, $680 million of which was deferred—to all three finalists. The Giants quickly agreed, but they knew Ohtani preferred Los Angeles. As the organization digested the thought of missing out yet again, Silvestri sought an answer to a question that had been gnawing at him. Ohtani had come straight from the airport to Oracle

Park and then headed back out after the meeting. At any point, had he happened to get up and visit the clubhouse's bathroom?

In the end, the Giants never actually installed the TOTO. They would have had to remodel their bathroom to drop power lines into an individual stall, and that wasn't a reasonable task, especially on short notice.

Ohtani, like other superstars before him, allowed the Giants to reach the podium before handing the gold medal to another franchise. The Giants made the best free-agent addition in the sport's history when Barry Bonds returned home in 1993, but in the years since, they have all too often finished second, a theme that's unavoidable when discussing their history of chasing and making notable additions.

As free agency started to explode and nine-figure deals became commonplace, assistant general manager Bobby Evans dropped a line that still echoes through the halls of Oracle Park. The Giants were two months removed from a third title and hoped to add All-Star Jon Lester to their rotation. They tended to have entertaining media sessions at the Winter Meetings under Brian Sabean, who often insisted that reporters grab a drink before starting their line of questioning, but on this night there was nothing but silence as team officials looked out over the San Diego harbor. Evans stepped out into a hallway of the Manchester Grand Hyatt and waited until the suite door closed behind him. Forty-five minutes earlier, Lester had called. "We did not receive a rose," Evans said.

Eight years later, the Giants found themselves back at the Grand Hyatt, this time with a much bigger prize in their sights. For most of the 2022 season they made no secret of the fact that they would chase Judge in the off-season. A native of nearby Linden, Judge seemed to be entering one of the great win-win situations in free-agency history. In his walk year, he set an American League record with 62 home runs and won his first MVP award, which set the stage for a bidding war between his hometown team and his current one. The Giants had spent months preparing for Judge to hit the market, and right before Thanksgiving, they finally got their chance to show off.

They hosted Judge for two days, taking him to see possible future homes in Lafayette and putting him in touch with Steph Curry's camp in hopes that the Bay Area's biggest star could make a difference. They held a happy hour at the ballpark's Cloud Club and then dinner in the Gotham Club. Judge was engaged throughout, asking plenty of questions and giving the impression he was genuinely interested in coming home.

The visit was the first Judge had taken to a prospective new team, and team officials thought the night at Oracle Park went well. Another part of the trip, however, concerned them. They had gone to great lengths to keep the whole thing underground, but as their car service approached a posh downtown hotel, Judge's agent told the driver that the superstar would get out a few feet early and walk into the lobby by himself. Judge knew someone would be waiting for him, and a video soon hit Twitter showing him being asked what he was doing in San Francisco. "Just visiting some family and friends; that's about it," he said, smiling. It was a clear message to his former bosses across the country, and Giants officials watched it over and over again for a couple of days, trying to figure out what it all meant. Their main determination was that it wasn't good.

The Winter Meetings started with no decision and little clarity about which way Judge was leaning, putting those chasing him in an awkward spot. The first five questions of manager Gabe Kapler's required media session were about Judge, and when he was done talking in generalities, he left the ballroom and made the short walk to a television set that had been set up in the corner of a long hallway. It was a quiet spot, with just enough room for Kapler, a couple of journalists, a cameraman, and several members of the Giants public-relations staff. Every one of their phones buzzed right as Kapler was getting mic'd up.

"Arson Judge appears headed to Giants."

Kapler immediately found himself surrounded, and when a reporter showed him the infamous (and misspelled) tweet from national reporter Jon Heyman, he held up both hands and insisted, "I don't know anything about that," the frustration showing on his face. As he reached for his own iPhone, other reporters in the area inched closer to see if they could get confirmation from the Giants manager. Around the country, there were similar moments of chaos for members of two organizations.

Crawford was driving home from a workout at the team's facility in Scottsdale when his wife, Jalynne, texted him that Judge had chosen the Giants. He told her that the first reports on Twitter are often not accurate, but the more he saw, the more he thought maybe the Giants had actually pulled it off. A few miles away, Webb, the only other active Giant who had been at the Judge dinner, checked his phone during a break with a physical therapist.

"I was like, 'Holy shit, we got him,'" he said.

Webb opened up the team's group text and started going back and forth with other excited Giants, but that was short-lived. A few minutes after Heyman admitted he had jumped the gun, Webb replied on Twitter. "Not cool man," he wrote.

"I was mad at him a little bit, but it's all right; we've talked about it," he said. "I think everyone was pretty excited for like seven minutes in our group text, and then obviously the tone changed."

It took a bit longer for that to happen in Hawaii, where Duane Kuiper was on vacation with his grandchildren. As he sat on a deck chair and watched his two granddaughters splash around a hotel pool, his son texted him the good news. He got up and prepared to head into the water, but first he turned and announced to several nearby Giants fans that they had signed Judge. As they celebrated, his phone started buzzing over and over again. Cole was calling back with an update, but his father was already in the water.

The pursuits of the best free agents are so shrouded in secrecy that it didn't surprise any of the players that the Judge thunderbolt could come out of nowhere. But president of baseball operations Farhan Zaidi had been right in the middle of every conversation with Judge and agent Page Odle. The dialogue had been active, and Zaidi knew they were still in the bidding. But he also knew the Giants hadn't won. He was getting lunch when he saw the tweet. "I was pissed," Zaidi said. "I pretty immediately called Jon Heyman and said, 'That's not accurate.'"

While the Giants and their fans had seven minutes to dream, Yankees fans, players, and staffers briefly lived out their worst nightmare. Manager Aaron Boone had just showered and was getting ready for his own session with the media when he noticed his phone blowing up. That was the low point of an uneasy 24 hours for the organization.

During it all, Judge was on a flight to San Diego. His agent texted him to give him a heads-up that the rumor mill had gone crazy, and family members, friends, and teammates checked in to see if he had, in fact, made a decision. "It was funny . . . the one time I get to choose, I didn't get to choose," he later said on Mookie Betts's podcast.

When Giants officials saw the tweet, they had the same sinking feeling as when they had seen the lobby video.

Sometimes an incumbent needs a scare to bring a player back, and it had now happened twice to the Yankees. A few hours later, Judge returned to his comfort zone with the Yankees.

It was disappointing for the Giants but not that surprising. They knew it was an uphill climb the entire time but also that Judge was such a potential game changer that they had to be all in, even if they were likely to get hurt. "Look, Aaron is a Yankee, and I think he was born to be a Yankee," Webb said.

The Giants quickly pivoted to Carlos Correa, and that's when disappointment turned to embarrassment. The Correa chase provided an interesting dichotomy; after trying to get every detail right with Judge, the Giants simply offered Correa a deal he couldn't turn down. Six days after missing out on Judge, the Giants and Correa reached terms on a franchise-record 13-year, $350 million deal. They finally had their superstar, but the reports that night included an important caveat, three words that became infamous: *pending a physical.*

The Giants had failed others on physicals over the years, but they were always small deals. This was tied for the longest contract ever given to an MLB free agent, and after Correa went through a CT scan, X-ray, and MRI on his right ankle, the medical staff realized there was a problem. The file they had received from the Twins didn't include anything about the ankle because they had never looked at it. Correa had undergone surgery on the leg as a teenage prospect with the Astros, but he didn't believe it was a problem. The Giants, who were as well-versed as anyone after dealing with Posey's own leg injury years earlier, felt differently, and all of a sudden the length of the deal took on a very different feel.

Had it been a five-year contract, the risk would have been worthwhile. But 13 years was far too long, and the Giants felt strongly that the ankle would become a serious problem halfway through the deal. Ultimately it was an ownership call, and about three hours before a scheduled press conference at Oracle Park, the team announced a postponement of a whirlwind day that was supposed to end with a cable car ride in downtown San Francisco. What followed was perhaps the wildest month in free-agency history.

Correa quickly moved on, signing a deal with the Mets, who also failed his physical. Both teams checked in with the same foot specialist, one who primarily dealt with NFL players, and both came away with the same conclusion. As the Giants tried to make sense of it all, Zaidi met with his players over Zoom, accepting responsibility and taking questions from a confused group. Because of the sensitive nature of players' medicals, Giants officials could do nothing over the holidays but drop their hands and take all the punches. They were confident in their evaluation of the ankle, but that didn't ease the pain much. "I think the whole situation was really unfortunate," Zaidi said after Correa finally returned to the Twins for $200 million over six years. "And way more public than it should be if things are running in an ideal way."

The Correa debacle was more difficult than other near-signings for a number of reasons, including the fact that it became a public-relations nightmare on multiple fronts. Crawford had been at Disney World in Orlando when the Giants asked him to help recruit Judge, but he hopped on a flight and flew across the country. His weeklong family vacation was cut short, but nobody gave him a heads-up that plan B after Judge was a full-throttle chase of Correa. The best shortstop in franchise history found out about the agreement—and an apparent change of positions after 11 years—on social media, a communication mistake that angered teammates and fans.

More than anything, though, Correa hurt because he had said yes. Giancarlo Stanton, a star they chased in unsuccessful trade talks in 2017, had never given the organization a chance. Ohtani preferred the American League. Judge had at several points of the pursuit told Giants officials how impressive their pitch was, but ultimately he used the lure of his hometown team to pressure the Yankees.

But Correa had agreed to come, and it all fell apart in a shocking way. It was a finish nobody saw coming, but in the annals of Giants free-agency history, he doesn't quite stand out like the One That Got Away.

For all of the attention that was paid to the Lester chase, the Giants never really felt he was coming to San Francisco. Baer, Sabean, Evans, and Bruce Bochy flew to Atlanta to meet with Lester and Posey, who lived a few miles away, but it was pretty apparent he would choose the Cubs. As they walked out of the meeting, Bochy, as good a judge of body language as anyone in the sport, turned to the others and said Lester wasn't going to be a Giant.

Lester was high-profile, but over the years, the Giants had fallen just short on plenty of others, from Pudge Rodriguez to Zack Greinke. The first pursuit of Ohtani was a long shot, but the Giants did their best to stand out. Trainer Dave Groeschner laid out a plan for the Japanese superstar to pitch every six days and play the outfield. Bochy added a personal touch by learning some Japanese from bullpen catcher Taira Uematsu. But the Giants could tell Ohtani didn't love their plan to use him in the outfield, and he chose to play in Anaheim, where he could be a designated hitter.

The other target that off-season, Stanton, was also best suited to DH, but back then, he was an outfielder and the reigning NL MVP. The sides agreed to a deal that would send Stanton to San Francisco in exchange for Denard Span and minor leaguers Jacob Gonzalez and Andrew Suarez, with the Marlins potentially sending about $40 million over the next decade to help offset some of the $295 million left on his deal. But a week after meeting with the Giants at a hotel in Los Angeles, Stanton used his no-trade clause to rebuff them and the Cardinals and land in New York.

Falling short on Ohtani and Stanton helped usher in a new front office, and a few months in, Zaidi made a run at one of the game's best players. In just about every way, Bryce Harper was the perfect fit. He was just 26, making him the rare superstar who could chase another title with the existing core but also be around long enough to lead a future generation. While Harper had some of the worst numbers of his career at Oracle Park, he loved the atmosphere. Sure, he always found it chilly, but he had faced the Giants in the 2014 postseason and never forgot what it was like to play in front of that crowd.

The Giants were a late entrant in the sweepstakes, with Baer, Zaidi, and Bochy flying to Las Vegas to meet Harper, his wife, and agent Scott Boras at a casino near his home in early February. Years earlier, Harper had played on a travel team called the San Diego Stars that got field passes for a Padres game. He got to meet Bochy, and he remembered how all of his fingers disappeared in the former catcher's huge hands. When they met again in 2019, Harper told Bochy he would love to play for him, but he needed to know how long they might be together. He knew Bochy was going into the final year of his contract and had not announced his future plans. Harper's one shot at free agency was too big a decision for any uncertainty. "We had a great meeting. They're a great organization and they have been for a long time," Harper said. "The biggest thing for me was asking Bochy if he was going to be here, and he said no, he had just one year left. I think that was the thing that really scared me the most."

The question was still bouncing around Harper's head as he neared a decision a few weeks later. A night before it was announced, he called Crawford and asked about the team and the organization. He also asked if the shortstop had any insight into what the plan was after Bochy retired.

Nobody did at the time, and the next day, Harper reached a $330 million deal with the Phillies. The Giants had offered him $310 million over 12 years, and while they signaled to Boras that they could stretch higher if needed, there was a lot of ground to be made up because of the difference in state taxes. There was also another problem. "The key thing," Boras said, "is they were late to the event." Boras and Harper thought the meetings with the Giants went well, but they were always chasing offers from the Phillies and never caught up.

In a twist, the succession plan to Bochy ended up being to hire Kapler, who was Harper's manager in his first year in Philadelphia.

"You never know what's going to happen, right?" Harper said. "I love Philadelphia. I love where I'm at and I'm very happy with the decision. It came down to Philadelphia or San Francisco, and I just felt that for me and my family, it felt right that we were going to go to Philadelphia."

PART 4

HOMEGROWN

12
Buster Posey

John Barr had been in draft rooms for 23 years by the time Brian Sabean brought him up from Los Angeles to oversee amateur and international scouting. He was the scouting director in Baltimore when the Orioles picked Ben McDonald and Mike Mussina in back-to-back years, and during a decade with the Dodgers, he led the way in selecting Russell Martin, Jonathan Broxton, and many other future big leaguers. In the summer of 2009, he was inducted into the Professional Scouts Hall of Fame.

Barr had for years seen how the air could be sucked out of a room when a team's board emptied before it was their turn to make a selection. He also knew well the elation that would take over when it seemed everything had gone as well as it possibly could, and that's what he felt on June 5, 2008. When the draft was over, he walked up to Peter Magowan, who couldn't hide his excitement. Barr did nothing to temper it. "Peter," he said, "I think that's the greatest draft I've ever been a part of."

Barr and Magowan weren't the only ones in the room who were stunned by what had just transpired. With the fifth overall selection, the Giants drafted Buster Posey, a player they felt was the best in the country. And 32 picks later, they chose Conor Gillaspie, a Wichita State infielder who was a first-round talent and coveted enough that he was able to successfully negotiate a September call-up. In the third round, they selected powerful Texas Tech outfielder Roger Kieschnick. The Giants used their fourth-round pick on a UCLA shortstop named Brandon Crawford.

They had ended up with four of the top 20 players on their draft board, and as the Crawford pick was being turned in, Sabean turned to a trusted lieutenant and said out loud what many in the room were thinking: "We either had a great board or we're totally wrong."

San Francisco, of course, turned out to be well ahead of the pack that night. Gillaspie helped them win a playoff game, but they didn't end up getting much out of him or the oft-injured Kieschnick. As with any class, there were minor hits and surprising misses. But in Posey and Crawford, the Giants ended up with the two best players in the draft.

Posey nearly doubled the combined career Wins Above Replacement of the four players chosen in front of him, but for the Giants, his value went well beyond what he provided between the lines. The selection was a franchise-altering one in every way, and an incredible full-circle moment for Barr, who had kept an eye on Posey since he was a high school shortstop in Leesburg, Georgia.

Years before the draft, Barr had traveled to Fort Myers, Florida, for a Perfect Game Showcase. As he was leaving his room at the Hampton Inn one morning, he ran into Posey and his mother. Then a senior at Lee County High, Posey introduced himself and said he would be pitching and playing shortstop that night. Barr already knew who the young prospect was, and he promised to be watching from the stands. That was the first time he ever scouted Posey in person.

Barr continued to track Posey as he became a star at Florida State, and the two ran into each other again when Posey was playing in the Cape Cod Baseball League. When Posey asked if Barr would consider him in the first round the following summer, Barr smiled. He worked for the Dodgers at the time, and they would be picking 15th. Barr predicted that Posey would be gone long before the Dodgers would get a shot.

Barr was right about the Dodgers' fate, but a few months after he saw Posey, Sabean hired him away. As Barr settled in with the Giants and started preparing to make a crucial selection near the top of the first round, he couldn't stop thinking about Posey. He realized that in his new home, he would have a chance to draft him. "He was the guy all along," he said. "We were just hoping he would be there."

For as much as it seemed like fate at that point, Posey certainly did all he could to nearly scuttle those plans. He moved to catcher as a sophomore and a year later was the best player in the country, winning the Golden Spikes Award after hitting .472 and picking up six saves.

The Giants nervously watched the initial picks go by and breathed a huge sigh of relief when Tampa Bay selected shortstop Tim Beckham after weeks of debating whether to go with him or Posey. When the Pirates took Pedro Alvarez and the Royals selected Eric Hosmer, Giants officials broke out in smiles. The Orioles had taken catcher Matt Wieters with their first-round pick a year earlier, so this time they went with lefty Brian Matusz.

Barr had his guy, and two years later, the Giants had a rookie catcher leading them to their first title in 56 years. Posey went on to three of them, along with an MVP, Rookie of the Year Award, Gold Glove, and batting title. He made seven All-Star teams, and one day he'll give a speech in Cooperstown. It all started on that fateful day in 2008. Or maybe years earlier, when a promising 17-year-old bumped into one of the game's best scouts. When the Giants selected him, Posey immediately thought back to that first meeting. "It was meant to be," Barr said. "I really believe that."

In the worst moment of Posey's career, adrenaline took over. Or maybe it was stubbornness. Nobody is quite sure.

It was the 12th inning on May 25, 2011, and Posey had just been flattened at home plate. As Marlins outfielder Scott Cousins approached home on a sacrifice fly, he lowered a shoulder and slammed right into the game's best young catcher. It wasn't a baseball play—more like a linebacker flying in to try and dislodge a football as a running back hit the hole—and Posey knew right away that something was wrong. He slammed the dirt in front of the plate with his right hand and then attempted to crawl forward as trainers Dave Groeschner and Mark Gruesbeck raced from the dugout. Groeschner called for a cart to take Posey off the field.

"No," Posey said. "I'm walking off the field."

"Buster—" Groeschner started.

"I know," the catcher responded, "but I'm not getting on the cart."

The two trainers helped Posey off the field, his left leg bent at the knee so it wouldn't touch the ground. They hobbled through the dugout and took a break when they got out of sight of teammates and cameras. Then they slowly made their way up a long flight of stairs and to the clubhouse. The cart stayed behind the left-field wall.

"It was probably me being stubborn as much as anything," Posey said years later. "I don't think I understood that my foot was just dangling by the skin at that point."

X-rays taken at the ballpark confirmed Groeschner's worst fears. Posey had three torn ligaments in his ankle and a fractured fibula. Four days after the collision, he underwent a 90-minute procedure to stabilize and insert two screws in his lower leg. The Giants put on a brave face, but internally they all knew their repeat bid was over. They had lost not just their young leader behind the plate but also their cleanup hitter.

For Posey, the concerns went far beyond 2011. After doctors did tests and put Posey's leg in a splint, Groeschner drove him and his wife, Kristen, home. It was an emotional trip, one filled with questions about what was next, and when Groeschner glanced over at Posey, he could see the wheels spinning in his head. There was no question Posey would be back. But nobody could guarantee he would continue playing a position he had fallen in love with. "There was a lot of doubt," Posey said. "I had no idea if my ankle would allow me to get back in the squat or how it would feel blocking a ball."

Posey tried to be optimistic, but it wasn't hard to find reminders of how steep the climb ahead of him would be. Kristen was pregnant with twins at the time, and when they got home that night, Posey realized he couldn't make it up their house's stairs. A few days later, they decided to move. The rehab process would be difficult enough without having to hop up a staircase every day at home.

With the help of Groeschner, Posey attacked the rest of the summer and fall. When the Giants reported to camp the next spring, the only sign that something had happened was an ankle brace that he wore during batting practice. With every BP homer and bullpen session, he seemed to be nearing 100 percent, but behind the scenes, the Giants knew something still wasn't quite right. Posey was feeling pain when running to his left, a significant issue in a sport where all you do as you run the bases is make turns to your left. Sabean and Bruce Bochy kept asking Groeschner when the catcher would be cleared to play more often, and Posey started to wonder when he would finally feel like himself. "Turning to my left was difficult, I'd say up until a week to 10 days before the season started," he said. "And then luckily it just kind of got right at the right time."

Posey was behind the plate on Opening Day, catching Tim Lincecum and contributing a pair of singles. He hit .353 in his first month back, and in June he caught the only perfect game in franchise history. In July, 13 months after a career-threatening injury, he was voted an All-Star starter after garnering an NL-record 7.6 million votes.

The immediate success was somewhat surprising, but not to those who knew Posey best. Groeschner had watched as the 24-year-old altered his meal plan to make sure he didn't gain weight when he couldn't walk. He would instruct him to ride an exercise bike for half an hour and come back an hour later to find him still churning away. Posey examined every detail of his rehab, even meeting with the grounds crew to slightly alter the composition of the dirt around home plate. Heads groundskeeper Greg Elliott reworked the area, using black clay that soaked up water as a base, with a half-inch of brown clay on top, a mix that was softer on Posey's ankle but firm enough that he could still get his usual footing on throws down to second base. There was diligence to it all but also a competitiveness that was there long before the Giants handed in the draft card.

When Posey was a junior at Florida State, coach Mike Martin held him out of the lineup one day because of a tight hamstring. It was a meaningless game for a team headed for the NCAA Tournament, but Martin could feel Posey's eyes on his back the whole game. When the Seminoles got within two runs in the ninth, he turned and saw Posey staring at him. Martin finally gave in. Posey was sent up to pinch-hit and lined the second pitch he saw for a game-tying single. "The thing is," Martin said a few years later, "Buster doesn't know how to play a meaningless game."

Thanks to their star catcher, the 2012 Giants wouldn't either. Posey's return from injury was the best year of his career, and he led the Giants to a second title, turning it up a notch after the unexpected loss of Melky Cabrera. Following Cabrera's suspension, Posey hit .351 with a .975 OPS. When Cabrera asked that MLB disqualify him from the batting title, Posey became the first NL catcher in 70 years to win it. A year after he needed help just to walk, Posey ran away with the MVP award, picking up 27 of 32 first-place votes. "It was just a really unique year, because I had such a great perspective," he said. "I was happy to be on the field. Obviously to win an MVP and win a World Series is a dream come true, but honestly I feel like I could have had a very average year and it would have been a success in my eyes just to be back on the field."

In addition to the marquee awards, Posey was named the Comeback Player of the Year, an award he would win again in his final season. In the nine years in between, he left an indelible mark on the organization.

A few days into Ty Blach's career, a veteran walked into Bochy's office with an odd question. "Is this kid for real?" he asked. Blach was as nice and earnest a prospect as any of the longtime big leaguers had ever come across, and after three short appearances in September 2016, the Giants tabbed the rookie to start their biggest game of the year, an opportunity he was grateful for.

The Giants had a one-game lead over the Cardinals for the final playoff spot as they came to the ballpark on the season's final Saturday, but they had Blach, in his second career start, going up against a three-time Cy Young Award winner. As Blach sat down for a pregame meeting, Posey did his best to calm any nerves. "This is a great day for the Giants to clinch the postseason," he told him. "And for Ty Blach to get his first career win against Clayton Kershaw."

Blach went out and became the first Giants rookie in three decades to throw eight shutout innings against the Dodgers, leading the way in a stunning 3–0 win while never shaking his catcher. There were a couple of times, however, when he was tempted to.

In that pregame meeting to go over the scouting report, Blach was told not to even think about throwing a fastball away to Yasiel Puig, the Dodgers' most dangerous hitter. When Puig came up in the second inning, Blach looked up and saw Posey calling for an 0–1 fastball away. As he tried to sort through his confusion, Posey seemed to sense that the rookie was running through those pregame instructions in his mind. He put his finger back down and wiggled it. Blach hit his spot and Puig popped up softly down the first-base line. In the seventh, Posey called for the pitch again. Puig took it for strike three. "After the game, I was like, 'Buster, what was that?'" Blach recalled. "He was like, 'I just saw something.'"

There are five statues around Oracle Park representing Hall of Famers, and Posey will get one at some point too. The only question is what it will depict. The joyous Buster Hug, seen after

World Series wins and no-hitters is perhaps his most famous image. That simple swing that drove so many balls onto the center-field grass is a great candidate. Perhaps the Giants could capture Posey as he watched his grand slam soar into the seats in Cincinnati in 2012. The statue could be placed in front of a painting of disgusted Reds catcher Ryan Hanigan, who knew right away that his season was over.

But the most appropriate pose might be more subtle. It would be Posey in an athletic squat, his glove resting on his left knee as he glanced up at a hitter. His mind would be moving a mile a minute, because for as much pregame preparation as he did, the real work started once the opponent dug into the batter's box. That's when he would truly read intentions and adjust as needed. Posey wasn't sure when he started doing it, and he wasn't even really sure exactly what he was looking for. But as he thought of what pitch to call next, sometimes he would pick up on a cue. The obvious ones were where a hitter was standing, but Posey would study faces and body language to see whether an opponent looked locked in or anxious. Every piece of information could be used to get his pitcher through an inning.

The pose was that of a man who was in full control of his surroundings and ready to lead his teammates. Posey did so by setting an elevated bar for himself that raised the floor for everyone else, and those who knew him in high school and at Florida State can't remember a time when it was any different.

When Posey started his first full professional season with the San Jose Giants, Kevin Frandsen's parents were his host family. Frandsen's father was a longtime basketball coach and watched closely as the 22-year-old catcher began his journey to the big leagues. One day, he pulled his son, a Giants infielder, aside. "Kevin, I know leadership. I know leaders. That's different than a leader," he said of Posey. "That's the president. He could run for office right now."

It surprises nobody who knows Posey that he is the rare athlete who could quickly transition into an ownership position just a year after retiring, and two years later he became the club's president of baseball operations. It was a new challenge for a man who spent years helping others reach greater heights. Just about every pitcher who has thrown to Posey has an example of a time when he helped shape his career.

For Derek Law, that moment came one pitch into his first bullpen session in big-league camp. Posey left his spot catching Madison Bumgarner so he could introduce himself to the young right-handed reliever and let him know, "You're going to pitch big innings for us." Posey did the same that spring for Chris Heston, who had to find a way to keep his nerves in check when the catcher moved over to his slot in the bullpen at Scottsdale Stadium—and then Bochy and Sabean stood on either side of Posey. A year later, the right-hander didn't shake off Posey a single time as he no-hit the Mets.

It wasn't just young pitchers who felt the impact, either. Kevin Gausman was in his ninth big-league season when he pitched to Posey for the first time, and a few weeks into the season, he took a shutout into the ninth inning at PNC Park in Pittsburgh. Gausman gave up a couple of hits before getting pulled by manager Gabe Kapler, and the Giants went on to blow the lead and lose in extra innings. Afterward, Posey respectfully told Gausman that he needed to know when he wasn't at his best. "It was hard for me to hear at first, and it took me a couple of minutes of sitting at my locker to realize that he was right," Gausman said. "I was gassed, and we could have been sitting there with a win if we had called our closer. He was so good at being able to recognize the other side of the situation in the moment."

It was the kind of tough love that helped the Giants get through a 107-win season, but Posey wasn't just there for leadership when he returned from an unexpected year off. He made the All-Star team and returned to his prime form on both sides of the ball. After years of dealing with injuries, he looked like himself again, and he carried a heavy load on and off the field for a team that was in a dogfight for six straight months.

Only after it was over did his teammates get a true understanding of what was happening. Posey, they realized, was emptying the tank in every way.

There were no positives to the injury Posey suffered in 2011, but there was a silver lining. The twins Kristen was carrying arrived in the middle of August, and while their father was in a walking boot, he was by then able to get around and take in all that comes with being a first-time dad. Nine years later, Posey found himself doing that again, in a very different situation.

The Poseys had spent years trying to add to their family via adoption, and as COVID-19 shut the world down in 2020, they matched with a set of twin girls who were born as the Giants prepared for a shortened season. After a few days of camp, Posey announced that he would be opting out to care for his four children, including two girls who had just been born prematurely. It was an easy decision for Posey, but that didn't mean he wasn't anxious to return. As soon as the off-season started, Posey called director of hitting Dustin Lind and told him he wanted to get started earlier than usual, with specific goals in mind. He would return the next season at the age of 34, and he wanted to be more explosive. Lind and strength coach Brad Lawson mapped out an ambitious off-season that relied heavily on methods that hadn't been as pervasive early in Posey's career.

There was an emphasis on heavier lifting and then a program to work on moving his body at a much faster pace. Posey swung with light bats and hit tennis balls to work on moving quickly. As the calendar turned to 2021, hitting coaches Donnie Ecker and Justin Viele added new drills, including one in which he hit left-handed to build speed on both sides of his body. A lot was also taken off the table.

One of the most remarkable parts of Posey's second comeback was how little was often required to keep him sharp. He was a dozen years into his career at that point and never took on-field batting practice. He would walk into the cage at 5:20 PM every night and take a few swings off a tee that was placed way out in front, a way to adjust the swing that had worked incredibly well for so long. For years, Posey had tried to stay back on pitches, but the new coaches worked with him on getting off his backside.

After the tee, he would hit a few soft flips and then attack the pitching machine. The work never lasted long. Posey knew himself too well to waste any energy that would be better expended during the game. "Sometimes he would take two swings and then leave," Ecker said. "He never really took more than 20. If he felt good, he would be like, 'I'm good. It's not going to get any better than that.'"

Posey pulled a homer over the left-field wall in Seattle in his first game back and the next night crushed an outside fastball to dead center. To the outside world it looked like he was all the way back, but he knew better. When the Giants visited Miami a few weeks later, Posey came up in a big spot and grounded out weakly on a fastball right down the middle. He was seeing the ball well, but something was wrong. He felt stuck on his backside. "I was just so frustrated," he said. "I told J. V., 'I'm going to feel like my back foot is coming off the ground. That's what I want my mind's eye to see is my back foot coming off the ground,' which is so different than the way I traditionally hit. I would stay on my backside and rotate, but when I did that, it just freed up my hips so much."

The swing that changed Posey's season came against a pitcher who was once supposed to join him as a franchise cornerstone. After the 2011 collision, the Giants traded top prospect Zack Wheeler in a failed attempt to bolster their diminishing title hopes with outfielder Carlos Beltran. A decade later, Wheeler, now the Phillies' ace, grooved a cutter and watched as Posey smoked it 428 feet. He crushed an elevated 98 mph fastball into the seats in left an inning later. The adjustments—which included standing more upright and lifting the starting point of his hands—had worked. "I can remember that moment in the cage," Posey said. "I was like, 'Whoa, the ball is actually coming off like it should be again.'"

Posey finished the year with 18 homers, his most in six years. His OPS was the second-highest of his career, and he won his fifth Silver Slugger Award and second Comeback Player of the Year Award. Almost everything about the organization had changed between the two, but when Posey returned, he picked up right where he left off. The new coaching staff quickly figured out that if someone was acting up or something needed to get done as a team, it was Posey, not Kapler, whom they should seek out.

Posey set a tone with a speech at the start of that season, and about a half dozen times over the course of the year, he approached the hitting coaches and said he wanted to speak during the daily hitters' meeting. The addresses were always short, sometimes just 20 seconds or so, with Posey reminding his teammates to stick to the team-first approach and keep the line moving. He always seemed to sense when the lineup was starting to veer off course, even by just a couple degrees.

The most impactful message might have been conveyed after one of the best wins of the season. The Giants stunned Dodgers ace Walker Buehler on *Sunday Night Baseball* in early September and took a one-game lead in the NL West. In an emotional clubhouse, Posey leaned over to a coach and whispered, "We can't have a letdown."

Members of the staff feared the ensuing road trip might be the week they finally fell behind the Dodgers, but Posey told his teammates that he knew they were tired but they needed to keep taking care of business. For six months, Posey had stuck to a strict two-games-on, one-game-off schedule, which was mapped out weeks in advance by Kapler. But with the division on the line, he played six straight games, the final one clinching his first NL West title since that first comeback.

It was a run that seemingly came out of nowhere, but in retrospect, Posey's resurgence makes plenty of sense. Before the season, he and Kristen decided they were at peace with 2021 being his final season. Both sets of twins were getting older, and Posey was eager to join their busy schedules. The physical challenges of the game had stripped him of some of his enjoyment, and he feared hanging on for too long. He had seen others grow bitter with how their own careers ended. Posey was content with going out when it seemed he had plenty left to give. "If I had not had a good year, I probably would have had an inkling to want to go back and at least try to finish on a high note," he said. "It was nice to finish on that high note and also feel like, *Okay, this is the right move for us.*"

Posey made 102 starts in the field during that final season, all of them behind the plate. He had spent plenty of time at first base in his prime, a way for Bochy to keep his bat in the lineup, and because he once played all nine positions in a college game and had grown up as a shortstop, it was often easy to wonder if he might ultimately end his career fielding grounders at one of the corners. Posey himself had to ponder that in 2011, but ultimately he finished his career the way he started it. He was one of the best catchers the game had ever seen, and that's how he went out. "It meant a lot," he said. "It's a position I really didn't start playing until later in life, my second year in college, but it's one that I came to love, and I'm happy that I got to do it as long as I did."

13
Will Clark

The assignment on Will Clark's first day in the big leagues could not have been tougher, but after just one pitch, he broke into a wide smile.

Clark had never faced a pitch as hard as Nolan Ryan's fastball, and when he walked up to the plate at the Astrodome on April 8, 1986, that's what he was looking for. When Ryan threw him a first-pitch curveball, Clark was stunned. Astros catcher Mark Bailey was too, but not by the pitch selection. He wanted to know why a 22-year-old was so giddy as he faced one of the most intimidating pitchers in the history of the game.

"What are you smiling at?" he asked.

"The Express is throwing me curveballs!" Clark replied, his eyes wide.

Two pitches later, Clark did get his fastball—and he didn't miss. He crushed the ball to dead center and broke into a sprint. Center field at the Astrodome was a graveyard, and he was just hoping the ball would smack the wall. It cleared easily, and the rookie started to glide around the bases.

Clark touched the plate and looked up in the seats to find his parents. He clapped his hands and dramatically pointed up at them before strolling back into the dugout, where 24 jaws remained dropped. "When he hit that everybody, collectively, in unison, went, 'Who the fuck is this guy?' Because that doesn't happen in the Astrodome. It doesn't happen against Nolan Ryan," said Mike Krukow, that day's other starting pitcher. "He floats around and he gets to the plate and does the point, and a star was born. The legend began that day."

As Clark sat down on the bench, he felt a calm come over his whole body. It was a sensation he had felt before and would feel many times during his big-league career, always in big moments. He was preternaturally comfortable in the spotlight, even as a rookie, but as he sat there, he started thinking about something else. Veteran Chili Davis was sitting to his left, and Clark looked over at him.

"Chili, he's going to drill me the next time up, isn't he?" Clark asked.

"Oh, hell yeah," Davis replied.

It's a sequence that remains crystal clear to Clark decades after it happened, and he's not the only one. Clark's debut was as memorable as any in franchise history, and it was a crucial turning point for an organization that had lost 96 and 100 games in back-to-back seasons, the former giving them the No. 2 overall pick in the 1985 draft, which they used on the sweet-swinging, brash first baseman from Mississippi State.

Krukow dreaded the start of camp the next spring, figuring that much of the focus would be on rehashing the only 100-loss season in the history of a franchise that had been around for a century, but Clark sucked the pessimism out of the room. He was immediately at ease in front of microphones and cameras. He was as cocky as a player who had not even made his big-league debut could possibly be, but the veterans didn't mind. It was a needed breath of fresh air, and Clark knew when not to cross a line.

Every rookie goes through some hazing, and the ones who stand out get it worse than others. One day, veterans took orange paint to Clark's fancy boots, adding a Nike swoosh to one and an Adidas logo to the other. Krukow later found out that the boots had been a gift for making the 1984 Olympic team, but Clark took the prank in stride. The veterans wanted to see how he handled himself, and Clark broke into a wide grin. It was clear the cocky rookie was going to fit in, partly because he didn't view it as cockiness. For Clark, it was just self-confidence, and it was hard to blame him.

Clark hit .287 as a rookie, and a team with no expectations finished with a winning record. The next year, the Giants reached their first postseason in 16 years, and two years later they were in the World Series for the first time in nearly three decades. Years later, as Krukow watched a dynasty form, he often thought back to that first day in 1986. He thought of Clark as he stepped up to speak to tens of thousands at city hall after the first title in 2010. From day one, Clark had changed the culture of an entire organization. Krukow credits him with making it cool to be a Giants fan again. "In 1986 we got everybody back on board, and it was the most powerful thing I've ever seen," he said. "It carried into '87 and then '89. We were back. He brought us back."

It started with one swing—one very memorable swing.

When the pandemic shut down the sports world and made face-to-face interaction difficult, Clark needed to find a new way to connect with a kid he was mentoring. The lessons weren't getting through, so one day Clark set up a tee in front of a 2001 Buick LeSabre in his garage and recorded a few swings on his phone. He was 56 years old, but the rhythm was still there and the swing had not changed at all. If you closed your eyes and listened to four cracks of the bat that sounded like gunshots, you could easily picture Clark lining RBI doubles into the gap at Candlestick Park.

Occasionally, in his role as a roving instructor for Giants minor league affiliates, Clark would find that he couldn't get a prospect to fully grasp what he was trying to pass on. To demonstrate it, he would hop back in the cage and take a handful of cuts. He often was met with wide eyes. "That's what it's supposed to look like, right there," he would crack.

The smooth left-handed stroke is one of the most famous swings in MLB history, and one of the closest to perfection. Few have ever made it look easier than Clark. "There was no tension," explained Dusty Baker, who was one of Clark's first hitting coaches in the big leagues. "Will, he had the most tension-free swing damn near of anybody."

It wasn't always that way for Clark, who was born and raised in New Orleans. But the game did always seem to come easy to him. He played in the Babe Ruth Baseball World Series when he was 15, and a year later he reached the American Legion World Series and helped Jesuit High School win a state title. Clark hit 10 home runs in just 14 games as a junior, but as he prepared for his senior year, he knew he needed to make some tweaks. He worked with a local hitting instructor named Barry Butera, who had once won a Triple A batting title with a Boston Red Sox affiliate. Butera found Clark to be the quickest learner he had ever worked with, and the minor tweaks led to big results. Clark initially stood right on top of the plate and had an approach that he described as "bailed and wailed." But Butera backed him off the plate and closed his stance. Immediately, Clark found that the middle of the field had opened up.

One of the game's most famous swings was born, and it carried Clark through successful runs at Mississippi State and with Team USA at the 1984 Olympics. His numbers jumped off the page, but it was a batting practice session that might have been most responsible for changing the course of the Giants in the 1980s. Team USA played an exhibition at Candlestick Park, and Giants general manager Al Rosen found himself intrigued by Clark's BP session. "What's your name, young man?" he asked Clark. "The ball makes a different sound coming off your bat."

The Giants selected Clark, finally fulfilling his lifelong dream that would have come true three years earlier had the Kansas City Royals just met a simple demand. The Royals drafted him in the fourth round out of Jesuit, and during negotiations, Clark asked that they pay for college, since at the time he intended to go back to school one day and get a degree in petroleum engineering. The Royals balked, Clark went to college for three years, and the Giants were the ones to strike gold.

Clark ended up getting more than 7,000 at-bats in the big leagues, but he took just 246 in the minors. He had just turned 22 when the Giants called him up, and the Ryan homer vaulted him to a strong rookie season. He hit 35 homers in 1987 and helped the Giants win the division, and a year later he hit 29 more and led the league in RBIs and walks. But Rosen wanted more. He called Clark into his office after the season and said he was hitting too many ground balls for a No. 3 hitter. Clark had never seriously altered the swing Butera had seemingly helped him perfect, but he took Rosen's words as a challenge, spending the off-season making changes with Baker.

For as good as Clark was in those three years, he knew he was getting caught in-between on fastballs. His first move was to stand straight up and then rock back, and often that kept him from being on time. Baker cut that whole move out, instructing Clark to rock back and forth on his front foot as a mechanism to find his timing against pitchers. The buttery swing seemingly was perfected, and over the next five years, Clark continued to be one of the league's most consistent hitters while providing two of the most memorable hits for that generation of Giants fans: a grand slam off Greg Maddux at Wrigley Field and a two-run single later in the series that helped the Giants win the 1989 pennant. Clark was 13-for-20 in the NLCS and won MVP honors.

The franchise's resurgence was seemingly complete. The Giants weren't just a threat again, they had a legitimate shot to finally bring a title to San Francisco. A year after Clark was taken second, a young third baseman named Matt Williams was drafted with the third pick, giving the Giants two of the league's best hitters at the corners. Another slugger was on the way, but Clark soon found that for all he had done to turn fortunes around, he was on the way out.

Throughout the 103-win season, which ended with the Giants missing the playoffs by one game, Clark tried to negotiate an extension. But the Giants were losing money and still trying to recover from nearly moving to Tampa Bay. They later would trade Williams because it was too cumbersome to carry both his salary and Bonds's, but first, it was Clark who felt the squeeze. Ownership made it clear he should focus on free agency, and Clark signed with the Texas Rangers on a five-year deal, two years more than the Giants were willing to guarantee.

The sweet swing never stopped producing, and Clark finished with a .303 batting average over 15 seasons, with 284 home runs and an .880 OPS. It wasn't enough for the Hall of Fame, which initially kept the Giants from retiring his popular No. 22 jersey, but when Barry Bonds got that honor, the door was opened for Clark, who had done more than enough to join him.

He never won a title as a Giant, but it's not hard to connect the dots from his generation to the one that paraded down Market Street. The Giants nearly left town a decade before Clark arrived, and they nearly left again after he had been there for a few seasons. The situation was so tenuous in the early 1990s that every win and slice of momentum seemed to matter. Clark made up more of that pie than anyone else. "If Will's not here, we're gone," Krukow said. "That was a big motivation for Peter Magowan keeping them here."

In 2010 Clark watched his first franchise beat his second one, finally winning it all. He did so with immense pride. "We got this thing turned around," he said, "but they put the nail in the coffin."

On July 30, 2022, No. 22 finally went up on the wall at Oracle Park. Willie Mays and Bonds were among those who helped the Giants celebrate, but the day was particularly meaningful for Krukow, who had let Clark live in his guesthouse as a rookie and watched one of the game's brightest young stars play Wiffle ball with his kids in the backyard. Krukow proudly announced that Clark deserved to "be remembered with the storied immortals of this franchise forever."

When it was his turn to take the microphone, Clark delighted the crowd with a gracious and emotional speech that led to a thunderous finish. "I am Will 'the Thrill' Clark," he yelled as the crowd roared. "I am part of San Francisco. And

I am forever a Giant." It was a flash of the type of energy that helped turn a franchise around, and a few minutes later, in a much quieter setting, he flashed the grin that was always there, even in that very first at-bat. "This," he said, "is my Hall of Fame."

14
Brandon Crawford

Three decades later, Lynn Crawford still smiles and shakes her head when she thinks of the photo. Her son would later take thousands of them with fans sitting in similar spots at ballparks, and for 14 summers he was on TV every night. But the photo that was taken of Brandon Crawford at Candlestick Park when he was just five years old remains one of the more famous images of his life.

The Giants were all set to leave San Francisco for Tampa Bay, and during that final series, the Crawford family went to say goodbye. Lynn took Brandon and his sister, Amy, to a game, and they both made signs. A day later, Mike Crawford took his son to what they thought would be their final Giants home game. A photographer from the *San Francisco Chronicle* caught Brandon leaning on the dugout rail, his hat turned backward and a Giants shirt tucked into red shorts. The look on his face said it all.

This is what the Giants were leaving behind, and when the *Sporting Green* came out the next day, Lynn's son was the face of the fan base's disappointment. "There he was, and my first reaction was, 'It looks like he's got ice cream on his shirt. You couldn't have cleaned him up a little bit?'" she said, laughing. "Oh my gosh, he looked a mess. And he looked so sad. He thought it was going to be the last day, and he was just so sad."

The boy from that photo was no different than any other five-year-old in the Bay Area. When he thought about what he would do when he grew up, Brandon Crawford wanted to be the shortstop for his hometown team. It was a dream millions of young boys across this country have had over the years, but few have ever lived it the way he did. All things considered, he might have had the coolest career of anyone ever to put on orange and black.

There were others who hit more homers or won more Gold Glove Awards. Crawford was worth nearly 30 Wins Above Replacement during his Giants career, but that didn't even give him bragging rights in his own draft class, not when Buster Posey was selected three rounds earlier. But nobody can match Crawford's story.

For 13 seasons, that young boy who wanted to be the shortstop of the San Francisco Giants got to do it better than anyone else ever has. He won two titles, made three All-Star teams, took home four Gold Glove Awards, and was a surprise MVP candidate during the best regular season in franchise history. He was so reliable at shortstop that he never moved, and when he said goodbye during an emotional final day at Oracle Park in 2023, he walked off the field having played 13,597⅔ innings as the Giants' shortstop, plus one scoreless inning on the mound, the latter being a goal he had chased for years. When Giants infielders gathered for their first drills of the spring, Crawford would take the mound for a few seconds and imitate teammates. In his mind, there was no doubt about what his second big-league position should be.

On paper, it would have been a phenomenal career had Crawford come to the Giants from Georgia or Texas or North Carolina, like the other stars of his generation. But he came, quite literally, from the organization's backyard. He fell in love with baseball at Candlestick and learned how to keep score at Scottsdale Stadium. Years before he became one of the most prolific autograph-signers in the game, he stood in those lines himself, extending a baseball and a pen. It seemed he was born to play baseball for the San Francisco Giants, and perhaps he was.

Mike and Lynn Crawford had Giants season tickets before they had children, and while Lynn was pregnant with their first child, they went to a game at Candlestick. A few months before Brandon Crawford was born, a foul ball landed in his mom's lap.

Late in his third year at UCLA, Crawford watched the first round of the MLB Draft on TV, wondering if a surprise was in store. His junior year hadn't quite gone as well as he had hoped, but he finished strong, and there was some thought that he could sneak into the end of the first round. That passed, and then the second round came and went, and the third. He saw other shortstops get called and knew he was better than them, and the disappointment started to set in. Then the phone rang.

A few picks into the fourth round, Crawford got a call from the Minnesota Twins. They wanted to know if he would sign if they selected him, and Crawford wasn't quite sure how to respond. He didn't want to slide any further but also didn't want to say yes right away, knowing he could always go back to UCLA and try to have a better year. As he was trying to figure out what to say, the Giants selected him with the fifth pick of the fourth round, nine spots ahead of where Minnesota was sitting. Crawford thanked the Twins for their interest and then hung up. It had been a difficult day, but he had a smile on his face.

"There was obviously a lot of disappointment about falling that far, and at the time you think that means everything—which obviously now I know that it meant very little—but there was excitement that it was the Giants," he said years later. "I couldn't believe that 30 teams had a chance to take me at least three times, and it ends up being the Giants. That part was really exciting for me and my family."

It was the realization of a journey that started when he learned how to crawl by trying to get to balls that were just out of reach. When the family got a plastic orange giveaway bat at a Giants game, he wouldn't let it out of his sight. It was so glued to his hand that on Halloween he was dressed as Bamm-Bamm from *The Flintstones*, which allowed him to make the bat part of his costume.

The early passion for baseball was stoked by yearly trips to spring training. Lynn would require that he make a book during every trip, which included research on players, facts about the state of Arizona, a page to keep score, and another page for autographs, which she hoped would encourage her shy son to come out of his shell a bit. Every hour that wasn't spent at school was dedicated to imaginary baseball games in the backyard. Crawford was a gifted soccer player as a child and would go on to play three sports at Foothill High, quarterbacking the football team, but there was never any doubt about which way he was leaning. "He said he was going to be a shortstop for the Giants by the time he was in first grade," Lynn said. "That was just the plan."

In that fourth round, Crawford finally became a Giant. Well, kind of. It was a stressful summer for team executives, who had to wait until the very last minute to reach an agreement with Posey, and Crawford took nearly as long. He was thrilled it was the Giants that finally called his name but was also confident that he could play his way into the first round if he went back to UCLA. Had the Twins been the ones to make the pick, it was much more likely that he ultimately would have ended up back at school, but it was the Giants, and that was impossible to turn down.

The first thing that everyone remembers is how quiet it got. The roar at PNC Park dissipated so quickly that it almost seemed someone had a remote control and clicked mute on 40,000 fans. The ballpark had been so loud in the early innings of the 2014 NL Wild Card Game that Giants outfielders couldn't hear each other calling for the ball and relievers sitting in the dugout had a hard time carrying conversations, but as Crawford rounded the bases in the fourth, all anyone could hear were the screams from the Giants family section.

Crawford reached the big leagues with his glove, and that reputation never changed over the years. He won three straight Gold Glove Awards in his prime and added a fourth in 2021, when he was so productive on both sides that he finished fourth in NL MVP voting at the age of 34. That season showed off just how far he had come at the plate since his rookie year, which ironically is remembered for a grand slam in his big-league debut. Three years later, he would do it in a much bigger spot.

With the bases loaded in a scoreless game, Crawford got a hanging curveball from right-hander Edinson Volquez and spun on it. He later joked that he was just trying to get a ball deep enough that Pablo Sandoval could score from third, but the ball kept carrying and carrying as he became the first shortstop in MLB history to hit a postseason grand slam. Madison Bumgarner did the rest that night.

A few months earlier, as Crawford slumped, the coaching staff quietly had conversations about giving some of his at-bats to rookie Matt Duffy. But as he often did, Crawford played his best baseball with his back against the wall. He hit nearly .300 the rest of the way.

Crawford was as competitive as any Giant, even if the fire burned in a less visible way. Giants executives learned that soon after drafting him. When Crawford was in A ball, he made a diving attempt on a foul ball and nearly slammed his head into a fence. What stood out wasn't the effort but the fact that he had made it in the eighth inning of a game his team trailed by 13 runs. A few years later, Bochy said publicly at the end of camp that he might sit Crawford against left-handers. The shortstop wore out left-handed batting practice pitcher Chad Chop, and when he hit a walk-off against hard-throwing Colorado Rockies lefty Rex Brothers a few weeks later, Bochy laughed and said he had changed his mind. Nearly a decade later, Crawford fought off a similar attempt from a different regime.

There was never a threat to his other main role at Oracle Park. For nearly his entire Giants career, Crawford was the clubhouse DJ, responsible not just for pregame music and batting practice soundtracks but also victory playlists for teams that did a whole lot of winning. Every version included "Bounce It" by Juicy J, which might have secretly been played at Oracle Park nearly as often as Tony Bennett and Journey.

Crawford hit 146 homers with the Giants, 24 of which came in 2021 when his career year helped the Giants upset a heavily favored Dodgers organization that he had been taught at an early age to dislike. He drove in 744 runs, 8 coming in a 2019 game, when he became the first shortstop in MLB history to record five hits and eight RBIs and tied Mays and Orlando Cepeda for the most runs driven in by a Giant in one game. That huge day came three years after he tied a National League record with seven hits in one game.

By far the most impressive number, though, was the one in the *games played* column. Even though he didn't become the full-time shortstop until 2012, Crawford led the NL in starts at the position in the 2010s. Every spring, the staff talked about finding more opportunities to rest Crawford. And every summer, his defense proved too important to take him off the field. Bochy once admitted he sort of forgot to find breaks for Crawford during seasons, but the shortstop wouldn't have wanted them anyway.

Crawford's shoulder acted up in 2014, and there were multiple springs when it seemed throwing might be a problem, but it never cost him time. During one two-week stretch before he was named an All-Star in 2018, he got treatment on his oblique, hamstring, knees, triceps, neck, and forearm, but none of the ailments kept him out of the lineup. One summer, he sprained two fingers on his throwing hand and responded by lifting his index finger off the bat when he swung. He might have spent more time with trainer Dave Groeschner than anyone else, but when the first pitch came around, he was always ready. Over his first 10 seasons, Crawford went on the Injured List just once, an impressive feat for any player but especially a 6'2" shortstop who seemed to hit the dirt at least once a night.

It all added up to 1,682 games and 6,318 regular-season plate appearances for the team he grew up rooting for. Three decades after he leaned on a railing at Candlestick Park and thought about his favorite team leaving for good, Crawford joined the two best players in franchise history—Bonds and

Mays—as the only San Francisco Giant to make 12 straight Opening Day starts at the same position.

At the end of the 2023 season, the Giants said goodbye to their longtime shortstop, whose final day started just like all of the others in orange and black. Crawford never lost his love of fielding grounders, and on his final morning, he walked out onto the dirt to field a few more from longtime coach Ron Wotus. As always, he brought out some flash for the final one. Then he signed a few autographs near the dugout, something he might have done more often than any player in franchise history. Crawford never forgot how cool it felt to gather his own signatures while waiting for players to walk out of the clubhouse at Scottsdale Stadium. "He noticed how some players were so nice and some were not," Lynn said. "I'm sure it registered in his head that when—not *if*, because this was always the plan—he was in this position, he was going to be somebody that was nice to these children."

The Crawfords had five of their own, and four of them took the field that last day to throw out ceremonial first pitches to their father. Nine innings later, he walked off the field trailing only Bonds, Mays, and Willie McCovey in appearances as a San Francisco Giant.

"A dream come true doesn't quite cover it," he said.

PART 5

THE ACES

15

Tim Lincecum

The life of a scout is spent on the road—in Marriotts, airports, and rental cars—all in search of the next big thing. It's a life Brian Sabean embraced when the Yankees hired him in 1984, and within two years he was the organization's director of scouting. Sabean, like all former scouts, has been on more airplanes than most could ever dream of. But the most important flight of his career might have been one he *didn't* take.

As the 2006 draft approached, Dick Tidrow went to Washington to get another look at a diminutive right-hander who was somehow the most dominant pitcher in the country. The industry expected the Giants to have Cal pitcher Brandon Morrow at the top of their board, and they did have plenty of interest, but Tidrow's mind was made up when he spent a weekend watching Tim Lincecum.

The Washington junior struck out 16 and completely blew away the gruff director of player personnel, who was watching from different vantage points of the ballpark. Tidrow was a former pitcher who had 100 wins and 55 saves in the big leagues, and for two decades he had shown off as good a scouting eye as there was in the game—but this felt different. The arm speed. The stride. The athleticism. The way the fastball burst from his fingertips. It was a unique package, but Tidrow knew immediately that it was special. There was just one problem: he had to convince his boss not to come and see for himself.

Sabean wanted to scout Lincecum the next weekend, but on the morning of his flight, Tidrow begged him not to go. He insisted he had seen enough, and not just in the 130-plus pitches Lincecum had thrown against a lineup that would go on to win the College World Series. As he was leaving the ballpark, an area scout asked if he was going to stick around for Sunday's game. Lincecum, he said, would come out of the bullpen as the closer if the Huskies were winning. Tidrow stayed in town and watched everything Lincecum did in pregame warm-ups the next day. "I've never seen anything quite like it," he told Sabean. "Not only the uniqueness of the delivery and the way he approaches pitching but the athleticism. I saw this guy throw 130 pitches, and the next day he's doing long-toss foul line to foul line. He's doing front flips and backflips, and he comes in and closes the game."

Tidrow was convinced that Lincecum was the one for the Giants. He was also convinced that Sabean flying up to see for himself would tip their hand. Whether that was true or not didn't matter. Tidrow had seen enough, and Sabean trusted him. When the Giants took Lincecum 10th overall a few weeks later, Sabean approved the pick without having ever seen him pitch live. "I put so much faith and trust in Dick," he said. "He told me he could be a fast flame, but as soon as he's ready, get those innings in the big leagues."

Looking back, the curious thing about Lincecum's draft stock is that if you ignored his size and mechanics—which was nearly impossible given the risk-averse nature of most front offices—he checked off all the boxes of a traditional top pick. He led Liberty High School in Renton to a state championship, winning Gatorade Player of the Year honors after striking out 183 batters in 91⅔ innings. The lightning-quick arm was already delivering 94 mph fastballs—it just happened to be attached to a body that was 5'9" and 135 pounds.

A year later, Lincecum became the first to be named both the Pac-10 Freshman of the Year and Pac-10 Pitcher of the Year. He led the league with 161 strikeouts, 13 of which came in a win over No. 1 Stanford. Two days before that game, he came out of the bullpen to pitch the final two frames of an extra-innings win. After his sophomore year, Lincecum posted a 0.69 ERA in the prestigious Cape Cod Baseball League, striking out nearly two batters per inning and holding some of the country's best prospects to a .104 average. He broke the Pac-10 career strikeouts record as a junior, finished with a 1.94 ERA, and won the Golden Spikes Award, given to the best amateur player in the country.

By any measure, Lincecum was the most dominant player in college baseball, but on draft day he waited as four other right-handers went in the first five picks. Luke Hochevar, who had reneged on an agreement the previous year, went first overall to the Royals. Collegiate right-handers Greg Reynolds and Brad Lincoln were second and fourth to the Rockies and Pirates, respectively. That set up what seemingly was a no-brainer.

Lincecum had grown up half an hour away from the Mariners' ballpark and stayed local for college. He was right in their backyard, but they chose Morrow, a right-hander who was pitching in the Giants' backyard. It was a nerve-racking few minutes for the Giants, who hadn't been able to get a read on how Mariners GM Bill Bavasi and scouting director Bob Fontaine were leaning. Years later, Lincecum's father, Chris, called that brain trust "idiots." Morrow ended up primarily being a reliever in Seattle before he was traded away. Bavasi was fired two years after the draft.

The Giants had interest in left-handers Andrew Miller and Clayton Kershaw, but they went to the Tigers and Dodgers, the latter of whom had Tim Lincecum high on their board in case they missed out on Kershaw. Baltimore, selecting ninth, reportedly took Lincecum off their board altogether because of concerns about his size. That left the Giants. "It was an easy call," Sabean said.

After signing, it didn't take long for Lincecum to make it clear to his new coaching staff that he was different—and not just on the field. He was taken into the clubhouse that first day and met pitching coach Dave Righetti, who looked up and saw a fresh-faced kid dressed like a skateboarder, with a backpack slung over his shoulder. The stressed-out staff was in the middle of another losing season, but Righetti couldn't help but smile when his future ace introduced himself. "He walked in and said, 'Hey, dude,'" Righetti recalled later, laughing. "We're pounding our heads against the wall trying to get better, and here he comes: 'Hey, dude!' I said, 'Oh, this is going to be interesting.'"

Righetti was already somewhat familiar with Lincecum. He wasn't generally involved with the draft process, but Lincecum was such a distinctive pitcher that the amateur scouting staff brought the pitching coach and bullpen coach Mark Gardner in one day to watch some of his clips at Washington and give thoughts on his delivery. The next year, Righetti got to introduce the first-rounder to his new manager. When Bruce Bochy went out to the field one day, Lincecum was playing catch. Righetti pointed him out. "I had heard about him, obviously, but I didn't know he was that small," Bochy said. "And then you saw him throw, and you knew he was special."

Bochy had not spent much time with Sabean, but he quickly learned he had some very specific beliefs about how to handle prospects. One of them was you don't waste your bullets in the minors if you're ready, and as Lincecum started to get comfortable in his first spring training, there were many within the organization who wanted him to go straight to the big leagues on Opening Day. Everything about what they were watching felt different. Even his bullpen sessions drew huge crowds.

The hype continued to build once Lincecum was sent to Triple A. The Giants knew his stuff was good enough for the big leagues, but they had some initial concerns about his command. In Fresno, it became clear that the quality of his pitches would carry him no matter where they were located. In five starts, Lincecum threw 31 innings and allowed just 12 hits and one run while striking out 46. He was so overpowering that teammates would see opposing hitters smile as they ran down the line after hitting grounders. Just making contact was a victory. Lincecum also showed off the competitiveness that would become one of his hallmarks. "The guys that would get a hit—you would look at Timmy, and he was almost like, 'I'm going to absolutely destroy you the next time,'" said former Giants infielder Kevin Frandsen, who came up with Lincecum. "He had that killer in him, but it took a little bit for it to come out. People didn't realize it."

It took just a few weeks for the Giants to make a call. On May 6, 2007, Lincecum made his highly anticipated MLB debut, and while the first start was rough, it wasn't long before he started to live up to outsized expectations. He went seven strong at Coors Field in his second start, and five days later he struck out 10 in a win over the Astros. The Giants were headed for a last-place finish, but a superstar was taking over the Bay Area in front of their eyes, albeit in his own way.

As teammates were getting to know their new right-hander, they would marvel at how he would sit in a catcher's squat in his clubhouse chair as first pitch approached, seemingly oblivious to the fact that he was well behind a normal starting pitcher's schedule. It led to some panicked moments for his coaches at first, until they realized it didn't take long for Lincecum to get loose and that he was much better when he did it his way. Before one of his first starts, Righetti watched as Lincecum ran down to the bullpen without playing long-toss, threw 13 warm-up pitches, and then turned around and headed for the dugout. "Holy shit," the coach said to those around him. "Is he ready?"

He always was in those early years. It was different, but it led to two of the best years in franchise history. In his first full season, Lincecum went 18–5 with a 2.62 ERA and a San Francisco Giants record of 265 strikeouts. He became the first Giant since Mike McCormick in 1967 to win the Cy Young Award and the youngest in either league since Roger Clemens in 1986. The next year, he went out and did it all again. This time he was 15–7 with 261 strikeouts, but he lowered his ERA to 2.48 and became the first player to win back-to-back Cy Young Awards in his first two full seasons.

Tidrow had been right. From the first time he laid eyes on Lincecum, he saw a shooting star, but he may have actually been conservative in his evaluation. The Giants had not just the best pitcher in baseball but someone to build a franchise around, and for an encore to the two Cy Young seasons, he would lead a title push with one of the most dominant performances in postseason history.

Lincecum made his playoff debut with a performance for the ages, one that got the Giants rolling toward their first title on the West Coast. He struck out 14 Braves in a two-hit shutout to kick off the NLDS, but that doesn't tell the full story of his dominance. Lincecum whiffed the side in the second inning on nine swinging strikes and had 31 of them in all, the most by a Giant in the pitch-tracking era. With the Giants holding a 1–0 lead in the ninth, he ended the historic night with two more strikeouts, becoming just the second pitcher ever to strike out at least 14 and allow two or fewer hits in a postseason shutout.

"It was one of those nights where the ball was just dancing," catcher Buster Posey said. "He was all over the plate with the fastball. I don't know if he could tell you that he knew where it would go—it would cut, it would run, it had some sink. And you couple that with the change-up that's falling off the table, and he's flipping in that curveball. It was a challenge just to catch but probably more to hit."

A few weeks later, Lincecum got the ball for the World Series clincher and struck out 10 over 8 innings as the organization erased decades of disappointment. At the time, it seemed impossible that he would make just one more postseason start, although perhaps that's the way it always had to be. His prime was otherworldly, but it wasn't meant to last long. By the time Lincecum was 28, he was fighting to hold his rotation spot, but the Giants would never forget what he had meant to them. They couldn't even if they tried.

Lincecum was such an outlier that when he hit arbitration, his agents argued that he shouldn't be compared to other pitchers but rather to MVPs Albert Pujols and Ryan Howard. When Giants officials walked into a hearing, they looked up and saw both Cy Young Awards sitting on a big wooden table, a not-so-subtle nod to what Lincecum had already accomplished.

They soon learned that he wasn't done. The Cy Young days were over, but he still had ways to contribute to title runs, and to delight a fan base that made him one of the most popular athletes in Bay Area history.

If it weren't for his size, it would have been hard to recognize the reliever who was leaning up against the chain-link fence in the visiting bullpen at Great American Ball Park. His hands were jammed deep into the pockets of a gray hoodie, which was pulled so tight over his head that you couldn't see the color of his hair or the logo on his hat.

But at 5'11" and about 170 pounds, there was no doubt about who the figure in the shadows was. And there was no way to misinterpret the look in his eyes. Lincecum wanted the ball. It didn't matter that he was no longer in the rotation, or that the role was unfamiliar. He wanted to pitch, and as he watched the early innings of Game 4 of the 2012 NLDS in Cincinnati, he did nothing to hide that desire from Bochy, who stood 350 feet away with a direct line of sight into the bullpen.

In the bottom of the fourth inning, Bochy finally made his move. The Reds put two on with two outs, and Lincecum jogged to the mound, where he paused to tie his laces. He fell behind to Ryan Ludwick, then threw two diving change-ups, getting out of the jam without breaking a sweat. Lincecum threw 55 pitches over 4⅓ innings that afternoon. He allowed two hits and one run, and struck out six. On paper, it was similar to what another Giants ace would do when he came out of the bullpen two years later in Kansas City. But there was very little about the two circumstances that matched up.

Madison Bumgarner was at the peak of his powers when he did it, but in 2012, Lincecum was no longer himself. By the end of his 10-year career, it was clear that his time in the big leagues could be neatly separated into two halves. He was the best pitcher in the world for the first half, but the second half was turbulent, and the nights were never tougher than in 2012.

Lincecum had made his fourth consecutive All-Star team the previous season, and while his velocity was dipping and some of the advanced metrics were starting to indicate his Cy Young days were over, the Giants still came to camp in 2012 with the expectation that he would lead the way. The results weren't there early on, but Lincecum still had more than enough stuff and moxie to dominate on occasion. For weeks, there would be "What's going on with Timmy?" questions before and after starts. But all it took was one throwback appearance, and the narrative would switch to "Timmy is back."

Lincecum lasted just 3⅓ innings in each of his final first-half starts, hitting the All-Star break with a 6.42 ERA. After a blowout loss to the Pirates, Bochy faced previously unthinkable questions about whether his Opening Day starter would begin the second half in the rotation. As the summer went on, Lincecum finally grabbed a bit of momentum. There were a couple more blowups along the way, but he pitched to a 3.83 ERA in the second half, helping the Giants reach the postseason and also giving Bochy and Righetti a difficult decision to make. When they formed a postseason rotation, the overall struggles outweighed everything else, but the former staff ace took the decision in stride, saying, "It's not about what you've done; it's about what you've done lately."

Instead of pouting, Lincecum joined the relievers for early workouts. He said he planned to run on adrenaline when his name was called, and for the rest of October, that's what he did. In an odd way, the move became freeing. Lincecum spent long days between starts in 2012 trying to figure out what was happening to him. But as a reliever, he could turn his brain off.

He had just a few minutes of warning before each outing, and he loved the spontaneity. It allowed him to embrace what he had done better than anyone earlier in his career: just grab the ball and dominate.

The Giants tested the waters in Game 2, throwing Lincecum out for two relief innings in a loss, and doing so amid confusion. He came in on a double-switch and didn't get a chance to warm up, but he was still better suited to do that than any pitcher in the world. He was sharp, finding his old rhythm and swagger. Bochy would use him four more times that month, with his new bullpen weapon striking out 20 and allowing just five runs over 17⅔ innings.

The season had started with Lincecum sharing an *ESPN the Magazine* cover with Kershaw. The two-time Cy Young Award winner had bragging rights over Kershaw, who had just won his first, and the cover photo featured Lincecum holding Kershaw in a headlock. The headline read, "Cy vs. Cy," although seven months later only one of them could still reasonably claim to be pitching like an ace.

Back in 2006, Tidrow had told Righetti there was a clock on Lincecum, and six years later, his prime was quickly coming to an end. But because he so easily took to the bullpen, Lincecum was able to win a second ring, and soon he would add two more lines to one of the best résumés of his generation.

Bochy met dozens of fathers over the years, and their request was almost always the same. They would shake his hand, look him in the eye, and give some variation of, "Hey, take care of my son," which he fully understood as a father of two boys, including a pitcher who would reach the big leagues. But the message from Chris Lincecum was different. "Don't worry about Timmy," he told Bochy. "I trained him. He can handle the workload."

Throughout Lincecum's prime, his father's prediction held up. He threw 227 innings in his first full season and surpassed 200 in each of his first four, making the All-Star team each time. Chris Lincecum was the creator of the unique delivery, teaching his son to use every hinge and lever from his toes to the tips of his fingers.

Chris had been an undersized pitcher himself and believed strongly in the fluidity of a delivery that at times looked violent. Once his son was in motion, every inch of his body was working to deliver the baseball with maximum force, with the legs, hips, upper body, and arm moving as one. The last element almost resembled a jump toward the plate and included an ankle kick that came naturally to Lincecum when he was learning how to pitch. That move catapulted him down the mound with a stride of more than seven feet.

The power came from it all being in sync, and the mechanics got the absolute most out of a frame listed at 170 pounds—or a pound or two heavier after a visit to In-N-Out, where in his early years he would occasionally put down three Double-Doubles, two orders of fries, and a chocolate-strawberry milkshake. But the focus on his delivery overshadowed a key fact about the skinny pitcher who would often get stopped by security as he walked into visiting ballparks: he was the best athlete on the roster. Chris Lincecum at times described his son as having the lean strength of a Greek god. "His mobility was unbelievable. He just had this quick-twitch power that you don't see a lot of guys have," trainer Dave Groeschner said. "He had a lot of balance to him. He didn't look like it because of his stature, but he would jump on counters, he would do handstands in the training room or weight room and walk across the whole room on his hands. He could get out of bed and jump up and do 50 pull-ups. There was really a lot of athletic ability that people didn't get to see because he was a pitcher."

There was also an ability to recover that would make even Wolverine jealous. When starting pitchers come out of a game, they go straight back to the trainer's room to get wrapped in ice. Some, especially the older ones, look like mummies, their shoulders and elbows wrapped until the ice starts to melt and drip down their forearms. That wasn't Lincecum. He never iced, joking that his father taught him it was for injuries or drinks. It was unorthodox, but it worked, and Groeschner and his staff never forced the issue. The only time they would even ask Lincecum to ice was if he got hit by a line drive or had some sort of contusion, and even then the pitcher had to be talked into it. "Pitching-wise and for his arm, he never iced," Groeschner said.

The Freak, as Lincecum was nicknamed, was a physical marvel, but there was only so much the body could give. As it was breaking down, though, Lincecum was able to summon his early brilliance for two memorable performances, both against the Padres.

On July 13, 2013, Lincecum took the mound at Petco Park with a 4.61 ERA. Nine innings and 13 strikeouts later, he had his first career no-hitter. The next season, he did it again, this time at Oracle Park. The performances showed off the unpredictable brilliance of baseball. In his prime, Lincecum had been the most unhittable pitcher on earth, but it was only on his way down that he was actually able to throw a no-hitter in the big leagues.

Lincecum joined Hall of Famer Christy Mathewson as the only Giant to throw more than one and became the first player to no-hit the same opponent in back-to-back seasons. The only pitchers who have ever won multiple Cy Youngs, thrown multiple no-hitters, and won multiple titles are Lincecum and Sandy Koufax.

The second one was about as stress-free as a no-hitter can get. His pitch count was never an issue, and unlike in most historic games, there was never a line drive or slow ground ball in the late innings that required a memorable defensive play. Lincecum even added a pair of hits of his own, and he was preternaturally calm the entire time. In the late innings, he kicked tradition to the side and openly chatted with teammates in the dugout, laughing and even mimicking his own running style on the bases. "I figure it's more awkward when they don't talk to you than when they do," he pointed out later.

The no-hitter at Oracle Park was the third in a remarkable run for the Giants. It started with Matt Cain's perfect game in 2012 and ended with Chris Heston's no-hitter in New York in 2015. The most stressful of the bunch, however, was Lincecum's first, a 148-pitch marathon on a rowdy Saturday night in the Gaslamp Quarter.

Lincecum had spent that season making adjustments, studying more between starts, and spending additional time in the weight room. For so long, he had been able to rely on the overpowering nature of his stuff, but his fastball topped out at just 92 mph that night. He still had the darting change-up, though—which he threw 43 times—and sharp breaking balls. It was clear early that he had the full arsenal working, and he struck out six straight at one point. There were 29 swings-and-misses but they came with a cost. He wasn't getting quick outs, and when he mixed in a couple of walks in the sixth inning, his pitch count climbed to 102.

In the dugout, Bochy and Righetti started a back-and-forth that would continue for three stressful innings. Bochy would lean back after outs and smile. "Should we go get him?" he would ask, knowing that neither was inclined to do so, and that Lincecum wouldn't allow it, anyway. "He wouldn't have talked to me the rest of the year if I took him out," Bochy said. "There was no chance."

Bochy and Righetti had been through so much with Lincecum, so many highs and lows. They did all they could to protect him by having a reliever ready to go as soon as he gave up a hit, but they also knew what finishing the no-hitter would mean to a superstar who had taken some lumps over the previous 15 months. Lincecum got through the seventh on a dozen pitches, and Hunter Pence's diving stab of a sinking liner ended the eighth. Lincecum pumped his fist, a look of determination on his face. He had just thrown his 131st pitch, but there was no turning back now. "He was getting better and better," Posey said. "That's a rarity in baseball. Once you get to the 100-pitch mark, it's usually time to shut it down."

Righetti checked on Lincecum before the ninth, but there was never any doubt. Lincecum felt fluid, not fatigued, even as he shot into unfamiliar territory. His jersey was drenched in sweat, but his final change-up of the night induced a routine fly ball to left. He finally had his no-hitter, although he had to dig deeper than anyone ever could have imagined.

The pitch count was the highest by a Giant in 24 years, and nobody in MLB has topped even 135 since. There's a decent chance that Lincecum will be the last ever to throw 140 pitches in a big-league game, but he treated that night the same as any other. From a young age, he had been built specifically for these moments. "No ice," he said the next morning, smiling. "Not even in the drinks I didn't have last night."

Bochy has never regretted it, noting that he doesn't think Lincecum would take anything back from his career. "It was something special," he said a decade later. "I'll never stop believing that." He watched with pride that night as a beaming Lincecum was lifted off his feet by a Buster Hug. Righetti had tears in his eyes as he stood in the dugout and took in the entire scene. He thought about how a man who had been at the absolute top of his game had handled the ensuing struggles with as much grace as anyone possibly could. "It was almost like a gift to him," he said. "He had done so much to revitalize the organization in a lot of ways. We were going to let him go until he gave up a hit, because he deserved it."

16
Madison Bumgarner

For the first two decades of the ballpark's existence, the press conference room at Oracle Park was located a few feet from the home clubhouse, directly across a hallway from the Lori Gardner Family Room, where wives, children, parents, agents, and friends wait after games. Until the explosion of the analytics staff caused a remodel of the clubhouse, the podium was located in a convenient spot for players and managers.

The small room sits on the path that leads directly to the players' parking lot, making for an easy exit. A door in the back corner leads to the clubhouse, which allowed Bruce Bochy to make it from his office to the podium in less than a minute. During the championship era, Bochy's trip back to his desk would take him past the lockers of Buster Posey and the Brandons, and he often would stop to go over details of a game.

The press conference room was not in a convenient spot for opponents, though. There were two ways to get there from the visiting clubhouse, located down the first-base line because Dusty Baker preferred that the Giants move to the other side—which had better sightlines—as the ballpark was being built. One path was a straight shot down a corridor, but it wasn't a rational option for postseason opponents since fans were still milling about long after games. The other required walking across the field and through the home dugout and then going up a long flight of stairs. It was there, a few feet from the Giants' batting cage, that Royals manager Ned Yost encountered Madison Bumgarner after Game 5 of the 2014 World Series.

Bumgarner had just thrown his second shutout in 26 days to give the Giants a series lead. Bochy could have gone to his bullpen by hitting for Bumgarner with one out and a 5–0 lead in the eighth, but that wasn't the way either man operated. The manager never let off the gas in the postseason. The ace never worried about what a few saved bullets might mean down the line.

Bumgarner took a called third strike, then turned to home plate umpire Hunter Wendelstedt. The pitch had been high, an inch or two above the zone. Even in that situation, the best-hitting pitcher of his generation wasn't thrilled to be robbed of a chance to take a massive cut at a fastball.

Bumgarner needed just 10 pitches in the ninth to finish the 117-pitch masterpiece, and he did an on-field interview that twice had to be stopped so he could wave his cap to 43,087 fans who had stayed to chant "MVP!" As the roar died down, Yost crossed the field for his press conference. He saw Bumgarner walking up the dugout steps. "Hey, kid!" he yelled. "Great game!"

Bumgarner didn't hear him, so Yost tried again. This time, Bumgarner turned around, and Yost congratulated him for a historic month. "You know what?" Yost said. "I sure am glad I don't have to see you again."

Bumgarner smiled and shook the opposing manager's hand. Game 6 was two nights away, and he already had thrown 47⅔ innings and 634 pitches that month. But he knew something Yost didn't. "I think I just laughed it off," he said later. "But I was thinking in my head, *Man, I don't know if that's so true or not.*"

Every winter, the Bumgarners would pack up and start the caravan to spring training. Team officials would hold their breath as FanFest approached, knowing the odds were much better that their star would drive to Arizona than San Francisco. It would be a break from his sprawling ranch in North Carolina, but home was never far from mind.

After signing out of high school, Bumgarner was initially sent to Scottsdale for the instructional league. The days there can be long and boring for young players, with not much on the schedule other than workouts in the morning. Bumgarner would stand in the outfield grass to shag fly balls and look up every time a Southwest flight flew over the field. He couldn't help but wish he were on the plane, which might get him closer to home. He called assistant general manager Bobby Evans after a few days and told him he was homesick. He wanted to fly back to North Carolina and see Ali, not find ways to pass the hours at the Days Inn. "Things are going to get better," Evans told him. "We're going to start games. Check in with me in a few days and let me know if it's any better."

The phone never rang again. Bumgarner adjusted by bringing some of Hickory to Scottsdale and San Francisco. It was easier to find items to lasso in Arizona, but in the Bay Area, he found creative ways to practice. During the 2010 postseason, the Bumgarners stayed with Jeremy Affeldt and his family. "He was lassoing my pool furniture," Affeldt recalled. "He made me run one time and he got me too." Affeldt got his revenge by making the young lefty bake oatmeal raisin cookies.

Bumgarner eventually found his way, but he never let stardom change the teenager who showed enough promise to be taken 10th overall in the 2007 draft. He remained committed to his early hobbies, so much so that years later, after he signed a lucrative deal with the Diamondbacks, it was discovered that he was team-roping under the alias Mason Saunders. A low point of his career came because of his love for riding dirt bikes, one of which landed him in the hospital three weeks into the 2017 season and cost him several months on the mound. His favorite restaurant was the House of Prime Rib, the perfect comfort spot for the couple that would later sell cuts of beef from their ranch. Bumgarner never lost the raw honesty that made him such a refreshing interview, even if the answers were often short, and more than one young reporter melted under his steely gaze after a loss.

His final season in orange and black was 2019, and throughout the first half, there was speculation that the new president of baseball operations, Farhan Zaidi, would deal the team's ace and start a full teardown. The Giants seemed headed for a busy trade deadline, but they came together as it approached, winning 16 of their first 19 games in July. With fewer than two weeks to go until the deadline, Bumgarner pitched brilliantly against the Mets in a game the Giants won in the bottom of the 16th. A few minutes later, reporters took turns finding different ways to ask how concerned he was about potentially being traded. "I don't give a shit," he said. "I'm here to win games for this team, and that's what we're doing."

Bumgarner allowed just one run over nine innings, and he was happy the Giants had kept their run going, but as soon as that game ended, he ducked into Bochy's office. He had a bone to pick.

Three years earlier, Bumgarner had so thoroughly dominated the same Mets team that Bochy was planning to send him out for the 10th inning of the Wild Card Game before Conor Gillaspie's homer changed everything. During that 2019 game, Bumgarner was at just 94 pitches through the ninth and thought he would finally get his chance to push himself into extra innings. The dugout lobbying fell on deaf ears, but Bumgarner made sure to circle back after the game to let Bochy—who was worried about him getting hurt before free agency—know he was displeased.

There was so much trust between the two and so much faith from the manager that Bumgarner almost always got his way in those situations. On days when he wasn't pitching, he would sometimes stand behind Bochy in the dugout, spikes on just in case a pinch-hitter were needed. Bochy often obliged, most memorably against Aroldis Chapman, the hardest-throwing reliever the game has ever seen. He looked down at his scorecard one night and quickly realized that his best pitcher had a much better chance of catching up to Chapman's 103 mph fastball than any of his remaining position players. Bumgarner fouled one off before drawing a walk. Bochy later let Bumgarner make history and hit for himself instead of using a DH in an American League ballpark, and at times during the pitcher's prime, members of the coaching staff discussed whether it was worth actually using him as a designated hitter on days he wasn't pitching. One summer, there was serious talk of him doing the Home Run Derby.

Those moments, the ones in which he was larger than life, delighted Bumgarner. He did not seek attention and hardly ever gave interviews, but he certainly enjoyed showing that he was not your average ace. Bumgarner's batting practice shows were the stuff of legend, and he would come out once a series to take aim at the Western Metal Supply Co. building at Petco Park or the TGI Fridays restaurant at the very top of the upper deck at Chase Field.

Two days after Bumgarner blanked the Mets in the Wild Card Game, the Giants arrived at Wrigley Field for the NLDS. Before Game 1, Bumgarner walked onto the field in a hoodie, a bat in his hand. "Watch this," he said to a reporter, smiling as he stepped into the cage. He started peppering Waveland Avenue with home runs that easily cleared the bleachers. Bochy used him as a pinch-hitter later in the series.

The bravado that carried Bumgarner through all of those nights and his record-setting 2014 postseason was clear from an early age. It didn't take long for Dick Tidrow, the organization's most trusted voice when it came to pitching, to fall for the tall, lanky left-hander with a crossfire delivery. When Tidrow first laid eyes on Bumgarner, two things immediately stood out. "He was one of the few high school pitchers I had ever seen pitch inside," Tidrow said during the 2014 postseason. "I thought at the time that he wasn't afraid of much, and I don't think that's changed. He has always been fearless. It's how he was brought up. It's in his DNA. It's hard for a guy with his release point to pitch inside to right-handed hitters, but he just repeated it and repeated it. I had never seen that before."

The Giants couldn't have predicted that Bumgarner would later hit 19 big-league homers, but when Tidrow watched him hit in high school, he saw a ferocity that he felt would carry over to big moments on the mound. Bumgarner, he noted, wasn't afraid to swing for the fences at every chance, even if he often came up with nothing but air. "That showed me a guy that wasn't afraid," Tidrow said. "He was not afraid to look bad."

Once Bumgarner settled in as a professional, it didn't take long for him to show that trait in games. He was just 19 when the Giants threw him into a spring training contest against the Dodgers. It was the only time Giants staffers ever saw Bumgarner admit he was nervous, but as he departed minor league camp, coordinator Bert Bradley told him everything would be fine if he trusted his stuff. When Bumgarner arrived for the game, he asked Matt Cain how he should pitch to Manny Ramirez. Cain told him Ramirez could sometimes be vulnerable on the inside corner, thinking Bumgarner might try it once to keep the 12-time All-Star off the plate. His jaw dropped when Bumgarner went inside on Ramirez three straight times. "Sometimes," Cain said years later, "you wonder if he's got a pulse."

In the biggest moments, Bumgarner always seemed like he was back home in North Carolina, whipping a ball past overmatched classmates. His calm in Game 7 of the 2014 World Series made him a postseason legend, but Bumgarner showed it in just about every other big game too. He was, for some reason, initially nervous that he would be left off the 2010 postseason roster, and then he went out as a 21-year-old and threw eight shutout innings in the World Series. Afterward, he earnestly told teammates that it reminded him of pitching in his high school's state championship game.

Six years later, he threw his second Wild Card Game shutout, hardly seeming to break a sweat. He was the only player on the late bus to Citi Field that afternoon and was so relaxed that he fell asleep on the ride over from Manhattan. When Bumgarner snagged a line drive back to the mound to end the eighth, he screamed and pumped his fist. As he walked off the field, he looked up and found Ali sitting 30 rows up from the dugout. He calmly flipped the baseball into the family section. Gillaspie hit a go-ahead homer a few minutes later, and

Bumgarner sidled up to him in the dugout. "Conor," he said gently, "I appreciate the hell out of that."

What was so fascinating about the focus in those big spots was the dichotomy with some of his more memorable moments in the regular season. Yasiel Puig was his main foil but far from the only one. Bumgarner yelled at Max Muncy for pimping a home run into McCovey Cove and glowered at Carlos Gomez for reacting angrily to a foul ball on a fastball he felt he should have crushed. He once had a 20-second stare-down with umpire Joe West, and he sparked a benches-clearing incident with Wil Myers because—honestly, nobody was really sure. "I just wanted to get mad for a minute," Bumgarner explained. When the Giants added new switchable lights to their clubhouse, equipment and clubhouse manager Brad Grems would always ask the starting pitcher which color he wanted them to be. "Fucking red," Bumgarner would reply.

The stories from the minor leagues were just as memorable. A Giants executive once got a call saying Bumgarner was trashing a Double A clubhouse after coming out of a game. He looked at the box score and saw Bumgarner had dominated on the mound, which led to some confusion—until he realized he was upset about striking out at the plate. In Triple A, he got ejected from a game and had to be restrained by teammates and pulled back to the clubhouse, where a staff member was frantically searching for the keys to Bumgarner's truck out of fear that he might decide to drive it onto the field.

As he was led off, Bumgarner turned and angrily fired the baseball at the outfield wall. The incident led to a three-game suspension and fine, but the front office wasn't exactly disappointed. When Bumgarner was called up to the big leagues, Bochy searched for the clip on YouTube to see what kind of competitor he was getting. Asked years later about the incident, Tidrow smiled. "We thought that was a lot of arm strength," he said.

There was a reason Bumgarner warmed up to the Marshall Tucker Band's "Fire on the Mountain." It perfectly summed up the approach he brought every five days, and it worked. He won 119 games in 11 seasons in orange and black, posting a 3.13 ERA over more than 1,800 innings. Starting in 2011, his first full season, he threw at least 200 innings six consecutive times, a run that included four All-Star appearances and two top-five finishes in Cy Young voting. He won two Silver Slugger Awards and had four consecutive seasons with at least three homers. Of his 19 in the big leagues, two came against Clayton Kershaw, two against Zack Greinke, and one against Jacob deGrom.

Bumgarner made little effort to hide how much he enjoyed that track record. Matt Duffy was preparing for a game against the Dodgers ace one afternoon when Bumgarner walked into the video room. "You want me to teach you how to hit homers off Kershaw?" he quipped.

The exploits at the plate added to the legend, but it was in the postseason where Bumgarner really built his reputation. He made 16 playoff appearances, and the Giants won 13 of them. He had a 2.11 ERA, but that number became microscopic when a title was truly on the line. Bumgarner pitched 36 innings in the World Series and allowed just 1 run and 14 hits. His 0.25 World Series ERA is the lowest in MLB history.

The finishing touches on that record came in Game 7 of the 2014 World Series, the only save of his career. He ended that postseason with a 1.03 ERA and was an easy choice for MVP of both the NLCS and the World Series, but the dominance had really started in the Wild Card Game, nearly a full month before he threw the final pitch of the season.

On the first night of October, Bumgarner struck out 10 in a shutout of the Pirates. He then threw seven strong innings in his NLDS start, and a night later he insisted to Bochy that he could come out of the bullpen to get a tough lefty or two. "He was driving me nuts," Bochy said. "Three or four times, he said, 'I can get [Adam] LaRoche . . . I can get [Bryce] Harper.' Geez, every time I turned around, I bumped into him."

When Harper homered in the seventh inning of Game 4, Bochy turned to Bumgarner and jokingly told him to get his spikes on. Sergio Romo and Santiago Casilla ended up closing out the game, but the foundation had started to be poured for what was to come. Bumgarner had waited 25 years for this moment. There was nothing that would stand in his way.

Tim Flannery was leaning on the rail early in Game 7 when he heard two Royals fans screaming from right behind the dugout. "Give us Bumgarner! Give us Bumgarner!" they yelled. When the Giants took a 3–2 lead in the fourth inning, the duo picked it back up: "Give us Bumgarner! Give us Bumgarner!" Flannery knew a plan had been set in stone well before Tim Hudson had thrown his first pitch. He turned and found the two fans. "You're getting him now, motherfuckers!" he yelled.

Bumgarner was on just two days of rest, but there was no wavering in Bochy's office or the clubhouse. The lefty had deemed himself available in Game 6 too, but the Giants got blown out. Before Game 7, the staff decided that Bumgarner and Affeldt would get it to the eighth, where Romo and Casilla could take over. Righetti was confident Bumgarner could get stretched out to 70 pitches, but it wasn't the end of the night that concerned the staff.

The Giants learned early on that their confident cowboy was actually as meticulous as anybody on the team. He would spend hours working on his delivery in front of a weight room mirror. There was a different workout routine for each day, and occasionally Bumgarner would be sitting in the dugout during a game and realize he had forgotten a step. He would run back to the clubhouse to check it off before coming back to watch the rest of the game. Bumgarner spent more than an hour preparing for starts, putting a sheet down in the weight room and ticking off exercises and stretches one at a time. Then he would go out to the field 40 minutes before first pitch and finish preparing his body.

That would be hard to replicate as a reliever, and Bochy's only concern before Game 7 was whether Bumgarner would have enough time to properly warm up. Righetti was confident that adrenaline would kick in, but he also knew that sometimes could lead you to feel like you're properly warmed up when you're really not. The decision was made that Bumgarner would get a clean inning regardless. The only thing he asked of his manager and pitching coach was to give enough time to go through his whole routine, which in his mind meant giving him enough of a warning about which inning would be his first. "And they did *not* do that," he said later. "I had to rush through my warm-up. I had to rush through it while trying not to rush through it. I went through it a little faster than I wanted, but I did finish it in time."

If there were any nerves, Bumgarner didn't show them as he watched the first four innings from the visiting bullpen. At 8:46 PM at Kauffman Stadium, he finally took the mound to begin throwing to bullpen catcher Taira Uematsu. Eight minutes later, he tugged his belt into place, pulled his hat down a bit tighter, and took eight big steps out of the bullpen. As 40,000 fans and players from both teams watched, he began a slow jog to the mound. His mind was clear. It felt like just another day, even if that was the furthest thing from the truth. "I just remember the presence," Bochy said. "It was like John Wayne coming out of the bullpen."

The Giants all knew it was coming. It's what they wanted, and in the moments before Game 7, it's the scenario teammates played out in hushed conversations. But still, they found themselves mesmerized. As Bumgarner jogged through right field, Hunter Pence noticed the raucous crowd getting quieter and quieter. On the bench, Ron Wotus scanned the faces in the crowd and watched as demeanors quickly changed. A few feet away, Righetti felt the same chill as two years earlier, when Tim Lincecum jogged out of the bullpen in Cincinnati. The familiar din of a ballpark, a combination of loud discussions and pumped-in music, was fading away.

Posey had caught Bumgarner in A ball when they were 22 and 19 years old, respectively, their bond initially forming as they talked of missing their hometowns and families back in the South. They were together for Game 4 of the 2010 World Series, when they became the first rookie battery to start on the biggest stage in more than 60 years. Posey was there through seven shutout innings in the second game of the 2012 World Series. But this was something new. This was the best Bumgarner had ever been or would be. "People talk about the zone. That was it," Bumgarner said at the 10-year reunion. "I didn't have it before then, and I didn't have it after then. That was the spot for me."

The two stars worked as one for five innings, and when a mistake in the outfield put the tying run on third with two outs in the ninth, neither panicked. They knew that a two-strike curveball in the dirt to Salvador Perez could clinch a title, but Posey felt the risk of a wild pitch was too high given the stakes. He got taller and taller, and Bumgarner somehow found the energy to keep hitting the top of the zone. His 68th pitch of the night finally got the job done.

Bumgarner always knew he would go the distance once he entered Game 7, but that's not what the Giants had planned for. That's not what the Royals had planned for, either. They thought they were done with him after Game 5, but there he was three days later, calmly entering from the bullpen to end a season.

"My biggest memory is more auditory than visual," Posey said. "Out of any place I've ever been, the energy and life seemed to be sucked out of the crowd. There was a quiet, and you could tell there was a nervous energy that kind of came over them. I think it's something I'll remember the rest of my life, because it was a really cool moment. It just seemed like however many people were there kind of said, 'Oh, crap, this guy again. We didn't think we'd see him again.'"

17

Matt Cain

The game began the same way as so many others over Matt Cain's 13-year career. He blew a fastball past an overmatched hitter and took a slow walk around the mound, waiting for the ball to travel around the horn. From there, the outs kept melting away. A lazy pop-up to second. A strikeout on an elevated four-seamer and another on a diving change-up. When the opposing pitcher lined out to right in the third, Cain had gone nine up, nine down.

Cain was nicknamed the Horse, and from a young age, it was clear that he would consistently go deep for the Giants. He was called up as a 20-year-old, and a few days later he went to dinner at a local restaurant. Veteran outfielder Randy Winn was there at the same time, and he leaned over to his wife and nodded toward Cain. "See that kid?" he said. "He can't even drink yet." The Giants had inserted Cain in their rotation just three years after taking him out of Houston High School in Germantown, Tennessee, but it didn't take long for him to prove that he would be capable of leading champagne-soaked celebrations in the future.

In his third big-league start, Cain went the distance against the Chicago Cubs. He was the second-youngest player in the big leagues, but he already was pitching like a savvy veteran. The Cubs got only a solo homer and a single against Cain, who soon made it clear that he not only would make a habit of soaking up innings but also of flirting with history.

The next June, in his 11th big-league start, Cain took a perfect game into the sixth inning against the New York Mets. A month later, he allowed just one hit at the Coliseum in a 120-pitch shutout. And a month after that gem, Cain took a no-hitter into the eighth inning against the Los Angeles Angels, putting Bruce Bochy in an uncomfortable position. With two outs in the eighth, on the young right-hander's 128th pitch of the game, Chone Figgins broke up the no-hit bid with a single to center.

That ended up being one of six different games over Cain's first seven seasons in which he threw at least seven innings and allowed just one hit. Two of those games were one-hit shutouts, and as he prepared for 2012, his final season under team control, Cain already had four shutouts and 13 complete games in the big leagues. As the game was subtly changing and workloads were being closely watched, he threw at least one complete game in each of his first eight seasons.

He truly was the rotation's horse, as reliable an innings-eater as there was in the game, and as he looked poised to hit free agency at the age of 28, he was also a two-time All-Star and World Series champion. The Giants knew Cain was headed for a record-breaking contract, so they took care of it themselves.

The $127.5 million deal that he signed right before Opening Day was the richest ever for a right-handed pitcher, and he soon got to work trying to prove he was worth every penny. On that beautiful day at Oracle Park early in the season, Cain found his rhythm early. Three perfect innings turned into four, and then five. It was around that point that catcher Buster Posey started thinking about perfection, and in the dugout, Bochy thought about how this was as good as he had ever seen Cain pitch.

The sixth inning started with another strikeout on a change-up, the seventh of the day for Cain, who would reach double-digits. As a liner to center turned into the 17th consecutive out, Mike Krukow talked on the broadcast about how Cain had a great feel for all of his pitches and how manageable his pitch count was. And then the improbable happened.

Opposing pitcher James McDonald lined a clean single to left with two outs in the sixth. Once again, Cain was left to wonder about what might have been. In his first home start after signing the record deal, Cain would end up with another one-hitter. Afterward, he didn't try to hide his disappointment or pretend he didn't know what was at stake.

Throwing a perfect game had always been on his bucket list. On April 13, 2012, exactly two months before the best performance of his life, Cain stood in the clubhouse and talked openly about how his latest bid for perfection had fallen short. "I've always been kind of conscious of it," he said. "I've never had one."

When Cain finally did get his perfect game, the most surprising part might have come while he was sitting in the dugout: the Giants scored in each of the first five innings. Cain got 10 runs of support that night, which oftentimes was about what he could expect over the course of an entire calendar month. Among the many facets of his legacy is the fact that he brought "getting Cained" into the lexicon in San Francisco. It will forever be used to describe the rough luck of a pitcher who gets little to no support from his lineup. For years, Giants hitters tried to figure out what the issue was. Even their championship teams made a habit of Caining Cain, and his teammates would stand at their lockers afterward and attempt to make some sense of another disappointing 2–1 loss. To their credit, they at least made it clear right away that this might become a thing.

Cain had gone five solid innings against the Colorado Rockies in his big-league debut on August 29, 2005. He was a month shy of his 21st birthday, but the drive that would carry him through 331 starts was already shining through. With a runner on and two outs in the fifth, one of the best hitters of that generation stepped up to the plate. Cain went 3–1 on Todd Helton, and then the two Tennessee natives locked horns for one of the best one-on-one battles of either's career.

Helton fouled off nine consecutive pitches, but the young right-hander kept coming with his best stuff. He pumped fastball after fastball, going inside and out, up and down. Helton fouled them all off, along with a couple off-speed pitches. On the 14th pitch of the battle, and Cain's 103rd of the night, Helton hit a harmless fly ball to left-center. If you ignored the fact that the rookie was wearing No. 43 and not No. 18, it was a scene that would fit in at any other point of his career. Cain watched the ball fly as he quickly walked off the field. He let out one quick shout and then turned and marched back to the dugout, showing the stoicism of someone 10 years more experienced.

In the dugout, teammates glanced at one another. They had heard all of the hype about the first-round pick who rocketed through the minor leagues. It didn't take long for him to prove that he was, in fact, going to be a game changer for the organization. "Matt Cain had 'it.' . . . When you see a guy that has the stuff—the maturity and the competitiveness—at such a young age, you know that guy has all of the ingredients to become a really good longtime Major League pitcher," Winn said. "From day one, he had that same demeanor. He never got flustered. All he did was take the ball every fifth day and go out there and compete."

On that first day, Cain lived up to the sky-high expectations. He also got just one run of support. That was the first loss of a career that ended with a losing overall record despite a 3.68 ERA. Cain allowed two or fewer runs 191 times, doing so in more than half of his big-league starts. He took the loss in 29 of those games and had 64 no-decisions. He made 26 big-league starts in which he allowed one run and didn't get a win. There were 15 nights when he walked off the field without allowing a run and went home with a no-decision. From his debut through the night when he made history, no starter in baseball dealt with less run support.

The night before Cain's debut, the Giants won 4–1. The night after, they won 4–3. But Cain's first game in the big leagues was a 2–1 loss. He got Cained well before anyone even knew that was a thing.

On those nights when he would be left hanging, Cain would retreat to the clubhouse and sit quietly. He wouldn't throw chairs or curse up a storm, but others could see he was quietly steaming. When Cain was really mad, he wouldn't say a word. Trainer Dave Groeschner would apply ice to his pitching arm and then leave him alone, watching from across the room as Cain's insides churned. On the surface, though, there was nothing but composure, which got the longtime trainer excited for the future. Groeschner would think about how the right-hander would be ready to lead the way when the rest of the team caught up. From the start, he handled those disappointing nights as well as anyone could.

"He was just a pro," Posey said. "It was, 'I'm going to go out there and take care of my job.' That's the way he handled it. It wasn't ever about pointing fingers; it was just 'go out there and take care of my job.'"

Cain ended up making three All-Star teams and starting on one. He gave the Giants six consecutive 200-inning seasons as they became a contender and then started actually winning titles. On a staff full of pitchers who burnished their legacies in October, Cain stood toe to toe with just about everybody. He didn't allow an earned run during the 2010 title run and started the clinching game in all three rounds of the 2012 postseason.

He became Bochy's most reliable starting pitcher, and also the one who set the tone. He wasn't quite as intimidating as Madison Bumgarner, and his fastball didn't quite light up radar guns the way Tim Lincecum's did, but it had tremendous carry through the zone. A few years after he retired, Posey found himself pulling up some of Cain's old highlights. He was struck by how crisp the stuff was. The fastball sat in the mid-90s, and the sharp slider hit his glove at 89 mph, but Posey knew that on so many of those nights, Cain had dialed it back to 85 or 90 percent to ensure he could pitch as deep into the game as possible. He thought back to how Cain would occasionally give him instructions that would startle most modern coaching staffs. "I remember him telling me sometimes before the game that we were throwing all fastballs the first time through," Posey recalled. "Nothing but fastballs."

During the best game of his career, Cain started the Houston Astros off with five consecutive fastballs. That felt normal, but his day had actually gotten off to a very unusual start.

The U. S. Open was set to tee off on June 14, 2012, at the Olympic Club, so a day earlier, Taylor Made set up a box on top of the plate at Oracle Park and brought PGA Tour star Dustin Johnson out to smash some golf balls into McCovey Cove before batting practice. The Giants flocked to the field to watch, and Cain realized it was a once-in-a-lifetime opportunity. *How am I not going to try and at least take a swing?* he thought. There were a couple of problems, though.

Cain was starting in four hours, and this certainly was not part of his game day routine. He was also just two months removed from putting his signature on that contract, which came with tremendous responsibility. He was nervous about the thought of taking a swing, but he also loved golf, so he asked Bochy if it would be okay to tee one up. Bochy nodded at Brian Sabean, who was sitting in the seats alongside the dugout. Sabean didn't give Cain his approval, but he also didn't put up a stop sign. Cain took that as Sabean's way of saying, "Just don't get hurt." He stepped up and smoked a 300-yard drive into the water and then retreated to the clubhouse to begin preparing to face the Astros.

The Giants rewarded Cain with a rare first-inning rally, and by the end of the fifth, it was 10–0. Cain had noticed early that his fastball had a bit of extra life, so he took advantage. He blew another fastball past a helpless hitter to open the sixth with his 10th strikeout, but a pitch later, it appeared his latest bid for history had ended. Astros catcher Chris Snyder got a first-pitch fastball down the middle and blasted it to left. Cain dropped his head and walked off the mound, thinking the no-hitter and shutout had disappeared with one mistake, but the high fly ball died in the chilly air and seemed to drop straight down as it reached the wall. Melky Cabrera reached up and grabbed a 380-foot out as he bumped up against the wall. "It sounded like it was gone. I knew I threw it kind of right into his happy zone," Cain said. "That ball should have gone out."

On the mound, Cain started to think about how maybe that had been a sign. In the dugout, Bochy felt the same sensation. It seemed from his vantage point that the ball had gone over the wall and come back. The perfect game somehow lived on, but a bigger scare was on the way.

Bochy was always proactive when it seemed history might be at stake, making late defensive changes to provide his pitcher with the best possible opportunity to get through 27 outs. Late in the perfect game, he inserted Brandon Crawford and Emmanuel Burriss as defensive replacements, pushing Joaquin Arias to third base, where he replaced Pablo Sandoval.

There was nothing Bochy needed to do about his outfield that night. The Giants had one of the best alignments in the league and a secret weapon standing in right field. The front office had signed Gregor Blanco out of the Venezuelan Winter League at the urging of hitting coach Hensley Meulens, and from the start of camp, it became clear that the speedy and energetic outfielder would make an impact. Blanco was fond of saying the Giants had three center fielders in their outfield, and in the seventh inning, that helped Cain.

He had started the inning by going 3–2 on Astros outfielder Jordan Schafer, and because a perfect game was on the line and not just a no-hitter, he had little choice but to come in with a fastball. Schafer lined it into the gap in right-center, and the Giants all had the same thought. Bochy immediately glanced at center fielder Angel Pagan and saw that he was shaded toward left field and had no chance. He dropped his head. In the press box, a disappointed Duane Kuiper prepared to call the double. On the mound, Cain, for a second time, felt his bid was over. "I look up, and nobody is there, and then Blanco comes out of nowhere," he said. "It didn't make any sense."

It did to Blanco, though. With a full count, he figured Cain would throw an inside fastball to try and get a grounder to second. He repositioned himself four or five steps toward his right, and that made all the difference. Blanco made a diving catch on the warning track 400 feet away from the plate and in a spot that previously had been exclusively reserved for center fielders. Cain watched in disbelief as Blanco not only ran the ball down but held on to it as he hit the ground. He breathed a deep sigh of relief and then went back to work, striking out Jose Altuve and Jed Lowrie as butterflies continued to build.

Years later, after appearing in multiple must-win games and World Series clinchers, Cain's teammates said that was the most nervous they had ever been. Everybody wanted to help him get to the finish line, and nobody wanted to be responsible for screwing it up. That included Bochy, who wracked the brain inside his size 8⅛" cap for additional ways to contribute. Cain was already at 103 pitches through 7 innings, and it took 11 more to get through the eighth. Bochy felt comfortable with the durable right-hander getting to 130 or so, but he also wanted to make sure he was ready to protect his arm in case Cain did give up a hit. That left him with a dilemma. The bullpens at Oracle Park back then were down the lines, and because he started his delivery while facing the home dugout, Cain would notice right away if a reliever even walked down to start stretching.

There was no way Bochy or pitching coach Dave Righetti were putting that thought in Cain's head, so right-hander Shane Loux was instructed to slip into the batting cage behind the dugout to start getting loose. "I hadn't done that before," Bochy explained later, laughing. "But like everybody else during a perfect game, you're superstitious. Guys are sitting in the same place, they're staying away from Matt. I didn't want him to see us having somebody throwing in the bullpen. I didn't want to change any part of his mindset that he might have out there."

The plan presented a few minor problems. Loux didn't have a traditional 60-foot setup, instead playing catch in cramped quarters with nets hanging all around him. He also didn't really even want to be getting loose. He had grown close with Cain and was just as excited to watch him as the 42,298 fans who filled Oracle on a Wednesday night. He watched the beginning of the ninth on the cage's small TV, but after a half dozen warm-up pitches, he fibbed that he was ready to go and ran back to the dugout. The other minor problem was that asking a reliever to warm up in secret wasn't exactly allowed. "It is illegal, but it was 10–0," longtime bench coach Ron Wotus said. "I think everybody wants to see the perfect game over a legal warm-up in a 10–0 game."

By that point, fans around the world had tuned in to see if Cain could become the 22nd player in history to achieve perfection. Cain took a moment before the ninth to look around at a ballpark that was shaking, and then dug back into the mound. A fly ball to left calmed his nerves, and another fly ball got him within an out of history. With a 1–2 count on Jason Castro, he broke from his usual nature, and it nearly cost him.

Cain reached back for everything he had in search of a strikeout, so much so that he let out a grunt nobody else could hear because of the roars of the sellout crowd. The 94 mph fastball caught too much of the plate, but Castro bounced it the other way. The sure-handed Arias fielded it cleanly but then stumbled, causing hearts to leap into throats all around the infield and ballpark, but he recovered and made a strong flat-footed throw across the diamond.

Cain didn't get that final strikeout, but with 14, he tied Hall of Famer Sandy Koufax's record for the most in a perfect game. He became the first Giant to throw one, which was, well, perfect. For so many years, Cain had needed to chase perfection just to keep his team in games as the offense struggled to back him. "It was kind of a reward for all of the games that he pitched where nobody scored any runs," Kuiper said. "Like, all right, Matt, the baseball gods are going to give you this game where you're going to remember it for the rest of your life."

PART 6

THE CLOSE CALLS

18
1962

The *Peanuts* comic strip that appeared in hundreds of newspapers a few days before Christmas summed it up perfectly. Charlie Brown and his best friend, Linus, sat on a curb, staring off into the distance. In the final frame of the strip, Brown burst into tears. "Why couldn't McCovey have hit the ball just three feet higher?" he yelled. A few weeks later, an update appeared in newspapers across the country. "Or why couldn't McCovey have hit the ball even two feet higher?" Brown yelled this time.

The cartoonist Charles Schulz was a Giants fan, and with a few strokes of his pen, he put a voice to what so many others were still feeling in the aftermath of the 1962 World Series. In the ninth inning of Game 7, the Giants had the tying run on third and the winning run on second for one of the most feared sluggers who ever lived. Willie McCovey hit a rocket, but it was right at New York Yankees second baseman Bobby Richardson. Young Charlie Brown was perhaps not fully accurate in his gripes. Richardson didn't have to extend at all for the line drive. It was shoulder height, and he tucked it away with two hands. Had it been a bit higher, he still would have made the catch. But three feet to his left or three feet to his right? In that case, the Giants would have been champions just four years after they moved to the West Coast.

The fabulous World Series capped a season in which the city's new baseball team fully won hearts and minds across the region. The Giants trailed the rival Los Angeles Dodgers all summer and were four back with a week to go, but they forced a playoff on the season's final day on a Willie Mays homer in the late innings and then stormed back again in the three-game series, winning the pennant with a ninth-inning rally at Dodger Stadium. It was such a sudden turn that even the unshakable Mays admitted to being shocked. As the Giants sprayed champagne around the visiting clubhouse at Dodger Stadium, Mays laughed and admitted to reporters that he "never thought [they]'d come back to win—never in a million years."

The comeback set up the first cross-country World Series, and it lived up to the hype. On one side there was a roster with five future Hall of Famers. On the other was Mickey Mantle and Roger Maris and a pitching staff led by Whitey Ford. It was a series meant to go seven games and come down to the final pitch, but a few minutes before McCovey's line drive, the Giants had another close call that has gone down as one of the great what-if moments in franchise history.

Trailing 1–0 in the bottom of the ninth, manager Alvin Dark sent Matty Alou up to pinch-hit. Alou dragged a bunt along the muddy grass for a leadoff single, but the next two Giants struck out. That set the stage for Mays, who shot an outside pitch toward the right-field corner. Under normal

Candlestick conditions the ball would have gotten to the fence, but the series had been delayed several days by a downpour of rain, and the wet grass slowed the ball enough for Maris, who got over quickly to cut it off and then rifled a strong throw to Richardson. As he relayed it to the plate, Alou rounded third, but coach Whitey Lockman put up the stop sign. It was a decision Lockman had to defend after the game, but he had support. Dark said Alou would have been a "dead duck" at the plate, and the 23-year-old outfielder insisted he had no chance of scoring.

The decision was made easier by the fact that McCovey was due up next. As he strolled to the plate, Yankees manager Ralph Houk visited the mound to see if Ralph Terry wanted to walk McCovey, who had homered off him in Game 2 and had a triple already in that game. Terry had gone the distance, and he told his manager he wanted McCovey. "If that's what you want, go ahead," Houk replied. Immediately, McCovey took a swing that nearly had them regretting their choice.

He crushed the first pitch, but it curled into the seats down the right-field line for a long strike. Two pitches later, McCovey again hit the ball on the screws. Dark later called it one of the hardest line drives ever to be caught, but it found Richardson's glove. Three feet to his left or three feet to his right, and the Giants would have been celebrating in front of their home crowd.

It was a disappointing experience, but the true pain in baseball comes with years upon years of similar results getting piled on until the drought itself becomes the story. The 1962 Giants were too fresh to fully grasp what had just happened, and nobody could have possibly predicted what was to come. McCovey later said that much of the sting was taken out of the loss because the Giants figured they would be back for the rest of the decade. As players walked off the field at Candlestick that day, fans could be heard yelling, "We'll get 'em next year."

Of course they would, right?

For years, Giants minor leaguers would gather in a large room in Scottsdale and listen to stories and advice from a group of five Hall of Famers who incredibly all shared the field once Gaylord Perry reached the big leagues in 1962. They were at different stages of their careers, but when you look back at those lineups, it's one of the greatest collections of talent in MLB history.

Mays hit 49 homers, Orlando Cepeda had 35, and McCovey crushed 20. Right fielder Felipe Alou and third baseman Jim Davenport both made the All-Star team, joining Mays, Cepeda, and Juan Marichal. The Giants even got 35 homers out of their catching duo of Ed Bailey and Tom Haller. Right-hander Jack Sanford finished second in Cy Young Award voting. In the off-season, a trade with the Chicago White Sox had brought in two experienced arms in Billy Pierce and Don Larsen. Pierce, who had dealt with a staggering lack of run support while with the White Sox, proved to be a perfect fit in front of a powerful lineup at Candlestick Park. In 12 home starts, he went 12–0.

The roster was a perfect blend of old and young, but so many of the team's key players were in their primes that it was impossible to imagine 1962 being their last shot at a title.

The Giants won the most games in the National League in the 1960s but didn't reach the postseason again. They became known for falling just short in the standings during that decade, even as individual accomplishments piled up. Mays won his second MVP award in 1965, and Mike McCormick won the franchise's first Cy Young in 1967. In 1963, Felipe, Matty, and Jesus Alou made up the first all-brother outfield in MLB history, and a year later, Masanori Murakami became the first Japanese player to play in the majors.

In the last year of the decade, McCovey had his best all-around season and won his lone MVP award. Mays hit his 600th homer that season, and the lineup got a boost from a young right fielder named Bobby Bonds, but once again it wasn't enough. For a fifth consecutive year, the Giants finished in second place.

With Mays 40 by then and McCovey, Marichal, and Perry all approaching their mid-thirties, the Giants made one last run in 1971, reaching the postseason for the first time in nine years but falling to a Pittsburgh Pirates team that included Willie Stargell and Roberto Clemente. What followed was the darkest stretch in the franchise's San Francisco history.

The Giants didn't make the playoffs again until 1986, and over 15 seasons, they never finished better than third place. For so long they had been reliant on superstars, but one after another ended up elsewhere. Mays was traded to the New York Mets in 1972, and McCovey was dealt to the San Diego Padres. Marichal was sold to the Boston Red Sox, completing owner Horace Stoneham's efforts to rid the roster of its high-priced veterans. The Giants were bleeding money, and Stoneham had no outside businesses to make up the gap. Within a span of 19 months, three future Hall of Famers were sent packing.

With a diminished product on the field and the A's now playing—and winning—across the bay, the Giants saw their attendance drop to about 500,000. Late in September 1974, they drew just 748 fans to a Monday game at Candlestick. Struggling on the field and at the box office, they didn't just attempt to leave a major city for the second time; they attempted to leave the country.

The Giants had reported $6 million in losses over the previous eight years, and with serious questions about whether the market could support two teams, they didn't appear to have a future in San Francisco. In January 1976 word spread that they had been sold for $13.25 million to a group that would move them to Toronto, but the city of San Francisco won a restraining order to halt the process and keep the team from breaking a lease at Candlestick.

Attorneys for the Giants argued that denying the move would lead to bankruptcy for the franchise, which was $2 million in debt. "The Giants are broke," one of them argued during the hearing. "They are living on handouts from the National League." At the last second, a solution was found. In early March, National League owners approved an $8 million sale to Bob Lurie, a San Francisco financier who brought in meatpacking magnate Bud Herseth to help the finances line up.

The Giants would be staying at Candlestick, but it would be another decade before they were back to relevance on the national scene. The franchise went 27 seasons between appearances in the World Series and waited much longer to actually win one in San Francisco. It was a painful stretch for players and fans, with an added twist of the knife for those who remembered just how close they had come to winning it all within a few years of moving west.

A night before the first game of the 1962 World Series, the Giants looked helplessly out of airplane windows as their flight circled the Bay Area. They had put the finishing touches on an epic Dodgers collapse earlier in the day, scoring four runs in the top of the ninth inning to wipe out a two-run deficit and win the pennant. Mays's single drove in the first run, and Cepeda tied it with a sacrifice fly. A bases-loaded walk of Davenport gave the Giants the lead, and 400 miles up the coast, fans started racing toward San Francisco International Airport.

As the plane carrying the NL champions started to descend, the pilot delivered a message: "Fellows," he said, "there's a little disturbance down there." It was estimated that 50,000 Giants fans had arrived at the airport to welcome the newly crowned heroes, and the crowd had kept another jet from taxiing off the runway. The Giants initially diverted their plane to Oakland but then started circling as they waited for a resolution. Finally, they landed at a hidden runway alongside United Airlines maintenance facilities and boarded a bus, which didn't fare much better.

As raucous fans chased the bus down and shook it, Giants vice president Chub Feeney cracked, "Somebody better tell them we won." When a few bus windows were broken in the chaos, Feeney pivoted and had the driver head to a nearby hotel. It was there that his players waited for cabs that would finally take them home—all except Mays, who somehow had slipped away at the maintenance building and found the only cab in sight.

A night before the start of the World Series, that delirious riot caused a delay of more than an hour for the Giants, many of whom realized that their wives weren't home as their cabs arrived. They had gotten stuck in traffic around the airport and never gotten within a mile of the arriving flight.

The teams split the first two games in San Francisco, and the Yankees took two of three when the series moved to New York. As everyone flew back to the West Coast, a typhoon slammed into the Pacific Northwest, leading to 100 mph winds in Oregon and dropping seven inches of rain on San Francisco. Candlestick's parking lot and outfield flooded, with the playing surface taking on so much water that helicopters were used to try and make the field playable. Against the wishes of the grounds crew, the field had been constructed with an adobe soil base, which was so hard that the rainwater sat on top of it rather than soaking through.

The World Series was delayed for three days, and in the midst of it, as the rain continued to fall on Candlestick, Pierce handed a catcher's mitt to a 20-year-old clubhouse employee named Mike Murphy and asked him to meet under the right-field seats. They played catch for 10 minutes to keep the lefty loose for Game 6, a wet seat cushion serving as home plate. When they returned to the clubhouse, others looked up from their game of cards and asked if it was still raining. Pierce joked that he had seen some guys building an ark.

When the World Series resumed, Pierce was brilliant, throwing a three-hitter in Game 6 and watching as Cepeda led an attack that knocked Ford out in the fifth inning. The seventh game came on the 13th day of the series, tying a record set because of a similar storm in 1911. Sanford and Terry matched up in one of the best-pitched games in postseason history, but the Yankees scratched a run across in the fifth on what proved to be a fateful decision by Dark. With the bases loaded and no outs in the fifth, he played the infield back. Sanford got the needed double-play ball to short, but a run scored. Dark didn't think one run would be the difference, but Terry was brilliant, cruising until Alou reached to lead off the ninth and went to third on Mays's double. So many times over his career, McCovey would be walked in similar situations, but with Cepeda on deck, he got a pitch to hit. His rocket was right at an infielder positioned perfectly.

It was disappointing, but the Giants weren't crushed. While chilled bottles of champagne sat unopened in the clubhouse, a party eventually picked up elsewhere at Candlestick. Stoneham had planned an event for after Game 7 and figured there was no use in wasting all of that alcohol, so 400 people gathered in the ballpark's Stadium Club a few hours after the final out. Players and wives attended, sipping champagne side by side with team employees and local politicians.

As the group had circled the airport a few days earlier, ripped-up phone books and files had rained down from offices in the financial district. So many cars gathered on Market Street that night that traffic was shut down for five blocks. The city was ready for a parade, and the team was so overwhelmingly talented that everyone figured it was coming soon. After Game 7, the great baseball writer Nick Peters ended his story with the line, "Congratulations Giants . . . Wait 'til next year."

Nobody could have envisioned it taking nearly three decades for the World Series to return to San Francisco. And when it did, Mother Nature once again took on a leading role.

19

1989

An hour before the first pitch of Game 3 of the 1989 World Series, pixels on the scoreboard at Candlestick Park started flashing. Then an entire panel went out. The Giants were about to host their first World Series game in 27 years. This was no time for even the most minor of mechanical difficulties, so GiantsVision producer Jeff Kuiper and technician Kevin Skillings walked out to center field and started traversing the metal catwalks behind the scoreboard to see if they could find the issue.

They thought that maybe something had simply come unplugged, or perhaps power was being siphoned away by a party in a massive tent set up in the parking lot. As Skillings poked around, the catwalks started swaying back and forth. He and Kuiper both went into a wide stance and grabbed on to railings to ride it out, something that was much more natural to the California-born Skillings than to his coworker. Kuiper had grown up in Wisconsin and had been working in California for just three years. That was his first earthquake, and it was a big one.

The epicenter of the Loma Prieta Earthquake was about 10 miles north of Santa Cruz and had a magnitude of 6.9. It caused 63 deaths, nearly 4,000 injuries, and more than $6 billion in damages. The heaviest shaking lasted about 20 seconds in the Santa Cruz Mountains, and because of the magnitude and depth, the quake was felt across the state, even registering in San Diego. At Candlestick Park, players were getting ready to line up for pregame introductions. The ground started shaking at 5:04 PM, and it took several seconds for many of them to realize what was going on.

Mike Krukow was born in Long Beach and had experienced several earthquakes in his time with the Giants. He knew right away what was happening, but as the ground kept shaking, he realized this quake was different. "It felt like I had a 600-pound gopher going underneath my feet at 40 miles per hour," he said. He had gone out onto the field to see if his wife and family members had reached their seats. As he looked into the stands, he couldn't take his eyes off the backstop at Candlestick. It was small and freestanding, with no wires to support it, but it was solidly built. Krukow had never seen it budge even an inch, but it was swaying back and forth as the ground shook.

Will Clark was running sprints in the outfield and thought the initial sound was an F-15 jet flying above. That changed when he looked at the light towers, which were rocking back and forth. Atlee Hammaker, Bob Knepper, and Dave Dravecky were having a conversation in the clubhouse when the rumbling started. Hammaker asked what was happening and Knepper screamed for everyone to get outside and into the players' parking lot. As they reached fresh air, they saw the asphalt rolling. Dennis Eckersley was combing his famous hair in the bathroom of the visiting clubhouse and all of a sudden felt that a train was coming through the door. The Oakland native yelled "Earthquake!" and bolted for the exit. In the home dugout, Matt Williams waited for the shaking to stop and stepped out onto the dirt. "There was dust coming down from the upper deck, but then the whole crowd started singing 'We Will Rock You.' It was nuts," he said. "My most vivid memory is what happened afterward. All the families came down to the field so we could go out to the parking lot, but none of us had our keys. The scariest part was walking back into the clubhouse to get our keys. There [were] no lights; the power [was] out. We didn't know if an aftershock was going to come. That was freaky."

This was a time not just before social media but before the internet and cell phones. Information was hard to come by, and as players reunited with family members, many assumed the first pitch would simply be delayed a bit. That changed when police radios kicked back in. The Giants had an officer named Bobby stationed in their dugout all season, and as players gathered on the field, he walked a few feet away from the group. The new communication system on his radio was supposed to be infallible, but it had gone out. When Bobby's feed finally returned, Krukow watched his face drop. He listened in as reports came in about different parts of the Bay Area that had been hit hard. A few feet away, Kevin Mitchell's eyes widened when Willie Mays told him part of the Bay Bridge had collapsed.

It took hours for players to get home from Candlestick, even if they lived just a couple miles away. The Giants had waited 27 years for the World Series to return to their ballpark, and when it finally happened, they had a team that looked to be building something special and long-lasting. When the ground started shaking, their historic matchup with the A's had to be put on pause, and as players settled into their beds that night and looked out into the darkness, they wondered if the 1989 World Series would ever actually resume.

On July 5, 1987, the Giants traded four players to the San Diego Padres for outfielder Kevin Mitchell and left-handers Dave Dravecky and Craig Lefferts. Krukow was waiting when they walked into the clubhouse for the first time. "Man, we are so excited to have you as part of this organization," he said, shaking their hands. The trade ended up changing the trajectory of a franchise that already was starting to show that much better days were ahead.

Dravecky made 27 strong starts for the Giants, including two after a remarkable return from a tumor in his pitching arm. Lefferts turned into a reliable closer. It was Mitchell, though, who really changed the ceiling for the Giants. He had been a good player in San Diego, but up the coast, he became an MVP, the first in San Francisco since Willie McCovey in 1969. Mitchell led the majors with 47 homers and 125 RBIs in 1989, winning the MVP award over Will Clark, who had 23 homers, 111 RBIs, and a .333 batting average. Off the field, they teamed up for one of the best posters in baseball history. Wearing suits and holding bats, they stood in front of stockbrokers and under a sign that said PACIFIC SOCK EXCHANGE.

Clark was joined on the right side of the infield by reliable second baseman Robby Thompson, and the lineup got a boost when Williams finally found his footing in his third big-league season. The Giants finished second in the NL in runs scored and third in ERA behind Rick Reuschel, Don Robinson, and Scott Garrelts. They played strong defense, and they had an ideal mix of veteran experience and youthful exuberance. They had lost the NLCS in seven games two years earlier, but that had been a valuable experience. "There was a closeness to that team," Krukow said. "It was just so wonderful to go through with that group because everywhere you looked in the clubhouse, there was somebody who was losing his mind because he was having so much fun."

The Giants went 92–70, winning the division by three games. Clark led them past the Chicago Cubs in the NLCS, but then they ran into a buzz saw. After losing the previous World Series to the Los Angeles Dodgers, the A's won 99 games and cruised through the ALCS. They had power and speed, but most important, they had the type of pitching that can choke the life out of a postseason series. It started with Dave Stewart, one of the game's most intimidating right-handers. He got the ball in Game 1 at the Coliseum and threw a five-hit shutout. A night later, Mike Moore threw seven dominant innings and the A's won 5–1.

The Giants were quickly in a hole, but they remained confident. Bob Welch had won 17 games, but the hitters were sure they would get to him in Game 3. That would bring momentum back to their dugout, and if the Series went long, they felt they had the stronger overall pitching staff. Plus, they were headed home, where they had been dominant all year.

From a purely baseball standpoint, the earthquake benefited the A's. There were 11 days between the second and third games, allowing both teams to reset their pitching plans. Stewart came back for Game 3 and went seven strong, and Moore pitched well in Game 4. The A's had stayed sharp by working out and playing intrasquad games at their spring training facility in Phoenix, and they scored 22 runs over two games when the series finally resumed.

For much of that layoff, there had been questions about whether there ever would be a Game 3 at Candlestick. Krukow waited an hour in line the day after the quake to get the *San Francisco Chronicle* and see how much damage had been done, and as he scanned the headlines, he figured the series was over. Clark felt the same way after hearing about the structural damage throughout San Francisco. The decision was discussed every day in meetings between team executives, Mayor Art Agnos, and MLB commissioner Fay Vincent. ABC was putting pressure on the league to resume play, and after a few days, Vincent floated the idea of playing neutral-site games in San Diego. Giants owner Bob Lurie jumped out of his chair. "I've never seen him so agitated," former Giants vice president Corey Busch said. "He said, 'Over my dead body. There's no way you're taking this World Series away from our fans. They've waited too long. We're not going to restart until this community is ready.' Vincent backed down right away."

As the delay went on, players from both sides met to discuss whether they even should resume. Ultimately they decided that a return to play could be part of the healing process for a region that had just been through an unimaginable tragedy, as long as it was safe to do so. Every inch of Candlestick was checked by engineers, and the ballpark was found to have suffered very little damage. There was one man who didn't need to read a report to know that, and it's not hard to guess who that was. Longtime clubhouse manager Mike Murphy had slept in the clubhouse for the first few days of the layoff, protecting an area that had no power and thus no ability to turn some locks on.

Finally, on October 27, the World Series returned to Candlestick Park. There was a moment of silence at exactly 5:04, and then loud celebration from a crowd of 62,038. The Giants had set up a program to provide refunds for fans who did not feel comfortable returning, but it was quickly shut down when only 50 people asked for their money back. The ushers around the ballpark had flashlights just in case, and some fans wore hard hats with Giants logos on the front. Mays had been set to throw out the first pitch nearly two weeks earlier, but when play resumed, that honor went to first responders.

In the days leading up to the resumption, Giants manager Roger Craig noted that perhaps the layoff would halt Oakland's momentum. That wouldn't be the case, but the Giants still found plenty to celebrate while getting swept. They went out in the community and visited shelters at the Moscone Center and local schools. The needs of displaced families were overwhelming, but the Giants tried their best to bring smiles back to faces, handing out baseballs, posters, backpacks, and whatever else they could find in orange and black. It was a powerful experience for all involved, and the players on that team have never forgotten what it meant to have some time with fans who were overjoyed to spend a few minutes talking baseball in the midst of a difficult, emotional process.

"What we did in staying here was one of the most incredible things that ever happened to me in my life," Krukow said. "We started every day at the ballpark, and then we would go into the city and visit shelters. They just wanted to talk baseball, just to get away from the reality of what was happening around them. These were people that had lost everything, but you walked in and they lit up, and it was incredible."

20

2002

A few days after the final out of the 2002 World Series, Kirk Rueter and Jeff Kent sat quietly on a couch at Kent's house. It was Halloween, the perfect time of year to celebrate anything associated with orange and black, but the two veterans were in a somber mood. Kent wasn't particularly talkative at any time, but on this night he was especially quiet, until he looked up and asked his teammate a question that had been bugging him. "Why didn't you start Game 7?" he asked.

Rueter had been ready for the assignment. With the season on the line, he wanted the ball, and ultimately he got it. After Livan Hernandez gave up four runs after facing just five batters in Anaheim, Rueter took over. Over four innings, he allowed just one hit, a performance that alternately gave his teammates hope and left them regretting that their intuition had not been followed.

As they sat on the couch and tried to digest it, Rueter told Kent how eager he had been to start Game 7. Kent nodded. "That was the only way I think we thought we could have won after what happened in Game 6," he replied. "Everybody thought we would win when you were pitching."

It took the Giants 52 years to finally bring a title to San Francisco, but on October 26, 2002, they were so close that the plastic sheeting went up to protect the lockers in the visiting clubhouse at Edison Field from champagne and beer. Furniture had been moved from the center of the room to clear space for a podium. The Commissioner's Trophy was brought down to a hallway, close enough that some players saw it as they went back and forth to the dugout. And then it all fell apart.

Most of a five-run lead in Game 6 disappeared in the seventh, one of the most infamous innings in franchise history. Dependable right-hander Russ Ortiz had allowed just two hits through six: an infield single and a broken-bat flare that was almost caught by Kent and came on such an ugly swing that the man who took it nearly fell to his knees in the batter's box. But with one out in the seventh, Ortiz gave up back-to-back singles. Dusty Baker emerged from the dugout. "We just thought he was coming out to give him a little rest, a little breather, a little pep talk," said shortstop Rich Aurilia, who was part of the mound meeting. "Dusty would do that sometimes. He would tell the pitching coach, 'I've got this. Let me go talk to him. I'm not taking him out. I'm just going to talk to him.'"

Baker had a lefty and a righty warming up, but for a second it did look like he was just coming out to chat with Ortiz, a Southern California native who was having the night of his life against a franchise he grew up watching. When Baker's right hand finally went up, Ortiz started to walk off the mound, but his manager called him back. He rubbed up the baseball, placed it in Ortiz's hand, and patted him on the back. The moment was initially an afterthought, but when the Giants blew the lead and lost again the next night, it took on a life of its own.

For all of the analytical and technological advances over the years, baseball can often still resort to the most basic of explanations. Many around the game, particularly in clubhouses, are obsessed with the concept of jinxes. Sure, it makes some sense for teammates to avoid a pitcher when he's working on a no-hitter, but there's no reason why that should extend to the fans or the media, as it always does. There's no putting down a bunt when you're up or down big. There's no stealing, either. In general, there's no doing anything that might anger the baseball gods.

Baker, in the months and years that followed, found that many believed he had done just that. The Giants had supposedly prematurely celebrated, but in reality Baker was just trying to show his appreciation for a player who had given his all on the biggest stage. It was a personal gesture, not one meant to rile up the Angels or rub the score in their faces. It was the kind of thing he did often through 26 years and 2,183 managerial wins with five different franchises. He never forgot that his job was to take care of his players, and at times that meant very publicly showing how proud he was. "I would get called a player's manager," he said after he retired. "And I would say, 'There's no other kind!' What's the opposite of that?"

Baker was there for *his players*, and the gesture was meaningful to Ortiz. If that riled up the Angels and led to the stirring comeback, it wasn't all that apparent in the moment. In the years that followed, some members of the 2002 Angels team said they were pissed while others admitted they never even saw the handoff. It's clear that the moment became a moment only after the Angels rallied and then won again the next night.

The FOX broadcast did show a replay of the handoff, but Joe Buck and Tim McCarver didn't make anything of it, noting that Baker had simply shown Ortiz that he deserved a game ball. The newspapers all focused on other details. Most of the Giants didn't know about the ball being given away until after Game 6. "At the time, nobody thought anything of it," Aurilia said. "Nobody was paying attention."

The focus was on getting through the final eight outs, which ordinarily wouldn't have been all that difficult. But when you're trying to end a five-decade drought, every step feels like you're winding up Lombard Street. The Angels scored three runs in the seventh and three more in the eighth, staving off elimination and leaving the Giants with just a few hours to try to bounce back from an epic punch to the gut. As they walked back to the clubhouse, their heads were spinning. "I was out there thinking we were going to be the first team in San Francisco to get a ring, and then it just went sideways," first baseman J. T. Snow said. "It all happened so fast. Me and Barry walked in, and they were rolling the plastic tarp up and moving furniture back into place. It just happened so fast."

In a quiet clubhouse, players knew they had let a ring slip through their fingers, but the length of a big-league season teaches you to turn the page quickly. Infielder Shawon Dunston turned music on to try and bring energy back to the room. As Snow and Bonds tried to make sense of what had just happened, they looked at each other. "Let's get them tomorrow," Snow said.

The Giants would have one more shot at that elusive title, but they weren't sure what Game 7 would look like. There was a pull from many players to go with Rueter, the lovable lefty who not only had luck on his side but also had an approach that might be a good fit against an aggressive Angels lineup in a pressure-packed game. But they knew that many on staff preferred Hernandez. As was often the case in his career, the manager had a difficult decision to make.

Only seven men have managed more Major League Baseball games than Dusty Baker, but that was irrelevant when Al Rosen tracked him down in 1987. In April of that year, Los Angeles Dodgers general manager Al Campanis had been fired after going on ABC's *Nightline* and responding to a question about the paucity of Black managers and executives by saying they might not "have some of the necessities" for the jobs. That was still fresh for Baker when Rosen asked him what kind of role he would like with the Giants. "I told him I wanted to be his assistant, because I thought I could have more impact on hiring and firing," Baker recalled. "I wanted to be his assistant GM, but Al told me no."

Rosen had other ideas. He had been watching Baker over his 19 big-league seasons and wanted him on the field working with players. Baker was hired as first-base coach and then became the team's hitting coach. When the organization was sold to a group led by Peter Magowan before the 1993 season, new leadership was brought in. Many of the team's best players, including Will Clark and Robby Thompson, vouched for Baker, who won over incoming general manager Bob Quinn and was hired as the manager of the team.

It didn't take long for the new ownership group and front office to realize they had made the right hire. The Giants won 103 games in Baker's first season as manager and competed for division titles throughout the latter part of the decade as they worked to get their finances under control and build a new ballpark.

The 2001 team got 73 homers out of Bonds and All-Star campaigns out of Kent and Aurilia but finished two games short in the NL West. As a veteran group gathered in Scottsdale the next spring, there was a sense that this was the last dance. Kent was two years removed from being NL MVP, and teammates knew he was about to leave as a free agent. Baker's relationship with ownership had run its course, and it was an open secret that this was going to be his final year too.

Despite the building storm and the sense that change was on the way, Baker did his best to keep the clubhouse pulling in the same direction for 162 games. General manager Brian Sabean had traded for David Bell and outfielders Reggie Sanders, Tsuyoshi Shinjo, and Kenny Lofton. Power right-hander Jason Schmidt bolstered a deep rotation. Robb Nen, Tim Worrell, and Felix Rodriguez gave Baker three reliable options late in games. And, of course, he still had Bonds, who led the league in batting average, on-base percentage, and slugging while winning the second of four straight MVP awards.

Bonds homered twice on Opening Day at Dodger Stadium and twice more a day later. The pitching staff allowed just five total runs over the first six games of the season, all of which the Giants won, but by the end of April, they had dropped to third place. It was a three-team race between the Giants, Arizona Diamondbacks, and Los Angeles Dodgers for much of the summer, but by late August it was clear the Giants would have to chase a Wild Card spot.

They gave up just nine total runs during a season-ending nine-game winning streak. It was too late to catch the Diamondbacks, but they locked up the final postseason spot in the NL and then rode three homers from Bonds to an NLDS win over the Atlanta Braves. Aurilia and veteran catcher Benito Santiago caught fire in the next round as Baker leaned heavily on his high-leverage relievers. When the Giants beat St. Louis in five games, players got congratulatory messages from former

Giants who had years earlier grown to hate the Cardinals. They were moving on to their first World Series in 13 years and were up against a deep Angels team that had won 99 games before sailing through the American League side of the bracket.

But the Angels players weren't the only ones the Giants had to worry about.

On June 6, 2000, the Giants jumped out to an early lead over the Angels behind solo blasts from Bonds and Marvin Benard. They were up 5–4 heading into the bottom of the ninth—and then the monkey appeared. Hoping to fire up the crowd, two members of the stadium's entertainment crew put a clip from the Jim Carrey movie *Ace Ventura: Pet Detective* up on the video board and included the words RALLY MONKEY. The little monkey jumped up and down. The crowd went nuts. The Angels scored two runs to win the game. A star was born.

The Rally Monkey was so immediately popular that the organization worked with a white-faced capuchin named Katie, best known for appearing on *Friends*, to create a series of clips they could use late in games. The gimmick fit the 2002 team to a *T*. The Angels lost 14 of their first 20 games but rallied to make the postseason. That's when the monkey became a national phenomenon, one the Giants and their fans found massively annoying but that they at times also had to respect. During a pitching change in the World Series, the infielders watched as the Rally Monkey started jumping up and down on the video board. "You know what," Santiago said. "I hate that fucking monkey, but it's pretty funny."

Whether because of the power of the monkey or—more likely—their dominant bullpen, the Angels went 24–16 when their good luck charm appeared late in games in which they were trailing or tied. That's the position they found themselves in late in Game 6, when Baker needed just eight outs from his best relievers. He first called on Rodriguez, who pumped one 95 mph fastball after another at a good fastball hitter. On a 3–2 count, Scott Spiezio got one down and in, the happy zone for most left-handed hitters, and found the seats in right.

When the Angels cut the deficit to one in the eighth and put two runners in scoring position, Baker called for Nen. The closer was a perfect seven-for-seven in the postseason, but he had injured his shoulder during the season and would never throw another big-league pitch after the World Series. When Troy Glaus ripped a go-ahead double into the gap, Mike Murphy scrambled to tear down the plastic that was covering 25 lockers in the visiting clubhouse.

As he prepared for Game 7, Baker thought back to his playing days. He had been in Los Angeles when the Dodgers had a one-game playoff in 1980 and manager Tommy Lasorda had chosen veteran right-hander Dave Goltz over rookie Fernando Valenzuela, the preferred starter for the players. Goltz got rocked, and Baker never forgot how important it was to have premium stuff in must-win games.

Hernandez had better stuff than Rueter, but for Baker, something else gave him the edge. Rueter would run all of the Final Four and Kentucky Derby pools in the clubhouse and always seemed to win. He was seemingly unbeatable in a head-to-head card game. Most of all, teammates marveled at how he won 130 games in the big leagues despite mostly just going at hitters with a two-seamer. They figured you had to be the luckiest person in the world to win that many games with that kind of stuff, and when they needed a little luck of their own, they would find the man they all called Woody and rub his distinctive ears.

Rueter simply gave his teammates the impression that he would always find a way to win, but Hernandez's résumé spoke for itself. As a 22-year-old with the Florida Marlins, he struck out 15 in his first postseason start. Later that postseason, he was named World Series MVP. Hernandez had done it on the biggest stage, but in his most important game as a Giant, he couldn't replicate his previous success.

The Angels knocked him out before he could record an out in the third inning. Rueter entered in the fourth and dominated, but there would be no luck on this night. For all of the attention that has been paid over the years to what happened on the mound during the final two games, it was in the batter's box where the Giants truly came up short. In their first Game 7 since 1962, they scored just one run.

The franchise would end the drought eight years later, but many on that 2002 roster, including Bonds, never experienced a parade. Dunston won three of them as a Giants coach, but it wasn't until the third that he truly felt he was over the sting of his toughest loss as a player. Baker had to wait 20 years before finally winning with the Houston Astros. A short time later, as he sat in the seats at a ballpark in San Francisco he helped bring to life, he said there were no regrets. Even with the most difficult decisions, there's sometimes only so much you can do. "It's easy after the fact, but I can only make one decision," he said. "It's either going to work or it's not."

21

2016

At 7:00 on the morning of the 2014 trade deadline, Matt Duffy was pulled off a bus headed from Richmond, Virginia, to Altoona, Pennsylvania. For hours, Duffy sat and stared at his phone, thinking there was only one possibility: he was getting traded, and he had a pretty good idea of his destination. Finally, Duffy got tired of thinking about his fate and took a nap. At 4:30 PM the call finally came, but he wasn't headed for another organization; he was going to the big leagues.

Over the next two years, Duffy won hearts inside and outside of the clubhouse. The skinny 18th-round pick wasn't supposed to be playing in the postseason that first year, and yet there he was, using his speed and instincts to race around from second on a wild pitch and score the tying run in the ninth inning of an NLCS game. He wasn't supposed to be a big part of the 2015 season, but he was too good in the spring to keep off the roster, and he finished second in Rookie of the Year voting.

At the end of his first full season, he was selected as the Willie Mac Award winner.

Duffy was durable and energetic, showing up early every day for extra drills as he learned third base on the fly. He played through injuries and stared down challenges. When Dodgers closer Kenley Jansen buzzed him with a high fastball one night, Duffy responded by smacking a single up the middle—and then immediately stealing second base. He always had a smile on his face, and that, combined with his stature and underdog story, made him an easy sell to the fan base. When they discovered that he stuck decals of *The Simpsons*' Duffman on the knobs of his bats and had a fat cat who would join him for video game sessions, his popularity soared.

Duffy seemed like another cornerstone infielder, but exactly two years after that nervous day in Richmond, he again found himself staring at his phone. When Bobby Evans's name showed up on his screen, he knew his life was changing. Duffy was headed to Tampa Bay in a deal that would bring left-hander Matt Moore to San Francisco.

The Giants had been the best team in baseball in the first half, but their season fell apart after the break, and they struggled even to make the postseason. When they got there for a fourth consecutive even year, they suffered one of the worst losses in postseason history. It was easy for fans to connect the dots.

To this day there are plenty who still believe in the Curse of Matt Duffy. Others call it the Curse of Skeeter, a reference to Duffy's popular 27-pound cat. There's no doubt that the trade helped the Giants on the field, but in the clubhouse, it was deflating. The affable infielder felt like he was everybody's little brother, and other young Giants viewed him as an important bridge piece to the veterans. Even manager Bruce

Bochy hated the trade; he felt like Duffy was becoming his roster's heart and soul.

Throughout the championship years, the front office had been fiercely loyal—not just with veterans such as Angel Pagan and Marco Scutaro but also with young homegrown talent. Brandon Crawford received a six-year deal that kept him from ever testing free agency in his prime. The next April, Brandon Belt got his own six-year deal. They were locked into a core led by Buster Posey, Matt Cain, and Madison Bumgarner, all of whom had been signed long-term. It was preached to minor leaguers that the Giants won by letting homegrown prospects flourish.

The players knew, of course, that the core wouldn't stay together forever. But because there had been so little roster upheaval, many didn't think about the possibility of a massive shakeup, especially given how well the first three months of the 2016 season had gone. Duffy had taken over at third after a failed Casey McGehee experiment in 2015, and it seemed like the Giants would build around a young infield filled with popular homegrown players. It was a shock when Duffy was dealt. It just wasn't a move players had ever seriously considered being possible.

That all came crashing down with that call from Evans, who admitted the day was emotional for the front office too. Throughout their negotiations with Tampa Bay, the front office had tried to make it a prospect-driven deal with first-rounder Christian Arroyo as the centerpiece. A few hours before the deadline, the Rays called back and said it had to be Duffy. The Giants grimaced and relented. They loved him on the field and off, but there were concerns about whether he would ever hit for enough power to stick at third base. And most important, they felt Moore would be a game changer, the type of addition who would be worth making a painful trade.

An hour before the deadline, Duffy's future wife asked if they were about to be traded. He assured her that players on the IL rarely got dealt, but he had an ominous feeling. He knew the Rays had tried to trade for him in each of the previous two years. They were the team he first thought of when he got pulled off the bus two years earlier. When Evans made that final call, he thanked Duffy for all he had done. The young infielder was devastated, but on deadline day, there's not much time to digest. The next morning, he headed to Florida. "I felt like I was getting ripped from my family," he said. "I had felt protected by all of the older guys, but now it was like I was a baby duck getting thrown out into the pond. Like, 'All right, we taught you some things; now go figure it out. You're on your own now.'"

It was a jarring turn of events for the Giants and an easily identified pivot point as their season started to spiral. In truth, however, the slide started before Duffy ever boarded that flight. The Giants lost seven of eight while visiting San Diego, Boston, and the Bronx on their first trip of the second half, and Bochy all of a sudden found he had too many leaks to plug. His best hitters went ice-cold, and nobody in the lineup could do a thing with runners in scoring position. The rotation started to backslide and the defense imploded. One game was lost on a walk-off balk when Santiago Casilla tripped going down the mound. In the first half, their struggles in the ninth inning had been an annoying pebble sliding around in their shoe. By the end of July, it was a boulder threatening to knock them right off their path to the postseason.

In September some in the clubhouse found comfort in the fact that at least they had Bumgarner ready for another Wild Card Game. Plus, they just had a knack for figuring it out in October, something their opponents in the NLDS were well aware of. "We definitely knew all the even year stuff," Cubs star

Anthony Rizzo said. "It was '10, '12, and '14, so when we saw them in 2016, we were like, 'Fuck . . .'"

This time, however, things would be different. The 2016 Giants had an Achilles' heel they would never fully overcome.

The big story as Opening Day approached in 2016 was the theft of Hunter Pence's scooter. A few days earlier, the focus in the clubhouse had been a conversation about which left-handed hitter would get Splash Hit No. 69 after the first season in the ballpark's history without a home run into McCovey Cove.

It was an even year, and as Bochy prepared for spring training, he had to work hard to find ways to keep roster battles competitive. In all his years as a manager, he had never before felt that the roster was so set heading into camp. The Giants had spent $251 million on veterans Denard Span, Johnny Cueto, and Jeff Samardzija, and after an inconsistent April, they took off.

The Giants won 13 of 14 in late May and then went 17–10 in June, extending the division lead to six games. The stretch set Cueto up to start the All-Star Game and throw to Posey. Bumgarner joined them in San Diego, and for weeks there were whispers that he might be included with the game's best sluggers in the Home Run Derby. Bumgarner was ready to do it, but the MLB Players Association nixed the idea because it would take a spot from a position player. Bumgarner settled for becoming the first starting pitcher in 40 years to hit for himself in an American League ballpark. In what may have been the most rhetorical question of his career, Bochy approached Bumgarner a few days before his final start of June and asked if he wanted to do it at the Coliseum in Oakland. Bumgarner was honored, and he lined a double to set off a six-run rally that clinched the 50th win of the season.

The Giants entered the break 24 games above .500 and three games clear of the next-best team in the majors. It seemed they could do no wrong, a sense that was perhaps best exemplified by a mind-blowing twist on a play that happens hundreds of times a game. During a game against the Arizona Diamondbacks in June, Jake Peavy didn't get a checked-swing call and started to yell at the third-base umpire. Posey threw the ball back to the mound and immediately realized Peavy wasn't looking at him. Posey jumped out of his squat and hitter Jake Lamb grimaced, but the ball banked softly off Peavy's shoulder and settled into his glove. Posey started laughing as Peavy tried to figure out what had happened.

Literally everything was coming up Giants, but it was another first-half moment that foreshadowed what was to come. In May, Casilla stormed off the mound when Bochy came out to remove him from a save situation that had turned hairy. For the first time since the even-year magic had started, the bullpen was showing serious cracks, and it was keeping Bochy up at night. He couldn't shake the feeling that the Giants weren't as good as they looked.

Bochy knew relievers preferred set roles, and sticking to that was a big reason he became known as one of the game's great tacticians. But because of Casilla's struggles in the first half, he turned to a committee. The relievers met with Bochy multiple times that summer to express that they preferred having a set plan, but the staff felt it was the best path.

As the deadline approached, Brian Sabean and Evans scoured the league for reinforcements. They fell short in attempts to acquire Mark Melancon, Andrew Miller, and Aroldis Chapman. Ultimately they decided to take another approach. Given enough starting depth, perhaps Bochy could work his usual late-innings magic in October. As he got a sense of the trade market, Sabean said it was time to make a move for a meaningful piece. "You know you're going to hurt somewhere," he said. "It's just how much pain you're going to take."

After one and a half seasons with the Giants, Moore was traded again, this time to the Texas Rangers. Eight months later, he returned to San Francisco as a visitor and went for a jog around Oracle Park. He stopped on the portwalk when he noticed plaques commemorating some of the best individual performances in the ballpark's history. Moore stared at bronze plaques for Cain's perfect game and Tim Lincecum's no-hitters, and he couldn't help but think back to August 25, 2016. As Moore stood along the Cove, he thought about how close he had come to his own slice of history. "Man, I could have come here with my kid one day and showed him," he said the next day. "That would have been pretty cool."

For all that was made of the Duffy-Moore trade, there's no doubt the Giants got the better end. Moore had been the No. 1 prospect in the game at one point, ranking right ahead of two guys named Bryce Harper and Mike Trout, and the Tampa Bay Rays had wisely locked him up to a below-market deal that included team options through the 2019 season. The Giants needed Moore in 2016, but they also had hopes that he could help lead their rotation through the rest of that decade, making it a worthwhile call to send such a big trade package the other way.

Duffy had Achilles surgery that September and played just 199 games over four seasons for his second franchise. The other key to the deal was Lucius Fox, a Bahamian shortstop the Giants had signed for $6.5 million. He never reached the big leagues with the Rays and was out of affiliated ball by his mid-twenties.

Moore had such a rough second season in orange and black that the front office gave up on the long-term hopes and dumped his salary on the Rangers, but in 2016, he added valuable innings to a staff that was leaking oil, and he made two starts that were just a few breaks from making him a franchise legend.

In his fifth appearance after the 2016 trade deadline, Moore came one out away from becoming the first Giant to no-hit the Dodgers. Corey Seager blooped a single into right on Moore's 133rd pitch, and he smiled as Bochy came out for the ball. In the visiting clubhouse at Dodger Stadium, he insisted his arm felt great. "They used to not even count pitches, right?" he said. That turned out to be a prescient statement.

Moore's only postseason start with the Giants ended after 120 pitches, and he could do nothing but watch as the bullpen collapsed in the ninth. It is a night many in the organization will never get over, but it should have been known as the Matt Moore Game.

The Giants entered the night trailing 2–1 in a series, but they felt good about their odds. Cueto had been brilliant in Game 1 and was set for a Game 5 back at Wrigley Field. Bumgarner was ready to come out of the bullpen behind him, and the Cubs knew it. But first the Giants needed to get the series back to Chicago.

Before Game 4, Bochy smiled when asked who would close out a potential win. "I'll let you know in the ninth," he said. The Giants had become the first team to blow 30 saves and still reach the postseason, and there was only one way for this season to end. They had won three titles in large part because of Bochy's deft handling of a lockdown bullpen, but the inability to close out games in 2016 led to the only postseason series loss for the winningest group of players in franchise history.

Sergio Romo was the closest thing the Giants had to a closer at that point, but he had thrown two innings the night before and Bochy was worried about his workload. He decided to play the matchups with a 5–2 lead, starting with rookie right-hander Derek Law. Pretty much from the start, it was a disaster.

Law gave up a single to Kris Bryant and was done after four pitches. From there it was Javier Lopez, Romo, Will Smith, and Hunter Strickland. For three straight Octobers, the Giants had seemingly won every battle of inches, but every single in that ninth inning seemed to be just out of reach. A rare mistake from Crawford kept the Cubs rolling, and when Javier Baez ripped a 100 mph fastball from Strickland into center, the nightmare was complete.

Many on that team had already won multiple titles, and others would go on to take part in parades elsewhere. But the sting of Game 4 will never go away. Some longtime Giants employees view the collapse as even more painful than the World Series loss in 2002.

Part of what made it so difficult was that it was so easy to see coming. The late-game issues were such a concern, even in the strong first half, that in July team officials contacted Jeremy Affeldt to see if he would come out of retirement. As the trade deadline approached, Affeldt sat with Evans one night at Oracle Park. The GM needed an answer, and Affeldt told him he needed to go out and acquire someone. Evans pivoted and traded for Smith, and many on that team wished the staff would have turned to him for the entire ninth inning in Game 4. The versatile lefty had just one career save when the Giants acquired him, but he had not allowed a run in 19 appearances dating back to August.

Most, however, preferred Romo, who allowed three runs just nine times in 515 appearances for the Giants and never did it in the postseason. He had thrown 32 pitches a night earlier, but he also built an entire career on heart and guts. In the minds of the 2016 Giants, Romo would have found a way to get those three outs without giving up the lead. That's just what he did.

Players can sometimes take solace in the fact that at least they lost to the eventual World Series champs, but in 2016 that just seemed to be extra salt sprinkled on the wound. The Cubs went on to win their first title in 108 years, and at a team gathering a few weeks later, manager Joe Maddon mentioned to Cubs employees how grateful he was that he never had to face Cueto and Bumgarner in a must-win game at Wrigley Field.

Bochy found it difficult to watch the first couple of postseason games after the Giants had been eliminated and admitted that Game 4 was his toughest loss as a big-league manager. When he looks back on it these days, he thinks of the matchups, wishing he had played some of them differently. And he wonders about what might have been with a more streamlined approach. "If I look back, I probably would have stuck with one guy a little bit more," he said years later. "But what could go wrong did go wrong."

22
2021

In the spring of 2020, the Giants opened the doors of their new $50 million spring training headquarters. The stunning 40,000-square-foot building has a multifloor weight room, a clubhouse with 10 TVs and mood lighting, and an event space that doubles as an indoor infield on rainy mornings. There is a float tank for recovery and the booth that Mike Murphy used to eat at every night at Don & Charlie's. On the third floor, two decks overlook the playing fields and offer stunning views of Camelback Mountain. A lounge is set up with Ping-Pong tables and leather couches for team meetings. It was in that room where Buster Posey reset expectations for the 2021 Giants.

It had been five years since the organization's last postseason appearance, and the Giants finished with a losing record during the shortened 2020 season, which Posey opted out of. With their catcher back to lead a rebuilt starting staff, the Giants were internally optimistic about being in the thick of the Wild Card race. There was no talk of winning the NL West, which had been taken eight consecutive times by the Dodgers. The new staff took a measured approach as camp kicked off, but Posey, as was so often said when he made a perfect throw down to second base, wasn't having it.

As the entire team met in the lounge on the first day of camp, Posey had a sense that expectations needed to change. He stood up and talked about the importance of going game by game, series by series, and he talked passionately about how the lineup should focus on becoming the toughest set of nine outs possible. Then he turned to the big picture.

Posey knew that each season gets broken up into sections, and overlooked teams often wait to see how they are faring later in the summer before taking a serious run at a division crown. But he felt the group in front of him had the talent to be pretty good, and he thought it was important to get in front of that from day one. "The bar is not to sneak into a Wild Card spot; the bar for us with the Giants is to go out and win the division. There's freedom in that, I think. It's like, 'All right, here's the standard,' and it's a high bar, but I think it also leads to confidence," he said later. "Guys are like, 'Well, shoot, the manager and these players believe we can do this,' instead of just thinking we're going to try to sneak in. I think it kind of rallied the guys early. The first day of camp, it was like, 'All right, we've got to set the bar high.'"

The short speech struck the right chord, although there were still plenty who viewed the climb as impossibly steep. "I'd say probably half the people in the room would admit to taking that with a grain of salt, like, 'Yeah, but the Dodgers . . .'" said backup catcher Curt Casali.

But Posey had reminded them that it was a challenge worth tackling. "That was important for us. At that point, nobody had given us a chance for a few years—nobody ever picked us to be first in that division," Brandon Belt said. "But to hear it out loud from a leader of the team, it gives everybody else a bunch of confidence and gets their heads in the right space. He got me in the right frame of mind. We had a few veterans speak up. I think that meeting in spring training was the turning point for us that year."

It was a message that was particularly powerful coming from a player, but Posey might not have fully grasped how important it was to shift the tone. He had not been in the clubhouse a summer earlier when players started having long conversations about how seemingly everything about the Giants was changing. The new front office and staff embraced openers, platoons, and cutting-edge training and recovery methods. The lingo changed, with manager Gabe Kapler talking of putting his arms in buckets. There were "bulk innings pitchers" but also "sprinters." The Giants irritated fans by announcing their starting pitchers at the last possible moment, and opposing managers rolled their eyes at how late the lineup card would be sent over. At times it seemed the staff was trying to challenge every tradition and method the game of baseball had, and not always for the better. Early in the 2020 season, a few veterans called a team meeting after a game to make sure that for the players, at least, the priority was always on winning games.

The next spring, that was made clear from the start. An unlikely goal had been set, and seven months later, when Posey caught a 97 mph fastball to end the regular season, he raised both arms and looked to the sky. It took everything they had, but the Giants had won the NL West, and done so in historic fashion.

They set a franchise record with 107 wins, edging the Dodgers by one game in the first divisional race in which both teams won at least 105 games. It was the closest race in MLB history, with the Giants becoming the first to win 107 games but clinch their division on the final day, and the Dodgers setting a record for wins by a second-place team. After 162 games, the Giants made good on a message that Posey teased publicly shortly after he spoke to teammates. "As much as I think the sports world loves to try to predict everything, there's still some parts of it that can't be predicted," he had told reporters at the start of camp.

His team ended up becoming the greatest outlier in franchise history. In MLB history, that type of win total is generally preceded by years of postseason performances or tanking to stockpile top picks. But the Giants went 29–31 in 2020 and then came back the next year and spent 125 days with the best record in baseball. They got contributions from every corner of the roster, winning endlessly at the margins, something president of baseball operations Farhan Zaidi preached when ownership hired him in 2018.

If ever there were a time for the Giants to take a full step back and tear it down to the studs, that winter of 2018 had seemed to be it. The Giants had lost 98 games a season earlier and then doubled down with expensive trades, but they seemed allergic to the word *rebuild*.

Larry Baer interviewed 10 candidates to lead the baseball operations department, but Zaidi was always a front runner. He built a glowing reputation in Oakland and then Los Angeles, and his vision aligned with what the Giants' board had always embraced. He had no interest in tearing things down. "Our ownership group has always been constructed in a way that we want to try to win every year and also develop. That's probably the hardest thing in sports to do," Baer said. "Some teams have done that—the Patriots, the Spurs, the Yankees to some extent—and our ownership group is aspirational about trying to do that. Farhan matched those aspirations. That's really what it came down to."

Perhaps the Giants should have taken a step back. That might have put them in a better position over the long haul, but with key veterans such as Posey and the Brandons still in the lineup, that was never really an option. Over the previous four seasons, the Giants won just 45 percent of their games, with GM Bobby Evans getting dismissed. Over the following three seasons, they went 240–246, a run of mediocrity that cost Zaidi and Kapler their jobs. But in the middle of it all is a remarkable 162-game season. For six months, just about everything went right.

Aside from their mothers and significant others, nobody knows more about the players on a 26-man roster than the clubhouse manager. They are equal parts concierge and confidant. They oversee an incredibly hardworking group that clothes and feeds players, and not just for 162 games. They take care of everything from supplying packs of gum to making sure cars get shipped to the right off-season homes. They bring in equipment makers, sunglasses vendors, tailors, and even barbers. The goal is to make life as comfortable as possible so players can focus simply on playing, and that work starts early every morning and ends hours after the 27th out.

The clubhouse manager is perhaps the single-most-indispensable employee in the entire organization, but at times is also oddly invisible. For decades, Mike Murphy saw everything and heard everything, but he was a vault. When he retired, Duane Kuiper joked that Murphy knew as many secrets as former FBI director J. Edgar Hoover.

Murphy had the pulse of the roster like nobody else, and early in 2010 he started telling people that the group had a different vibe. Eleven years later, Brad Grems felt the same way.

Grems took over for Murphy in 2015. He has been in baseball clubhouses since 2001, when he was a student at Arizona State, and two decades into his career he felt something he hadn't seen before. He started quietly telling those he trusted that the 2021 Giants were special. "There was a different energy," he said. "They gelled early, and I haven't seen as cohesive a unit as that one. We just had a special group, a good balance of veterans and young guys. They knew what it took to win ballgames. Obviously it's a lot easier to have fun when you're winning, but everyone was excited to get to the ballpark every day. Guys were showing up early; guys were staying late. It was like, 'We can't wait to get to the ballpark tomorrow,' because you knew you were going to have a good chance of winning."

Grems first noticed it at the end of camp. In April, as the late-game wins started to pile up, he became convinced something was brewing. The Giants would go down four runs and assume they were still going to win—and they did. They weren't just winning at the margins; they were winning at everything.

The Giants handled their roster much differently under Zaidi and Kapler, an executive who loved to churn through waiver claims in hopes of striking gold and a manager who wasn't afraid to go with a newcomer over a familiar face if he felt it gave him even a 51–49 edge. They made 376 transactions, and even moves that seemed like failures on paper ended up being highly impactful. In late April, Zaidi sent a spare reliever to the Yankees for outfielder Mike Tauchman, who hit just .178 before he was released. But that doesn't tell the full story.

Tauchman made the catch of the year a month after the deal, robbing Albert Pujols of a walk-off homer at Dodger

Stadium in a game the Giants would go on to win. Two weeks later, he robbed Juan Soto of a game-tying homer in a Giants win. The catch at Dodger Stadium prevented what would have been a fifth straight loss to the rival, and by the end of that weekend, the Giants were in first place. They would spend just one night out of the division lead the rest of the season, surprising a heavily favored Dodgers team that was coming off a title. "Everybody was taken off guard. We knew they were going to be a decent team, but I don't think anybody thought they were going to do that," Dodgers ace Clayton Kershaw said. "Everything went right for one year, which was really impressive."

That wasn't sour grapes from the other side. When looking back, even the Giants admit that literally everything went right. They won with power, hitting a franchise-record 241 homers, an MLB-record 18 of which came from pinch-hitters. They also won on the dirt. Their pitchers led the majors in ground ball rate, their massive coaching staff orchestrated the most effective shifts in baseball, and Crawford won his fourth Gold Glove Award.

They were a nightmare late in games, with Kapler using a record 406 pinch-hitters and Austin Slater tying a franchise record with four pinch-hit blasts. Kapler used "line changes"—sending up two or three pinch-hitters in a row to exploit matchups—and they almost always worked. The Giants had 43 comeback wins, including six when they trailed after eight innings. On the other side, they became the first team in history to have six relievers throw at least 50 innings with an ERA under 3.00.

Kapler's aggression early in games would occasionally lead to an empty bench when things got tight, but even that didn't seem to matter. He ran out of position players against the Braves in September but won in the 11th when co-ace Kevin Gausman drove a pinch-hit, walk-off sacrifice fly to right.

Gausman was the epitome of what the Giants sought to do on the pitching side. A former fourth overall pick, he struggled to harness his stuff at three previous stops and pitched out of the Reds' bullpen a year before he signed with the Giants. They had him lean on his strengths, and by riding an elevated fastball and nasty splitter, he made his first All-Star team. Veterans Anthony DeSclafani and Alex Wood signed for a total of $9 million and solidified the rotation. When the reclamation projects started to fade, the rotation followed the lead of Logan Webb, a right-hander from Rocklin, California, who had a streak of 20 consecutive starts without a loss.

The deep 26-man roster was able to overpower and outlast flashier groups, but the Giants also had their existing stars performing at high levels. Belt had never hit 20 homers before but slugged 29 in just 97 games. Posey's 18 were his most since 2015. Crawford took the biggest leap, setting career highs in average, OPS, homers, RBIs, and runs. Nine years after they first teamed up for a World Series title, Posey and the Brandons combined for 15.1 Wins Above Replacement, their most in any of the 10 seasons they played together.

It was a stunning run given the outlook at the end of March. On Opening Day, the 34-year-old Posey hit seventh for the first time in 11 years. Crawford, also 34, was a spot behind him, and the 32-year-old Belt was fifth. It was no secret that the new regime had different timelines for moving on from the veterans than the fan base did, particularly at shortstop, but the trio had one more run in them.

Posey had set the division title as the goal. After winning 107 games, it was time to think bigger.

At some point during the 2021 season, the breakout hitter on the roster ceased to be LaMonte Wade Jr. The young outfielder became known as "Late Night" LaMonte. Acquired in a minor trade a few days before spring training, Wade was known for having a good eye but not much power. He hit double-digit homers just once in the minor leagues, but in his first season in San Francisco, he hit 18 and became the first player in 40 years to have six game-tying or go-ahead hits in the ninth inning or later. That earned him the nickname, as well as the Willie Mac Award.

Wade had spent months giving fans late-night jolts of adrenaline that made it difficult to go to sleep. When he returned to Maryland in the off-season, he found that he was having the same problem. The final at-bat of Wade's dream season haunted him for his first two weeks back home, keeping him from fully enjoying all that he had accomplished. One swing in particular stuck with him. "All I could think about was the Scherzer at-bat," he said the next spring. "I lost a lot of sleep over that."

Max Scherzer came out of the bullpen for the final inning of the NLDS, making a rare relief appearance three days after a Game 3 start. He closed out the Giants on 13 pitches, and while Wilmer Flores's checked swing on the final pitch is the memorable one, the Giants' best shot to win the game came during the Wade at-bat.

A fielding error by Justin Turner put the tying run on base, and in the home dugout, the Giants felt a familiar surge of adrenaline. Kapler had already used three pinch-hitters, but he had one more card to play. Wade, his best late-game weapon, came off the bench. Everything seemed to be lining up perfectly.

Scherzer began the battle with a curveball in the dirt, and when a 95 mph fastball cut too far inside, Wade had the count leverage he always sought. Scherzer came back with another curveball, this one a called strike. It was a crucial pitch. He hoped that throwing a curve in a 2–0 count would set up the rest of the at-bat and put it in Wade's mind that he could throw any pitch at any time. Thinking he might have messed with the young hitter's mind, Scherzer came back inside with another fastball.

The pitch was supposed to be at the top of the zone, but it bore in on Wade's back hip. As catcher Will Smith reached across the plate, Wade took a massive cut. The Dodgers had pitched him inside all series and he was ready for it. The ball left the bat with the proper launch angle to clear the bricks in right field and traveled 313 feet—but it hooked a few feet foul. "I recognized the pitch and I cheated toward it, and I went to it the wrong way. If I would have stayed within myself and my approach, I would have been able to keep it fair," he said. "That's what I lost sleep over, because I know that I recognized the pitch and I got too excited."

If the swing rattled Scherzer, it didn't show. He turned for a new ball before the loud strike even landed and then struck out Wade. Had he been able to hold his bat back just a split second longer, Wade would have had his Travis Ishikawa moment. Instead, it was umpire Gabe Morales who became the most notable figure from that ninth inning.

The series and the season ended when Morales rung up Flores on a controversial checked-swing call, ending an at-bat that exemplified not just how the teams got there but how close it had been along the way. It was perfect that it came down to Flores versus Scherzer. All season long it had been David vs. Goliath, and in the final moments, that's what it was, a future Hall of Famer who came over in a deadline blockbuster against an overlooked veteran who had thrived in the special environment the Giants cooked up that season.

As disappointing as it was, it was also somewhat apropos that the season-long back-and-forth ended on a checked swing. At Dodger Stadium in July, Darin Ruf had gone around on a swing with two outs and two strikes in the ninth, but he was given a reprieve and the Giants went on to win. In the end, the Giants got the call in the regular season and the Dodgers in the postseason. They played 24 times over seven months, each winning 12 games. The rivalry had never been closer, but the Dodgers were the ones to advance.

Scherzer had only been part of it for a few months, but it didn't take long after the deadline for him to realize that this Giants-Dodgers back-and-forth was something special. Something unique. Something wholly exhausting. "It felt like we were winning every single ballgame, but the Giants were winning every . . . single . . . game," he said. "You couldn't make up any ground, and then to go at each other like that in the Division Series, I felt like we both burned each other out. It took absolutely everything we had to be able to beat that team. I pitched so much that I got dead arm because of it. It literally took everything we had, and if you don't do that, you don't win that series."

The conventional wisdom as the Braves went on to win the World Series was that either NL West squad would have been too beaten up to give them much of a challenge. But the Giants didn't quite buy that. How could they after the remarkable season they had just had? "I truly believe that if we beat the Dodgers, we make it to the World Series," Gausman said. "Now, what happens then, who knows, but they were our kryptonite. That was our World Series. We beat them in the division, but man, it took everything. If we get through that, I think we were in a better position after that game than they were, because they used a lot more pitchers and threw everybody. I truly believe that all of our mindset was, 'If we win this, it's downhill.' They were the only team that we thought could beat us, honestly."

The Giants were left to wonder what might have been. What if Wade's ball had stayed true? What if Flores had been given another shot? What if another break had swung Game 5 somewhere along the way? Some Giants have wondered if it was worth it to give so much to chase the division title, although it's hard to have too many regrets. It was a magical run, and down the stretch, a star was born. Webb emerged as one of the best pitchers in baseball and capped the division run by hitting his first career homer on the final day of the season, becoming the last pitcher to do so before the NL moved to the designated hitter. He dominated the Dodgers twice in the postseason, and when the series was over, Posey declared it was Webb who would lead the Giants into the future.

It was a painful ending to as close a division race as the game will ever see, but that's the way it had to be for one team. The margins were paper-thin for seven months, so of course the back-and-forth ended on a coin-flip call. In San Francisco, Wilmer didn't go. In Los Angeles, it was a different story. But was it the right call?

"It doesn't matter," Scherzer said a couple years later. "Because I've got to look back on other moments in my career when I lost. I've lost games because of crazy stuff, and I don't look back at those and sit there and say, 'Oh, I should have won that one.' No. I lost. When you have a moment where maybe it broke in your favor, it's, 'Okay, I won, but I've been in that situation on the other side where I've lost.'

"It does you no good to sit there and cry about umpires. You can't do that at this level. You've got to take any break you can get."

PART 7

FOREVER GIANTS

23
Candlestick Park

Will Clark played more than 600 games at Candlestick Park. At some point, he started to know how the conversation at first base was going to go before the opposing hitter touched the bag. It was always the same—some combination of "It's freezing," "This is terrible," and "How do you play here?" Clark would smirk. "Hang with 'em, big boy," he would reply. "You're only here for three games; I've got 81 here."

Since April 2000 the Giants have played at the most scenic ballpark the game has ever seen. But for the previous four decades, they lived five miles away in Hunter's Point, a run-down neighborhood located on the edge of the bay.

Candlestick Park opened on April 12, 1960, and was christened with a win against the Cardinals in front of 42,000 fans, including Vice President Richard Nixon, who noted how beautiful it was. A story in the *San Francisco Chronicle* that day called it "the Taj Mahal of games." It took just a year, however, for the gleaming new ballpark to become infamous.

With two on in the ninth inning of the 1961 All-Star Game, Giants pitcher Stu Miller found himself confronted by the type of wind gust players discovered as soon as they moved in. Miller's body wobbled a few inches, and he was called for a balk, which moved the runners over and led to an unfortunate newspaper headline the next day: MILLER BLOWN OFF MOUND. It wasn't quite accurate, but given what players and fans dealt with on a nightly basis, it might as well have been.

Candlestick's location was chosen in part because Horace Stoneham wanted a spot where 10,000 cars could park, an impossibility in the heart of the city. But once they got out of their cars, fans were greeted by winds that were so harsh and bone-chilling that the city soon commissioned a study to examine the ballpark's elements. It was determined that the wind could blow upward of 60 miles per hour in that corner of town, which didn't surprise players, who watched hot dog wrappers whip through the grass and pin themselves on the walls.

As the years went on, the stories piled up. The bench once completely lost sight of center fielder Brett Butler after the fog rolled in and enveloped him. Bobby Murcer would keep his bats in a clubhouse sauna to keep them warm. Center fielder Dan Gladden had to jog to the track one night and pick up Johnnie LeMaster's cap, which had blown off and was whipping against the fence. LeMaster, it should be noted, played shortstop.

The Giants leaned into the absurdity, with marketing director Pat Gallagher creating the Croix de Candlestick, a small pin awarded to fans who survived a night game that went into extra innings. The elements were so intolerable that at multiple points in its existence, there were conversations about putting a dome over the ballpark. The cold and wind became what Candlestick was known for, but the story of the ballpark can't be told without an understanding of what all of those miserable nights nearly led to. Candlestick became such a blight that the Giants tried to leave San Francisco altogether. Not once, but twice.

The first close call came in 1976, when the Canadian brewing company Labatt agreed to purchase the team and move it to Toronto. It was the first political crisis for new mayor George Moscone, and as spring training approached, it became increasingly evident that the Giants were headed back east. Real estate developer Bob Lurie was ready to put up half of the $8 million needed to keep the Giants in town, but a partnership with former Rangers owner Bob Short fell apart because of some questionable decisions Short had made at his previous stop. National League owners insisted that Lurie be the point person for the ownership group, so Short backed out.

Moscone and Lurie scoured the city looking for a replacement. Salvation came in the form of a last-second cold call to Corey Busch, Moscone's press secretary. For weeks, Busch had taken calls from city residents who thought they could chip in, including kids who promised to empty their piggy banks to keep the Giants in town. He called everyone back but had no promising leads until he returned from lunch one day before the deadline and found a message waiting from an Arizona resident named Bud Herseth. He claimed he had $4 million available, the exact amount the new ownership group needed, and he wanted to know more about real estate in Arizona that would be part of the package. Herseth had heard incorrectly, but he didn't balk when Busch told him that land wasn't included. Within minutes, Herseth was on the phone with Moscone. In the middle of that conversation, the mayor signaled for Busch to get Lurie on the phone.

It seemed too good to be true, but Herseth's financing checked out. Lurie held a press conference the next day with Herseth, whose only experience with baseball had come as a high school player. He was bought out a few years later, but his infusion of cash kept the Giants around, at least until Lurie ran into his own financial troubles.

For all of Candlestick's faults, it proved to be a hell of a home-field advantage when the Giants viewed it that way. After Al Rosen and Roger Craig took over, they insisted that players embrace the elements, and they got rid of those who couldn't. Craig taught pitchers splitters to get more ground balls, and the Giants grew the grass out to further help their pitching staff. Craig would even instruct the ballpark's grounds crew to water down the area in front of the plate to deaden balls hit on the grass.

The wind was unpredictable, but Giants fielders at least had the benefit of experience. Infielders learned to back each other up more often in case a teammate lost track of the ball. Outfielders learned that you could never drop your head and run to a spot as you would elsewhere, because you would look back up and the ball would be somewhere unexpected.

There wasn't much they could do about the cold, but it was a lot more jarring if you weren't used to it. The Giants pitched inside with more regularity, further annoying opposing hitters who were pissed off from the moment they walked out of the clubhouse. It didn't help that there was no bathroom in the visiting dugout and that opponents had to go to the right-field corner to get into their clubhouse. "They'd come out of the tunnel with their parkas on. It was cold, windy, the grass was wet," recalled outfielder Darren Lewis. "They were just miserable."

When embraced, Candlestick gave the Giants a psychological edge. They would laugh before a series against a loaded lineup, knowing that opposing stars specifically scheduled their off days for San Francisco so they could avoid playing in the cold for at least nine innings. Pitcher Dave Dravecky was emboldened by memories of former Padres teammate Tony Gwynn, one of the greatest pure hitters the game has ever seen, telling him that he hated hitting at Candlestick. If Gwynn was uncomfortable, Dravecky reminded himself, every batter he faced must be feeling the same way. For as much as he would commiserate with opponents who met him at first, Clark grew to love the Stick. "Candlestick made me a man, and it made me the player that I was," he said. "You had to concentrate every day, because if you didn't, that place would just chew you up. Playing at Candlestick was one of the best things that ever happened to me."

In good times and bad, the Giants were able to find a decisive home-field advantage. They lost a franchise-record 100 games in 1985 but finished just five games under .500 at home. The 1962 World Series team went 61–21 at Candlestick. The 1989 World Series team had a losing record on the road but was 53–28 at home.

Candlestick provided an edge, but in the end, baseball is a business, and there are only so many ways you can sell being miserable in the seats. The Giants tried four times in the late 1980s and early '90s to get public approval and financing for a new ballpark, but they fell short with voters each time.

A 1987 proposal for a new downtown ballpark at Seventh and Townsend was rushed and didn't pass. Two years later, the Giants hired an architectural firm and zeroed in on a plot of land at China Basin as part of an ambitious attempt to build a $115 million waterfront ballpark. An outside firm was going to finance most of the deal while also building an arena on the Embarcadero, quietly hoping that the Warriors might cross the bay. Many parts of the deal were similar to what the Giants ultimately would do with Oracle Park, but they again fell short at the ballot box, this time by only about 2,000 votes, and in part because of another natural act they couldn't control: campaigning was halted by the Loma Prieta Earthquake. Voters in Santa Clara narrowly rejected a referendum in 1990, and San Jose voters did the same two years later.

Lurie had saved the Giants once, but he was out of options. There were concerns that a strike was coming, and the financial losses had become unsustainable. He put the team on the market hoping to find a local buyer, but for months he was met with silence. Finally, a group from Tampa Bay stepped up, crushing fans and putting players in an awkward position as they played the final home game of the 1992 season. For the first time in two decades, it appeared an MLB franchise was being relocated. "We were going to Tampa, which for so many of us was heartbreaking," former Giants pitcher Bud Black said. "That last weekend, we were asked to wave and say goodbye to the fans. We had Tampa Bay writers around; we were getting literature about housing in Tampa Bay and St. Petersburg. It was awful."

The deal was so far along that officials from Tampa had flown out to San Francisco to go over inventory with Mike Murphy, but quietly a group was forming to try and stand in the way. The members of what would later become the ownership group that saved the franchise knew they had one card to play. The sale had to be approved at the owners' meetings after the World Series, giving San Francisco politicians and businessmen a window to try and put a deal together. With one foot already on the flight to Tampa Bay, the bids from locals finally got serious.

The new group would be led by two men with ties to the Giants. Larry Baer was born in the city and worked for the organization after graduating from Cal, but he departed to attend business school and was working as a CBS executive in New York when the Giants went up for sale. Peter Magowan was a heartbroken young fan in New York when the Giants left, and he saw firsthand the damage that did to a community. After attending Stanford, he went to work at Safeway, the massive grocery store chain run by his father, who had been at the Polo Grounds for Bobby Thomson's Shot Heard 'Round the World. Magowan followed in his father's footsteps as CEO and served on the Giants' board of directors, a position he had to resign from in order to try and fight Lurie's sale.

Lurie had agreed to sell the Giants to a group led by Vince Naimoli for $115 million, but the burgeoning competition got signals from people involved in the process that other NL owners would likely vote no if $100 million could be raised to keep the Giants in San Francisco. They were losing money every year at Candlestick, but Bank of America agreed to loan the new investors $40 million if they could raise the remaining $60 million. The plan was to put together a group of small investors and one "whale," who would contribute the largest single sum and serve as the primary owner, but it wasn't easy to find the right leader.

This was years before sports ownership became glamorous and wildly lucrative, and the potential investors were all busy with their own business empires. Magowan was running Safeway, Don Fisher was busy with Gap, and Charles Schwab had a financial behemoth to look after. Charlotte Hornets owner George Shinn flew to San Francisco and briefly emerged as the leading option, but he couldn't get the finances together. He also turned off minority investors by announcing at a meeting that the team's colors reminded him of Halloween and he would prefer a switch to teal. Another potential whale took a look under the hood of the organization and announced to the others that they were pursuing "a dog with fleas."

As the deadline approached, the prospective minority owners continued to meet, and one night they looked around real estate mogul Walter Shorenstein's office and all came to the same realization: Magowan was an obvious choice to lead the way. He was not only a successful businessman who understood customer service but also a past member of the board, and at the age of 50, he was perfectly positioned to dive in to the tough financial battles that were ahead for the organization. Magowan said he would think about it, and later that night he called Baer, telling him he would lead if Baer would move back to be second in command. "We'll do this together," Magowan told Baer. "And we'll have a lot of fun."

The new group still had no firm plans for a sorely needed replacement for Candlestick, but the finances were strong and the ties to San Francisco were even stronger. That was enough for the other National League owners, who didn't want baseball to leave the city but did want to be working with an ownership group that could finally put a potential jewel franchise in a ballpark to match. By a 9–4 vote, owners chose to block a proposed sale and relocation for the first time.

It was a joyous moment on the West Coast, and not just for the Giants and their fans. Dodgers owner Peter O'Malley had been instrumental behind the scenes, leading other owners in an effort to keep an important rivalry intact. But across the country, a region seethed.

The aftermath of the late change was ugly in Florida. The Giants were one of eight franchises to flirt with the Tampa Bay–St. Petersburg area before it finally was awarded the expansion Devil Rays, and they got by far the closest to actually making the move. About 30,000 fans in the area had committed to season tickets if the Giants arrived, and Naimoli was so confident that he started working on uniforms for his new team. They had a similar look to the Giants' existing set, except with TAMPA BAY in big lettering across the front.

As local politicians and businessmen took turns ridiculing the process, senator Connie Mack III—the grandson of the legendary manager—cosponsored a bill to challenge MLB's long-running and valuable antitrust exemption. Mack felt other MLB teams were using the area and existing ballpark to leverage their own communities for better deals, ballparks, and tax breaks.

The ordeal even inspired a *60 Minutes* segment that started with the famous clip from *Field of Dreams* when Kevin Costner hears the words "If you build it, he will come." In 1990 construction had been completed on what would later be known as Tropicana Field, a $140 million domed stadium that was meant to entice Major League Baseball to Florida's Gulf Coast. In the piece, local officials and politicians used phrases such as "feudal lords," "cartel," and "emotionally wrenching fraud" to describe the process and MLB owners. "It's the first time I have ever seen anything sold to the lowest bidder," Naimoli said.

There was nothing he could do, though. Lawsuits were filed and hearings were held, but the Giants were staying in San Francisco. It had been an arduous process, but Magowan's ownership group succeeded in saving the franchise, for better or worse. As news of the initial vote started to spread, Shorenstein gave Baer a summary he would never forget. "We've got good news and we've got bad news," he said. "The good news is we just bought the team. The bad news is we just bought the team. What the hell do we do now?"

For the new owners of the Giants, there was only one thing to do. Somehow, some way, it was time for the city to get a new ballpark.

24
Oracle Park

A few months before the Giants opened their spectacular new ballpark, Shawn Estes and Barry Bonds took part in a promotional event on a field that was nearing completion. The left-hander was to lob a pitch to the left fielder, who would smack it over the wall, reenacting a scene from the groundbreaking on December 11, 1997, when Bonds took some cuts wearing a dress shirt and slacks with a beeper on his right hip. As Estes walked into the ballpark, he peered out at a right-field wall that looked almost as if you could reach out and touch it from the mound. *Oh my gosh,* he thought. *Barry must have designed this place.*

That seemed as good an explanation as any to the pitchers, who all had the same sense of trepidation as they looked around for the first time. Bonds must have secretly joined architect Joe Spear in designing an outfield that was just 309 feet in the right-field corner. Estes stared at the wall and imagined right-handed hitters splashing homers into what would become McCovey Cove. They did the same. Earlier that off-season, Bonds and Rich Aurilia had been brought in to take batting practice as construction workers hammered away. It was a beautiful fall afternoon, with the sun shining and no wind. "We were launching balls," Aurilia said. "I was like, 'I'm going to hit 30 homers to right.'"

Pitchers weren't the only ones who were concerned when they saw the planned dimensions. The original design called for the right-field wall to extend all the way to the water, but the San Francisco Bay Conservation and Development Commission objected, so a portwalk was added. That meant the right-field wall would be just 309 feet from the plate, and this time Major League Baseball officials were the ones to hit pause. They weren't swayed by the Giants' insistence that the corner would play fair since the right-field wall is 24 feet high and quickly juts out into Triples Alley, which originally extended to 421 feet. MLB sent representatives out to run tests, and the Giants provided data about how few balls were actually hit right down the line. Those diagrams, the high wall, and the potential for thick maritime air holding up homers finally calmed the league's fears.

In retrospect, all of the concerns seem silly. The atmosphere has proven harsh for hitters, and dozens of potential homers get knocked down by the moist air every season. It took 25 seasons for Heliot Ramos to become the first righty to reach McCovey Cove, and there have been only 104 Splash Hits from lefties, 35 of them from Bonds. The Giants built a pitcher's park and then built title teams around pitching, but it wasn't easy.

The new ownership group took over in 1993 with 18 initial investors and Peter Magowan as managing general partner. Publicly the group took an optimistic approach to their unpopular existing ballpark, knowing fans had been turned off by how often the organization and players complained in previous decades. They stopped pointing out the many flaws of Candlestick Park and instead upgraded the concession stands and bleachers. Magowan came from a customer service background and dug deep into how the Giants could make small improvements to a park they knew they would have to call home for the rest of the decade. It wasn't a nice house, but it was their house. Privately, meanwhile, they worked on a grand plan to build a new ballpark without financing from taxpayers.

Baer and Magowan toured Santa Clara County and drove around at night to see if they could find a warmer spot for Candlestick's replacement. The area where the 49ers would later build Levi's Stadium was a potential option, but ultimately the draw of an urban ballpark was too strong. Others around the league were focusing on unique downtown ballparks that were rapidly replacing the boring circular ones that had gone up in so many cities in the 1970s, with Camden Yards, Jacobs Field, and Coors Field ushering in a new wave. The Giants used all three as models, even hiring the same architect, HOK Sport, but they faced financial challenges that didn't exist elsewhere.

Bob Lurie had taken an 0-for-4 in his bid to get taxpayer approval, and surveys the Magowan group leaned on all painted the same picture: about 75 percent of voters in the city thought the Giants deserved a new ballpark, and about 75 percent of voters also said they didn't want to pay for it. The decision was made to finance it privately, which had not been done in baseball since Dodger Stadium opened four decades earlier.

Even with help from the city in acquiring and rezoning the land, the Giants figured they needed to raise about $350 million, about half of which could be borrowed from a bank. That left a massive sum, especially for an ownership group that had just scrambled to put together a $100 million bid to purchase the team, so the Giants turned to unique methods. They took up-front payments from sponsors and also from fans, setting up a charter seat license program. It was a method being used in the NFL at the time, and there was so much demand for the licenses that the Giants ended up increasing their allotment to 15,000, which covered most of the best seats in the ballpark, including first-row tickets that were licensed for $7,500 a seat. When the ballpark eventually opened, the Giants already had about 30,000 season ticket holders.

As they worked on their new ballpark, the Giants front office also worked out of a second location, which was home to a new sales team dedicated purely to drumming up revenue for a park that wouldn't open for several years. They rented office space on the 40th floor of a building along the Embarcadero and held meetings every Tuesday night to assess their progress and tackle issues. A detailed model of China Basin was built and shuttled around the Bay Area, showing off the planned waterfront to prospective investors and fans.

The Giants created the Winner's Circle, a program that would bring in the required contractually obligated income. They needed to show banks they had an income stream going several years into the future in order to pay off the loan, and the Winner's Circle was a group of major sponsors who provided the money up front in exchange for exclusivity and a unique approach to showing off the organization's top sponsors. Old Navy was an initial member and sponsored the Old Navy Splash Landing as well as Rusty, a mechanical mascot that was remarkably short-lived. Chevron got cars on the left-field wall that protruded above the rest of it, leading more than one hitter to threaten to come out with a saw if he ever got robbed of a homer. The most notable—and controversial—deal was with Coca-Cola.

About $25 million of the needed funding came from a deal with Coca-Cola to construct an 80-foot bottle behind the left-field bleachers. The company wanted to do something grand, but the Giants only had approval for advertising that faced inward, and while the label faces the field, the whole bottle can be seen from well outside the ballpark. After some back-and-forth with city commissions, the bottle—with a slide inside—was approved, albeit with a concession to the city, as well as a companion. The bottle became part of a fan lot that was open to the public on non-game days for several years. The Giants wanted to find a way to soften the image of the bottle, so they added a 20,000-pound glove, inspired by a four-finger version from the 1940s that had belonged to the father of Giants executive Jack Bair, who displayed it in his office.

It took a few months for Giants pitchers to figure out that McCovey Cove and the 309-foot wall couldn't really hurt them and they should pitch outside to right-handed hitters, but it was years before the organization fully grasped how unforgiving the other side of the ballpark could be. There was initial excitement over the possibility of right-handed sluggers taking aim at the Coke bottle and glove, and in the first season, the Giants ran a promotion in which a fan's name would be picked every game and they would win $1 million if a homer reached that area. No hitter even came close, so the organization ran some tests. It was determined that because of the elevated platform, it was the equivalent of hitting a homer that traveled nearly 600 feet. The promotion was quietly discontinued.

While the bottle and glove quickly became part of the charm of the ballpark, another planned landmark was immediately the subject of boos. Magowan wanted an old-time feel with unique and customized features, but the organization swung and missed on Rusty. The 14-foot mechanical man was supposed to come out between innings to celebrate homers, mimic stolen bases, and wave to fans, but he faced technical challenges from the start and was unable to get back into his shed quickly enough. The Giants tried different approaches to calm the hate for a mascot attached to a major sponsor, even seating young kids in the section right next to Rusty, but nothing worked. He retired quickly, and his shed became a luxury suite.

Rusty wasn't the only initial idea to be scrapped. Portuguese water dogs were trained to fetch balls from McCovey Cove, but the program—aptly named BARK, as in Baseball Aquatic Retrieval Korps—only lasted a couple seasons. The most notable change came in 2000, when the bullpens were moved from foul territory to center field, a decision that was made after years of outfielders tripping over the mounds. The alteration made the ballpark slightly friendlier to hitters, cutting it down five feet in center field and six in Triples Alley, which went from 421 to a still-imposing 415, the area code for the city. In left-center, the wall was brought in from 404 feet to 399. That portion of the ballpark already had seen one subtle change: Yahoo! was an early sponsor, and one year their advertisement ended up right next to a marker on the wall noting that the dimensions were 404 feet. A website that can't be found or no longer exists shows up as a 404 Error, and one of the world's largest search engines wasn't thrilled by the coincidence. The sign was quickly taken down. A few nights later, a ball was hit into the gap, and a confused Jon Miller wondered on the broadcast about where it had gone.

One final chunk of the initial financing came from a $50 million naming rights deal with Pacific Bell, a telecommunications company. The Giants had conversations with other corporations, including Ralph Lauren, which could have provided a potential way to create a new Polo Grounds, but Pacific Bell won the bidding and that felt appropriate given the ballpark's location. As with many elements of the new park, though, there proved to be an unexpected hurdle. A few months before the groundbreaking, Pacific Bell was purchased by SBC Communications, although it wasn't until 2002 that the companies took on a single name. The ballpark became SBC Park in 2004 and then AT&T Park three years later, after another corporate merger, and that's how it remained until the original naming rights deal ran out and Oracle took over.

The main issue the Giants had faced at Candlestick was the biting wind, so they commissioned a study by UC Davis. Oracle Park was originally supposed to have sweeping views of not just the water but also the Bay Bridge, but when a mechanical and aeronautical engineering specialist placed a scale model of the ballpark in a wind tunnel, it was clear that changes needed to be made. By slightly turning the entire ballpark, the exterior facade would serve as an effective shield for nearly 90 percent of the seats.

On April 11, 2000, Kirk Rueter took the mound and looked around at 40,930 fans. Pac Bell was finally ready. It was 61 degrees and sunny, with only a slight breeze out to right field. Longtime umpire Ed Montague was behind the plate, and the rival Dodgers were in the other dugout. Barry Bonds, as responsible as just about anyone for the ballpark existing, was in left and batting third for a Giants team with World Series aspirations. They had continued to lose tens of millions after the new ownership group took over, with the 1994 strike landing a massive blow to their finances. But they had expected to operate at a loss until a new ballpark opened, and Bonds had made sure that the product on the field remained compelling enough to keep fans interested.

As Rueter looked around, he thought the ballpark looked too good even to play in. Everything was perfect—and then the games started.

Bonds hit a homer to christen his new home, but light-hitting Dodgers shortstop Kevin Elster smashed three of them, seemingly confirming every fear about the way the ballpark would play. The Giants lost 6–5 and gave up 17 runs while dropping the next two games. When the Diamondbacks swept a two-game series, the Giants had a winless first home stand at a ballpark they had been dreaming of for more than a decade. They returned in late April and got blown out by the Expos the first night back. "We lost the first six games here," Duane Kuiper said. "I remember on the postgame wrap, all of us said, 'Let's go back to Candlestick! This place sucks.'"

It didn't take long for everything to change. The Giants went 55–20 at home the rest of the way, reaching the postseason and continuing to build on the momentum Bonds and Co. had built in the final years at Candlestick. They drew three million fans for the first time in franchise history and later sold out 530 consecutive regular-season games, a streak that lasted seven seasons and shattered the National League record. Those initial cash calls gave way to a windfall, and the ownership group that kept the Giants from moving to Tampa Bay is now sitting on an investment valued at roughly $4 billion. Most importantly, Oracle Park is home to three World Series trophies.

"It was like the renaissance," Jon Miller said one afternoon as he sat in the heated dugout. "All of a sudden people who had never been fans became fans. It became such an in thing, a great place to hang. People just wanted to come here. This changed everything."

25
Kruk and Kuip

It's impossible to imagine the Giants without Mike Krukow and Duane Kuiper. They are institutions, the voices of the franchise, but also in many ways the faces too. Two former players who combined for one All-Star appearance are so woven into the fabric of the organization that they're as likely as anyone who took an at-bat or threw a pitch for the three championship teams to one day get a statue at Oracle Park. If the process goes as it should, the best friends will one day stand side by side as they're inducted into the Hall of Fame. But if one of them had gotten his way in November 1981, Kruk and Kuip never would have come to be.

Kuiper was coming off his eighth season with the Cleveland Indians at the time, and it was a disappointing one, limited by an injury to his right knee. That didn't bother the Giants. Manager Frank Robinson had been with Kuiper in Cleveland and knew he could still be a dependable backup to Joe Morgan, as well as a valuable presence in the clubhouse. Kuiper was 31 and had planted roots in Cleveland, one of the closest MLB cities to his childhood hometown in Wisconsin. He owned a Wendy's franchise and had started doing a local radio show. So when Cleveland and San Francisco agreed on a swap of right-hander Ed Whitson for Kuiper, the mischievous infielder went to work. "I had to pass a physical, and I went to a number of my doctor friends in Cleveland to see if they would tell me how to flunk it, and they did," Kuiper said. "I flunked my physical."

He thought and hoped the discomfort in his knee would void the trade. As he sat in Giants general manager Tom Haller's office, he heard a doctor voice his concerns. "We want him anyway," Haller replied.

Kuiper was shocked. He was also, officially, a San Francisco Giant. "I did everything I could to make this not my permanent home," he said decades later, laughing.

Thirteen months later, the Giants added another veteran to the clubhouse, sending Morgan and pitcher Al Holland to the Philadelphia Phillies in exchange for three players, including right-hander Mike Krukow. If it seems like Kruk and Kuip have been best friends since the moment they first shook hands, well, that's because that's kind of the truth. "As soon as I walked into the clubhouse in '83, I knew," Krukow said. "I knew I was going to be hanging with him."

The Giants had a half dozen players on those teams in the 1980s who went on to become longtime analysts, but it was the second baseman from Wisconsin and the starting pitcher from Southern California who ended up sticking around to form a partnership that is in its fourth decade and has altered the franchise they once played for, as well as the conventional wisdom of television. You're not supposed to have two former players on the call, but the Giants wouldn't have it any other way.

Every night for six months, fans across the world invite two best friends into their living rooms. That's exactly the way Kruk and Kuip want it to feel. Why has it worked so well, and for so long? It's simple. "I just think it's two old ballplayers talking ball, and we have fun," Krukow said. "It's just fun. There hasn't been a day that I haven't come to work eager to get here. I just know it's going to be fun."

Kuiper goes to work every night with his best friend but also with his family. The producer on Giants broadcasts is his brother, Jeff. A third Kuiper brother, Glen, did play-by-play for the A's for nearly two decades. The brothers view it all as coming together sort of accidentally, but the roots of their passion for the game were planted early.

Their father, Henry Kuiper, never got to chase any sporting dreams, although he was known as a tremendous softball player. He became a farmer at the age of 17 and soon purchased his own plot of land in Racine, Wisconsin. The Kuipers had cattle and grew corn, soybeans, and wheat, and Henry put his sons to work from a young age. But he also realized early on that they had a love and aptitude for sports. The boys played baseball from May until September, and then it was football season, and then time for basketball, but all three really showed skill on the diamond. Glen was a minor league infielder for the Reds for a couple of seasons, but Duane was the star, getting drafted out of high school, community college, and Southern Illinois University before he finally signed with the Indians.

Kuiper reached the big leagues two years later, and by 1976 he was the starting second baseman for the Cleveland Indians. The next year, he accomplished an odd feat that put him in Major League Baseball's record books: Kuiper played 1,057 games in the big leagues over a dozen years. He hit just one homer. On August 29, 1977, he drove a slider from future Cy Young Award winner Steve Stone a few rows into the seats in right field at Cleveland Stadium, where it dented the seat it hit. "Hey, look at Duane run those bases!" one of the broadcasters exclaimed as the other shouted, "How about that!" To Kuiper's credit, he trotted around the bases like someone who did so on a daily basis.

No player in MLB history has more plate appearances with just one homer than Kuiper's 3,754, but that wasn't at all emblematic of his ability at the plate. He hit .271 in the big leagues, but from the start, Robinson made it clear that there was a specific way he wanted the quick and energetic Kuiper to play the game. Robinson was an intimidating man, and when he took charge in Cleveland in 1975, he had a stern message for his rookie second baseman. "He sat me down and said, 'If you hit the ball in the air, you're not going to play.' And I believed it, because who doesn't believe him?" Kuiper said. "I'd hit 5 balls out of 10 in the air, and he would pull me into his office and go, 'You're right on the edge of sitting down.' So I was really cognizant of just slashing it."

When the Indians visited Oracle Park in 2014, the Giants handed out 40,000 bobbleheads commemorating the blast, which, appropriately, was a solo shot. Kuiper kept the ball, bat, and jersey from that game, and he later was sent the seat that it hit. For a while, he was the proud owner of a black shirt that read OFFICIAL DUANE KUIPER HOME RUN T-SHIRT. The greatest souvenir, however, was a memory.

Henry Kuiper didn't get many opportunities to watch his son play, but that game was nationally televised, so he witnessed what ended up being a once-in-a-career moment. After the game, Duane gave an early indication of what life after baseball might look like. During an interview about what was then his first homer in 1,382 at-bats, he cracked, "This should put to rest forever the question of whether the ball is juiced up this year."

There is some irony in the long-ball lore, because as a broadcaster, Kuiper is perhaps best known for his home run call. Just about every signature homer by a Giant in the last three decades—from Bonds's record breakers to Brandon Belt's 18th-inning blast in the postseason—has been accompanied by one of the best calls in sports: "He hits it high . . . he hits it deep . . . it is outta here!"

The call is most closely associated with Bonds, but it was actually another Giants slugger who inspired it in the 1990s. Matt Williams's home runs were generally moonshots, giving an inexperienced broadcaster time to really get into the call. After Kuiper said it a few times, he started to get positive feedback from fans. "It just kind of morphed into part of my DNA," he said. "And Barry didn't hit many line-drive homers. So I got to do it a lot."

What is remarkable is that Kuiper is doing it at all. Every team employs former ballplayers as color commentators, but it's rare for athletes to do play-by-play. As his TV career was getting going, though, he found himself in a situation that called for experimentation.

Regional sports networks started to pop up around the country in the early 1980s, and the Giants wanted to get in on the action. It was a rough period on the field, and they couldn't convince any existing networks to come into the market, so vice president Corey Busch pitched owner Bob Lurie on the idea of the Giants creating their own product. At the time, teams feared televising too many games because they felt it might take away from their attendance numbers and ballpark revenue, but the Giants, with mounting troubles at Candlestick, were perfectly situated to take a leap. GiantsVision was born as a way to market the team to the region for three hours every night, and in 1986, 35 home games were shown in San Francisco and San Jose. A year later, 50 home games were broadcast, this time throughout Northern California and the Central Valley.

The problem with starting from scratch is that you need everything, but the Giants had a feeling that one of their two broadcasters was already working for them. Kuiper's media career had started with a five-minute show in Cleveland on a tiny 5,000-watt radio station run out of somebody's garage, but the humble beginnings taught him how to write a show every day, and he discovered he wasn't shy about talking into a microphone. With just about nobody listening, he was free to work on his inflection and tone, and when he arrived in San Francisco, he took over a pregame radio show Joe Morgan had on KNBR.

When Kuiper's playing career ended after four seasons with the Giants, he realized he would be spending a spring outside of Arizona for the first time in 15 years. That wasn't all that appealing, so he called an Indians executive and asked if he could come to camp as an instructor. His coaching career lasted just three weeks before Busch asked to meet in Phoenix for lunch. The organization was ready to launch GiantsVision, and Busch, who had grown up in Los Angeles listening to Vin Scully, thought Kuiper was the perfect fit. "One of the things I learned from listening to Vin was that this has to be somebody that fans are willing to invite into their homes 150 days a year. That's what you're asking fans to do," Busch said. "I had gotten to know Duane as a player, and the number one thing was that he was a very likable person. The fans liked him, and I felt like he would come across on the television screen as someone you would like to watch a ballgame with."

That was an easy box to check for the infielder nicknamed Smoothie, but Busch saw another trait. He had an inkling

Kuiper could be a great teacher during broadcasts, so he asked him if he had ever sat on the bench and done play-by-play in his head in addition to the fake games that he called with Krukow to the great enjoyment of teammates. Kuiper admitted he had, and the natural waves of enthusiasm in his voice made him well suited to try it on air, even if he had never done it for others before. Just by listening to him describe a play, you can tell whether the ball is going to be fair or foul, or whether it is a home run and not just a deep fly ball. That ability to paint a picture has been there from the start.

In the early years, Kuiper was paired with Morgan, his former teammate and a budding broadcasting star in his own right. Initially they both tried to do play-by-play, which wasn't easy for two newcomers who weren't far removed from standing on the dirt waiting for ground balls. Kuiper found comfort in the fact that GiantsVision was so new that he figured not many people were watching his mistakes, and it wasn't long before it morphed into Kuiper handling play-by-play and Morgan doing color commentary. When Kuiper added radio play-by-play to his duties, he felt everything click into place—but his second run with the Giants nearly ended before one of the game's most enduring partnerships could come together.

The franchise's attempted move to Tampa Bay came close to costing San Francisco its baseball team, and for a season, it did cost the city a man who has an approval rating as high as anybody. With the team on the verge of being sold, all employees were told to find new jobs, and Kuiper landed with the Colorado Rockies.

The ink on his Rockies contract wasn't even dry by the time Peter Magowan saved the day in San Francisco, but it was too late. Kuiper couldn't get out of his new deal, and he headed to Denver at a time when everything was starting to turn around for the Giants. He lived at the Westin downtown, and late in the year, his former team visited and stayed at the same hotel. Kuiper saw a few members of the new ownership group at the hotel bar after a game, and one thing led to another. They asked if he would like to come back. "Would I like to come back?" he replied. "Are you serious?"

Kuiper had two years left on his Rockies deal, but the Giants' minority owners convinced Larry Baer to try to bring him back anyway. Baer called Rockies owner Jerry McMorris, who gave Giants executives 48 hours to hammer out a new deal with Kuiper. He was headed back to the Bay Area, and this time he would be working with his closest friend in the world.

In the spring of his 14th big-league season, Krukow didn't pitch a single inning. He left camp feeling that the only thing he had to throw at big-league hitters was a 78 mph cutter, and for a while it somehow worked. The 37-year-old allowed two runs over five innings in his season debut, and the Giants won four of his first five starts. When the Montreal Expos came to Candlestick Park in late May, Krukow gutted his way through eight strong innings to lower his ERA to 3.00.

If you looked only at the box scores, everything seemed relatively normal for the tall right-hander who had ranked third in Cy Young Award voting two years earlier and finished his career with 124 wins and a 3.90 ERA. But Krukow was operating on fumes. It was getting harder and harder to bounce back after starts, and there was no way to make adjustments since he couldn't even play catch pain-free. It was a matter of when, not if, his right shoulder would give out, and it finally happened on June 4, 1989, at Atlanta–Fulton County Stadium.

In the bottom of the fifth, Krukow gave up a three-run homer to third baseman Darrell Evans, who tied Hall of Famer

Duke Snider on the all-time leaderboard. As the crowd cheered and Evans celebrated, Krukow stood in the middle of the diamond holding his arm. He had heard a pop, and he headed back to the clubhouse and sat alone. "That was it for me," he said. "I was sitting there in front of my locker and this big old paw comes over me, and it was Murph. I looked up at him, and he said, 'You did good, Otter. You did good, Otter. You did good.'"

Mike Murphy knew exactly what Krukow had done. He had already had three surgeries, and the rotator cuff had finally torn. His career was over, and he wasn't quite sure what would come next. It wouldn't be baseball, at least at first.

After the Giants lost the World Series, Roger Craig asked Krukow and Bob Brenly to come to camp the next year as members of his staff, with Krukow serving as a pitching coach. He promised to teach two of the clubhouse leaders how to manage, but Krukow couldn't do it. His family had four children already, and a fifth was on the way. It was time to help his wife, Jennifer, raise them all, so Krukow retired and went into the restaurant business. He was part of a group that ran seven establishments on the Central Coast, ranging from waterfront grills to a steakhouse in San Luis Obispo to a place on a golf course called the 19th Hole. The hours were long, but Krukow enjoyed it. This was not at all, however, what his teammates had expected.

While some would joke that the charismatic pitcher could go into acting, most just assumed he would one day stand on the top step of the dugout and run a game. He was the leader of those Giants teams in the 1980s, someone who even future managers looked up to. On Bob Melvin's first day with the Giants, Krukow grabbed his catcher and said they would be running the stairs at Candlestick Park. It's a tradition that Melvin carries on to this day.

Under different circumstances, perhaps it would have been Krukow who was a rising coaching star when a new ownership group was looking for a manager. By that point, he was already back in the game in a different role. When Morgan started doing national broadcasts on weekends, the Giants asked Krukow to be a guest analyst. He was given additional work in 1992, and in 1993 he took on the full schedule. It was the start of a second career that would elevate the former All-Star to even greater heights, but it wasn't quite the start of Kruk and Kuip.

Kuiper was in Colorado when Krukow took over, so much of the initial development came with Hank Greenwald and Ted Robinson. They worked to calm the energetic analyst who was showing plenty of potential but was rough around the edges. Over time, Krukow's ability to take dugout vernacular into the broadcast booth has become his trademark, but early on he leaned on that a bit too much. "People didn't know what the heck I was talking about at first," he said. "But we've all grown together, and fortunately the listening audience was patient and let me develop. I was pretty rough. I was raw, which is fine from a color analyst standpoint. You can be a little rough. They kind of want that, and it all worked out."

One of Krukow's greatest gifts as a player was his ability to make any new Giant feel immediately comfortable in the clubhouse, and that has carried over to listeners. Kuiper still sees it on a daily basis when fans or team employees stop by the booth, or when the two stand behind the cage and catch up with players and coaches from both teams. The magnetism that shines through the TV every night is there at all times. "He's got such a unique personality," Kuiper said. "He is the welcome wagon. He makes people feel good, and I think that came across right away when he was starting out as a broadcaster."

At times early on, though, Krukow was forced out of his own comfort zone. While working alongside Lon Simmons on a road trip, Krukow was stunned when Simmons announced he would be doing play-by-play for the third inning. He had never done it before and didn't know what he was doing, and naturally, the inning included a triple play. Krukow butchered it. "It was the worst call of a triple play in history," he said years later, but Simmons was there with encouragement.

There were a few different partners in those initial years, and Krukow learned from them all. But when Kuiper returned in 1994, everything about the game presentation changed for the Giants. It didn't take long before they realized they had one of the most popular duos the game has ever seen.

During the first home series of the shortened 2020 season, the Giants celebrated the 30th anniversary of Kruk and Kuip. They brought cupcakes into the press box and made commemorative T-shirts. Early in the game, Kuiper smiled after calling a strikeout. When his part was done, Krukow chimed in with his most famous saying. "He's been saying it for I don't know how many years. He just told some guy to 'Grab some pine, meat,'" Kuiper said. "It's perfect. It's just perfect. 'Grab some pine, meat!' That's always probably going to be my favorite because I heard him say that back in 1983 when we first became teammates."

The original intent behind hiring Kuiper has become true of both Giants broadcasters. Whether you're 6 years old or 56, there's not much that's better than sitting through nine innings with a friend, and that's what Kruk and Kuip bring. Their camaraderie elevates the whole broadcast, and it has always been that way. They can't recall a time when they ever didn't get along. "We know each other so well," Kuiper said. "It's like an old married couple."

The relationship has allowed both to flourish, and to do so with their own styles. They now broadcast games in front of a screen that went up during that 30th season and features their best catchphrases. For Kuiper, it's sayings such as "Got him!" and "He's giving him the stank eye." There's also a nod to one of his most curious calls. When Pablo Sandoval charged a slow roller to third one night and recorded an unlikely out, Kuiper yelled, "This is going to be a tough play. Sandovaaaaal . . . dag yabbel got 'em!" He has never been able to figure out what he meant by that. "Grab some pine, meat" is Krukow's most famous phrase, but his half of the backdrop also includes "Ownage is ownage," "In the squaaaaat," and many others that have become intimately familiar to Giants fans over the years.

The 30th anniversary party caught the two by surprise. They didn't realize they had hit three decades in the booth together until they got to the ballpark and saw commemorative cupcakes, but as the saying goes, time flies when you're having fun. They've been doing just that since 1983, and over the years they have added to their crew. Krukow talks proudly of the fact that they've worked with Jeff Kuiper, Jim and Alma Lynch, and others for just about their entire careers. Kuiper takes tremendous pride in the fact that the group has a good time every single night, no matter what life throws at them off the field or how the Giants might be playing.

That has put them in a class of their own, and made good on a prediction that longtime broadcaster Greenwald made to the two former ballplayers decades ago. "Hank always said the longer you do this, there's going to be a large group of people that never even know that you played," Kuiper said. "And he was right."

26
Jon and Dave

A day after the Giants clinched the 2012 NLDS, Ryan Theriot walked into the lobby of the Westin in downtown Cincinnati and plopped several large bags on the floor. The Giants had all day to kill as they waited for the result of the other Division Series, and the infielder had spent part of it shopping for fancy hats at a nearby Macy's. It was very much in character, and it was also hard to blame Theriot for needing to find creative ways to pass the time.

The Opening Day second baseman had been resigned to mostly pinch-hitting by the time the postseason rolled around, but for what would end up being the final game of the season, Bruce Bochy—as he always seemed to do in October—pushed the right button. Theriot was a surprise choice to be the designated hitter in Game 4 of the World Series, and in the 10th inning he knocked a fastball into shallow right for a leadoff single. When Marco Scutaro's single brought Theriot racing home, the Giants were three outs from a second title in three years.

In the press box at Comerica Park, four broadcasters exchanged smiles and fist pumps, but during the commercial break, Dave Flemming, the youngest of the group, couldn't shake the feeling that a change needed to be made. When the Giants clinched their first title, Duane Kuiper was on the call as Flemming and Mike Krukow sat alongside him. Jon Miller had been doing the ESPN radio broadcast, but two years later, he was sitting in the front row of the KNBR booth alongside Krukow and Miller.

The Giants were unique in putting all four of their popular broadcasters together in the postseason, and it led to some logistical challenges. Innings were mapped out in advance on spreadsheets so the three play-by-play announcers could all call part of a game. When Game 4 went into extra innings, the predetermined schedule called for Kuiper to move to the back row since only three microphones could be in use, and it had Flemming in line for play-by-play. As Sergio Romo warmed up, Flemming leaned back and quietly asked Kuiper if he should offer lead play-by-play duties to Miller, his longtime mentor and a legend in the industry. Kuiper thought it was a nice gesture. "Dave could see what was going to happen," he said later. "But Jon didn't hesitate."

Miller had been just a few feet away, separated by a pane of glass, in 2010, but it hadn't been the same. A national broadcast is much different from one aimed exclusively at Giants fans, and he hoped at the time that he would one day get to call the final out of a championship season for the people who listened to him night after night. But he also felt it was Flemming's turn. The format was that Flemming would get the 10th, and Miller didn't think it was right to stray from that. "I asked, and he was like, 'Heck no; this is your inning! You do it,'" Flemming said. "Not many guys get to call the final out of a World Series. That probably will ultimately always be my favorite moment of my career."

Miller listened as Flemming relayed every detail to nervous Giants fans and then raised his voice to meet the moment. Two years later, it was Miller's turn. When Madison Bumgarner got Salvador Perez to pop up in Kansas City, it was Miller on the call. The Hall of Famer has never lost his love for the job, in part because he has never lost his appreciation for the small details of a game or season, and the 2014 Giants provided one of his favorite facts: in San Francisco, the three titles were called by three different play-by-play men. "We came full circle," he said, smiling.

Miller did too. The third ring came 52 years after the Giants fell short in their first attempt after moving. Miller listened to the final game of the 1962 World Series as he sat in a dentist's chair on the other side of the Bay Area. Earlier that season, he had attended his first baseball game, sitting in the upper deck with his father and watching the Giants beat the Dodgers 19–8 behind a 15-hit complete game from Billy O'Dell. The day left such an impact on the young fan that six decades later, he can still recite the players who hit home runs, the box score totals, and the paid attendance.

But it was the action above the field that really changed Miller's life. His seats gave him a perfect view of the press box at Candlestick, and he looked down in amazement as Lon Simmons and Russ Hodges called the game with producer Bill King. All three have since been enshrined in the Hall of Fame. Miller has joined them—and it all started that day. "I was watching them almost as much as I was watching the game," he said.

When Miller was a teenager, he devoured magazines and books filled with bios of big leaguers. He was a decent player himself, but it didn't take long for him to come to a realization. "I'm reading about all of these ballplayers, and they all hit .650 in high school," he recalled. "I thought, *Well, I'm never going to make it. I'm not hitting .650!*"

It was time for a different path, although Miller probably would have taken it even if he were more successful at the plate. He grew up in a Hayward, California, home where Giants games were always on the radio. His parents got him subscriptions to *Sport* magazine and the *Chronicle* so he could embrace his new passion, and he spent hours with a Strat-O-Matic game, simulating seasons while he broadcast them—complete with crowd noise, commercials, shouts from hot dog vendors, and public address announcements. One day, when he was really young, he brought a pebble into the living room and started taking swings with a letter opener as he called a fake game. It was a creative way to practice, although his mother wasn't particularly pleased that a rock kept smacking against her wall. When Miller's father heard him, he could only laugh. For some reason, his son kept referring to a young Giants outfielder and future manager as Felipe Alou.

The pebble gave way to a reel-to-reel tape recorder Miller would talk into as he watched televised games. That led to doing announcements on his high school's intercom in the morning, and from there it was off to the College of San Mateo, because the closer choice, Chabot College, didn't have a radio program.

Miller was just 22 when he called his first MLB game, at least officially. He had been making tapes at Candlestick and sent one to A's broadcaster Monte Moore, who believed he was ready for a shot. The A's needed help too. Impetuous owner Charlie Finley had made 13 changes in the booth in 13 years, so Miller slid into the spot behind Moore and did three innings a night on the radio. He was living his dream, and when the A's won their third consecutive World Series, he found himself riding in a parade. Finley then decided to make his 14th change.

Miller moved on to a variety of sports, including hockey and soccer, but he returned to baseball with the Rangers in 1978, and he has been part of the soundtrack of the sport ever since. He jumped from the Rangers to the Red Sox, and when their radio station was sold, the Orioles came calling. It was during his time in Baltimore that Miller became the first voice of ESPN's *Sunday Night Baseball*, a run that lasted two decades.

He returned to the Bay Area, where he once recorded practice tapes he would send to any team with an opening, in 1997 to become the voice of the Giants in a broadcast booth. The homecoming was long overdue, but it had actually nearly happened 17 years earlier.

When the Giants called in 1980, it felt like a dream come true, but the more Miller thought about it, the more he realized the Giants of his youth no longer existed, at least at that time. He had grown up on Mays, McCovey, and Marichal, and he thought Candlestick was heaven on earth, but the Giants were a losing team in the 1980s and played in a ballpark that was ill-fit for baseball and didn't draw many fans. Miller stuck with the Red Sox, who not only were better but allowed him to call Fenway Park his office every night.

For all of the time that Miller spent in his youth preparing for this life, he never quite came up with what he felt was a signature home run call. But when Pablo Sandoval arrived, Miller finally found what he had been searching for. During an ESPN game earlier in his career, he wanted to do something special for a Sammy Sosa homer, so he came up with "Adiós, Señor Pelota" (meaning, "Goodbye, Mr. Ball"). That was shortened for Sandoval, who walked up the next day and told him he loved the call. It stuck, and it led to one of Miller's most memorable moments.

When Hunter Pence hit a grand slam early in 2016, Miller started to yell "Adiós, Pelota!" but quickly caught himself. It had always been used for Latin American ballplayers, with "Goodbye!" accompanying most of the other home runs he called. As the ball soared out to the bleachers, Miller realized he was going into the wrong call, and the extra moment of thought led him to accidentally say Buster Posey's name. That turned into "Adiós, Pelota! A grand slam for Buster Posey's... good friend Hunter Pence." Both players had fun with the new moniker on their social media accounts, which allowed Miller to feel better, although he would have had a laugh about it regardless.

As with the other half of the booth, part of what has made Miller and Flemming so effective is the clear realization that they're having a good time every night. "The key that keeps you fresh is to love the game," Miller said. "And you can't fake that. If it's not fun anymore, you definitely should retire."

Miller is perhaps at his best when things go awry and that energy is needed. His call of Ruben Rivera's blunder—"That was the worst base running in the history of the game!"—is one of the funniest and most truthful calls in recent memory. There is an endearing looseness to his broadcasts, which he'll often match by coming to chilly Oracle Park in shorts and flip-flops. "You only have to *sound* dressed up," he'll say, smiling. But the craft itself is one he has taken seriously since his Strat-O-Matic days, and that will never change.

When Miller was calling the final out in 2014, he thought back to a moment 12 years earlier. He was on the call for Kenny Lofton's pennant-clinching single, and afterward, *San Jose*

Mercury News columnist Bud Geracie asked him to recount what he had said. Miller couldn't remember, so they found an engineer, and as they played it back a few times, he realized that much of his call had been drowned out by Krukow and Kuiper's excited shouts.

As Bumgarner elevated fastballs to Perez, Miller remembered what he had told himself in 2002. If he got another chance, he needed to be clear but also efficiently sum up the gravity of the moment. His audience, after all, was listening on the radio. Sandoval camped under the pop-up, and Kuiper grabbed Miller's shoulders and started excitedly shaking him. Miller took a quick breath to collect himself. "Sandoval down the line in foul ground, he's got plenty of room—and he's got it!" he said. "And the Giants have won, they have won the World Series for the third time in five years, and Madison Bumgarner has firmly etched his name on the all-time World Series record books as one of the greatest World Series pitchers the game has ever seen." It was a moment that had been worth the wait.

The broadcasting industry is filled with announcers who spent their childhoods like Miller, calling fake games with Strat-O-Matic, LEGOs, or bobbleheads. They made makeshift microphones out of pens or kitchen spoons, and they recorded themselves. That is not at all how Flemming got his start.

He grew up playing basketball, baseball, and golf in Virginia, but because baseball and golf shared the same season in high school, he had to choose one, and he chose golf. His family had season tickets to the Washington Redskins and made regular trips to Camden Yards in Baltimore, but being a broadcaster wasn't a childhood dream. It didn't seem like a reasonable one to have, so he went across the country to study classics at Stanford. Flemming assumed he would eventually head back to

Washington, DC, perhaps to go to law school and follow in the footsteps of his parents, who met on Capitol Hill. It didn't take long, though, for a new passion to take hold.

Flemming told his freshman advisor that he was bummed to no longer be involved with sports. He was encouraged to check out the student radio station, KZSU, and as he searched for an informational meeting in the basement of Memorial Auditorium, he got a crash course in college radio. The concrete walls were covered with faded posters and rows of old cassettes. As Flemming walked down the hall, he saw a sound studio. "Someone was hanging an orange traffic cone and whacking it with a wood stick. That's what was going out over the air," he said. "I thought, *Well, that's college radio right there.* It was really a weird place but actually a really cool place."

It also turned out to be the perfect spot for a young broadcaster to begin a meteoric rise through the industry. KZSU's small staff allowed him to get experience with multiple sports right away, which wouldn't have been as easy at a school with a big journalism program. "I was terrible at first. Terrible," he said. "But you do enough games and you get to be decent, and then there is a little adrenaline and ego boost of positive feedback the first time somebody comes up to you and says, 'Hey, I listened to that game and I really enjoyed it.' Even just that, even just a little encouragement or push, that went a long way."

Two experiences stand out to Flemming for nudging him further down the path. On a small staff, Flemming was thrown right into the deep end, and he was behind the mic one night as eventual national champion Arizona visited Maples Pavilion for a men's basketball showdown. With the Cardinal down two in the final seconds, point guard Brevin Knight drove down the lane, waited for the defense to collapse, and fired a pass to Pete

Sauer, one of Flemming's classmates. Sauer hit the game winner, sending a sellout crowd into hysterics. Flemming replayed the call in his head as he walked out of Maples Pavilion later that night. He was pleased with his timing in an elevated moment. *I would like to do that again*, he thought to himself.

A few weeks later, he was at the College World Series in Omaha. Stanford played Cal State–Fullerton, and Fullerton alum and booster Kevin Costner was brought up to the booth to join ESPN's broadcast. Between innings, Flemming poked his head into the hall and asked an ESPN executive if Costner would be up for joining a one-man college radio broadcast. Costner said yes, and for an inning, one of the world's biggest movie stars bantered with a 20-year-old student broadcaster. They had a small audience over the air, but a key figure was tuning in. The exec had come into the booth with Costner to supervise, and when the inning was over, he handed Flemming his business card, told him he did a great job, and encouraged him to send some clips. "If Costner hadn't said yes, everyone would have left and I would have just kept calling the game, but the fact that he was nice enough to say that he would do it meant this ESPN guy stood in and listened, and he told me, 'Hey, I think you should do this, and you should stay in touch,'" Flemming said. "That was a big encouragement for me."

For those talented enough to go on to the next level, broadcasting actually follows a somewhat similar path to playing sports professionally. After a year at Syracuse to get his master's, Flemming went to the low minor leagues to call games for the Visalia Oaks. He was starting to live out his new dream but only on a part-time basis. On busy nights, calling games was often interrupted while he would run down to change out a keg at the concession stand. He would vacuum the visiting clubhouse after games, and when the team's clubbie quit during a road trip, he found himself washing uniforms, cutting watermelons, and making PB&J sandwiches. It wasn't glamorous, but Flemming told himself from the start that he would do at least a couple of seasons before reevaluating. Never was that plan more tested than on his 24th birthday.

Because Flemming had gone to college in Silicon Valley while the tech industry was exploding, many of his friends were already making huge salaries at startups and driving expensive cars. Occasionally he would hear about a classmate who had sold an idea for millions, but on May 30, 2000, he was as far from that as he could imagine.

The Oaks were staying at a casino in Lake Elsinore, and as midnight approached, Flemming wasn't thinking about birthday celebrations. He was waiting patiently for the window—2:00 AM to 6:00 AM—to get access to the washing machines. In the early hours of his birthday, he stood in a laundry room of a casino, watching gamblers chain-smoke as he waited for jerseys to go through a spin cycle. It was a low point, but it wouldn't last long.

The Triple A Pawtucket Red Sox hired Flemming after that season, putting him one step away from the big leagues. When the Giants needed a fill-in for Miller two years later, Flemming sent a demo, and on April 26, 2003, he debuted on the same day as top pitching prospect Jerome Williams. The first game went well, but a day later, Flemming had a sinking feeling that perhaps this wasn't actually meant to be.

The Giants had won 18 of their first 22 games before Flemming arrived, but Kevin Millwood no-hit them on his second day in the big leagues. Flemming feared he might never get invited back, but those who were listening felt differently. It was a tense 1–0 game, and in the next day's *Chronicle*, Flemming was praised for how he handled the tough assignment. He called 15 games that season, including a test-their-chemistry series with Miller, who years earlier had shared advice when Flemming reached out through a mutual acquaintance. At the end of the season, Larry Baer offered a full-time job.

Flemming has since called NBA, NFL, and national MLB games. The man who once gave up baseball for golf is now in the booth for the Masters. He is one of the more accomplished broadcasters in the country, but in his main role, he is still the youngest person in the longest-tenured booth in baseball. It's Kruk and Kuip and it's Jon and Dave, but occasionally, the others—especially the two former players—like to remind him that he's the junior member.

During his first season, Flemming tried to set up a beach volleyball tournament during a road trip to Miami. "Flem," Krukow said, "this isn't fucking camp," a line they still lovingly use to this day. Kuiper once grabbed a large watermelon from the clubhouse kitchen at Coors Field and dropped it into Flemming's travel bag. When Flemming got to the booth, he noted aloud how heavy the bag was. The TV cameras panned to the booth during the game, and Kuiper laughed as he saw Flemming had placed the watermelon on a counter, so it was in clear sight when Kruk and Kuip told the story on-air. From that moment, Kuiper knew they were working with the right guy. At the end of that first season, Flemming did rookie dress-up day with the players.

Flemming laughs as he retells stories from those early years now, but initially he was worried.

The team's broadcasters are reminded every night of the history that comes with their positions. They work in the Hodges-Simmons broadcast booth, where the walls are covered with photos of the team's current and former announcers—everyone from Tito Fuentes to Al Michaels to Joe Morgan.

There are plaques commemorating Russ Hodges, the Giants' broadcaster for 22 years in New York and San Francisco, and Lon Simmons, who called Bay Area baseball for 41 years.

In 2010 Miller joined them in the Hall of Fame as the Ford C. Frick Award winner. The Hall has been strict about not allowing partners to go in together, but both Kuiper and Krukow have been nominated separately. Flemming was afraid he wouldn't live up to that standard, but the others made him feel at home right away, elevating him with praise on-air but also jokes that made it clear he was one of them.

The youngest broadcaster fit in seamlessly, but the bond is particularly strong with Miller, whom Flemming would listen to as he stayed up at night in Virginia rooting for the Orioles. The two have made some of the best moments in franchise history come to life, helping to form indelible memories even on nights when they don't expect to. Flemming had such a bad cold before the clincher in the 2010 World Series that he considered not doing the broadcast at all. When Edgar Renteria hit the go-ahead homer, he couldn't hold back, providing a memorable call that included a crack in his voice.

The 2012 call is at the top of his list, though. It's hard to beat announcing the final out of a season, and the generosity shown by his partner made it all the more special. "Jon has done far more games with me than anyone else, and I take a lot of pride in that," Flemming said. "It would certainly be a great thing for me if—in the end of it all—we are associated together. Jon stands on his own, but our partnership—I hope it goes on for a long time."

27
The Rivalry

Bill Laskey was warming up in the bullpen at Candlestick Park when he heard someone screaming his name. Fernando Valenzuela was standing a few feet away, animatedly informing Laskey in Spanish that he was going to choke. The Giants' laid-back right-hander looked down at the Dodgers' lefty phenom and smiled. Laskey stands 6'5" and isn't easily intimidated, but Valenzuela tried his best, switching to a method that needed no translation. He put two fingers to his neck and again intimated that Laskey was going to choke. Pitching coach Don McMahon ran out to talk to Valenzuela, livid that the 21-year-old was trying to rattle his starter, but Laskey simply laughed. "Don," he said, "relax."

That should have been easy for the Giants. They had been eliminated from playoff contention before the final game of the 1982 season, but they had one last piece of business before heading home for the winter. The first goal for the Giants is always to Beat L.A. When that's no longer in play, keeping the Dodgers from reaching their own goals is a nice consolation prize.

The Dodgers entered the final day just one game behind the Braves, who did their part by losing. Needing a win to force a playoff, the Dodgers were tied with the Giants heading into the seventh. With two outs, Joe Morgan yanked a three-run homer over the wall in left, stunning the Dodgers and keeping them out of the postseason.

Morgan was 39 and had started 10 consecutive games leading up to the final day. Backup infielder Duane Kuiper was surprised when he arrived that morning and found Morgan wasn't taking the day off, but for the East Bay native, the work wasn't done. "He only played because he wanted to help the Giants knock out the Dodgers," Kuiper said. "He had no other reason to play. He was raised here, and he got the rivalry. If it couldn't be us, then he didn't want it to be them."

Just like the rest of the game, the rivalry has softened over the years. For the first five decades after they moved to California, only one player suited up for the Giants and Dodgers in the same season, but that has become much more common. Fan favorites such as Jason Schmidt, Brian Wilson, and Sergio Romo went from orange and black to Dodger blue, and when the Giants decided to overhaul their organization in 2018, they hired a Dodgers executive who brought in a manager he had worked with in L.A. and signed a lot of his former players.

Earlier in the decade, however, two men did their best to keep the vitriol flowing at a time when the Giants were winning titles and the Dodgers were kicking off their run of division crowns. The intensity between the teams ratcheted back up in May 2014, when Yasiel Puig hit a homer off Madison Bumgarner, flipped his bat, and found the lefty waiting for him as he finished rounding the bases. Bumgarner, his tongue firmly planted against the inside of his cheek, was ready when reporters entered the visiting clubhouse later that night. "I was just congratulating him. It was a really good hit," he said. "I don't know why everybody got so mad. It escalated quickly for no reason. I think he said, 'Thank you.' I don't speak Spanish very well."

As he walked out of the room a few minutes later, Bumgarner stopped at the door and smiled. "How good was that?" he asked a reporter. But the personal rivalry would soon take on a more heated tone.

Bumgarner and Puig went at it again that September, this time clearing the benches and bullpens. Two years later, they would repeat the exercise—benches cleared, words exchanged, no punches thrown—although that one might not have had much to do with Puig himself. After having the best record in baseball in the first half, the Giants went into such a funk that they were in danger of missing the postseason. Bumgarner, knowing his night was over anyway, saw an opportunity to try and inject some life into his club.

The Bumgarner-Puig antics added another chapter to a rivalry that has been burning for more than a century. It's one where half of the state curses Brian Johnson, while the other half cringes at any mention of Steve Finley. Older generations tell stories of Juan Marichal going up against John Roseboro, while more recent fans view Barry Bonds versus Eric Gagne as the best at-bat they've ever seen. If Giants-Dodgers isn't the best rivalry in sports, it's certainly on the short list, and a lot of that has to do with longevity.

More than 130 years before the San Francisco Giants and Los Angeles Dodgers squared off in a postseason for the first time, the New York Giants and Brooklyn Bridegrooms—so named after several players got married around the same time—met in the World Series. The Giants fell behind 3–1, then reeled off five straight wins. Brooklyn switched to the National League the next year, and a rivalry was born.

What made the 2021 season so special was the fact that two longtime rivals, separated by 380 miles, went head-to-head for six months, but for much of the early history of the rivalry, the teams were on different paths.

Sparked by the hiring of John McGraw, the Giants won 10 pennants and 3 titles from 1904 to 1924. They might have had a fourth, but a 106-win team in 1904 (the franchise record until 2021) did not participate in the World Series. Owner John T. Brush refused to face the Boston Pilgrims, whom he viewed as being from an inferior American League.

For most of the first quarter of the century, the Dodgers finished near the bottom of the standings. That didn't, however, mean the rivalry was dormant. Mel Ott and Carl Hubbell had the 1934 Giants tied for first with two games left in the season, but the Dodgers won their final two meetings, handing the pennant to the Cardinals. The losses were particularly painful for Giants manager Bill Terry, who had been asked about the struggling Dodgers before the season and cracked, "I was just wondering whether they were still in the league."

After World War II, it was the Dodgers who took control of the NL. They ran off 10 pennants in 20 years, a stretch that included two pivotal moments in the game's history. The Dodgers changed the game by introducing Jackie Robinson, and four years later, he was at the Polo Grounds for the Shot Heard 'Round the World.

Both franchises had high expectations heading into 1951, but it took a while for the Giants to get going. They lost 11 straight in April, and it wasn't until the end of May that they were even able to crawl back to .500. On May 25 Willie Mays arrived, and when the Giants hosted the Dodgers a month later, he hit the first of 98 career homers against the rival. The Giants trailed by 13 games in August, but they reeled off 16 straight wins to get back in the race and then won seven straight at the end of the season to force a three-game playoff.

The Giants won Game 1, and in the fourth inning, there was a bit of foreshadowing. Bobby Thomson took Ralph Branca deep, giving the Giants a lead that would hold up. The series shifted to the Polo Grounds, where the Giants got blown out. A night later, the Dodgers took a 4–1 lead into the ninth, with Don Newcombe looking to get them back to the World Series. The Giants opened the bottom of the inning with three straight hits, but as outfielder Don Mueller slid into third on Whitey Lockman's double, he injured his left ankle. The delay gave both sides a chance to regroup.

Dodgers manager Chuck Dressen came out to the mound. Years later, in a video series for MLB.com, Newcombe recalled how Dressen asked how he was feeling. Newcombe felt fine, but shortstop Pee Wee Reese suggested a fresh arm for the final two outs. Branca was chosen and met Newcombe on the mound. "He said, 'Don't worry about it, big fella; I'll take care of everything,'" Newcombe said. "And two pitches later, he took care of *everything*."

Thomson was so intent on psyching himself up that he didn't even realize it was Branca on the mound until he dug into the box. He took a first-pitch fastball, and when he got another one, he hit a low line drive to left that ducked under the overhang of the second deck. As Thomson leapt in the air, Russ Hodges delivered one of the most iconic calls in sports history: "The Giants win the pennant! The Giants win the pennant!" he yelled over and over.

They would go on to lose the World Series to the Yankees, but that's not what anyone remembers about 1951. "We beat the Dodgers, and that's all that mattered to me," Thomson said later.

Mays repeated the line when the Giants ran down the Dodgers in the final week in 1962. As he celebrated the first pennant in San Francisco, reporters asked for his thoughts on the upcoming World Series matchup with the Yankees. "Who cares about them?" he said, smiling. "The important thing was beating the Dodgers."

The move to the West Coast was initially much more fruitful for the team in Los Angeles than the one in San Francisco. The Dodgers won the World Series just two years after arriving, and again in 1963. The Giants had the best player in the state—Willie Mays—and led the league in victories in the decade, but the Dodgers were the ones to win it all, riding the historic one-two punch of Sandy Koufax and Don Drysdale.

While the 1970s were rough for the rebuilding Giants, the Dodgers reached three World Series. In 1981, led by the wildly popular Valenzuela, they ended their title drought. A year later, Morgan's heroics guaranteed there would be no repeat and reignited a rivalry.

The Dodgers got revenge in 1993, taking the final game of the season to keep the Giants at 103 wins, one behind the Braves. Four years later, it was Giants fans who again were back on top, and in a very surprising way. The Dodgers had one of the best rosters in baseball in 1997, but the Giants had Bonds, and general manager Brian Sabean bolstered the roster with the famous White Flag Trade, which was ridiculed in Chicago but brought three veteran pitchers to San Francisco.

The Giants were two back from the Dodgers when they met in San Francisco in mid-September, but on the first night of the series, they inched closer behind seven strong from Kirk Rueter and a homer by Bonds. The next afternoon, 52,000 arrived at the ballpark and were treated to a four-hour classic. Closer Rod Beck threw three gritty innings, setting the stage for Johnson. The Bay Area native crushed a walk-off homer to left and raised both hands as the ballpark shook. The Giants rode the energy from that day to a division title.

It took less than a decade for Finley to get revenge for the fans down south. The Giants trailed by three games when they arrived at Dodger Stadium for the final series of the 2004 season, but a win on the first night cut into the deficit, and they took a 3–0 lead into the ninth a day later. Then the unthinkable happened. Felipe Alou had pulled every lever in an effort to stave off elimination, but in Game 161, his bullpen finally ran out of gas.

Alou couldn't use reliable righty Jim Brower, who had pitched a mind-boggling 10 times over the previous 13 days. Dustin Hermanson entered for a fifth straight game, and the Dodgers quickly tied it up on three walks, two singles, and an error by shortstop Cody Ransom. With the bases loaded, Alou turned to lefty Wayne Franklin. Finley's grand slam was a no-doubter, crushing the Giants and a hopeful fan base. As 54,000 Dodgers fans celebrated, the Giants ran off the field and sat quietly in a cramped clubhouse that did nothing to muffle the noise around them.

Finley was an unlikely hero at that point of his career but also a perfect one given how the rivalry has gone. He spent one season in Los Angeles, but he managed to strike a blow that many Giants fans will never forget. Morgan played just two seasons in orange and black, and Johnson just one and a half. But they all came through when it mattered most. They did so in a heated rivalry game.

28

Murph

The Giants waited 56 years to have a ring ceremony in San Francisco. When they finally got to celebrate, before the second home game in 2011, it was clear no expense had been spared. The rings were designed by Tiffany & Co. and featured 77 diamonds set in white gold with yellow accents. The centerpiece was the SF logo, and there was a tribute to the Golden Gate Bridge on one side. On the other side was the recipient's name and an engraving of the World Series trophy. An orange spessartite garnet represented the first title in San Francisco, and five diamonds paid tribute to the five the franchise won in New York. On the inside of the ring, the results of all three postseason series were displayed.

Nearly 100 years earlier, the organization had held baseball's first World Series ring ceremony, replacing the previous tradition of handing out a memento of some kind. The 2010 ceremony paid tribute to that long history, and the Hall of

Famers who had come up just short were among those to get Tiffany & Co. boxes. But it wasn't Willie Mays who received the first ring. It wasn't the architect, Brian Sabean, or manager Bruce Bochy. It wasn't Buster Posey or Tim Lincecum or Brian Wilson. As they all smiled and applauded in the dugout, emcee Mike Krukow introduced the choice. "Our first honoree has waited a long time for this," he said, letting the anticipation build. "He has been with the Giants since the team moved to San Francisco in 1958. Ladies and gentlemen, it is only fitting that the first ring be presented to clubhouse manager, the legendary Mike Murphy."

It was a rare moment in the spotlight for a man who preferred to work tirelessly behind the scenes. As the Giants began a raucous celebration in the visiting clubhouse after clinching that first title, Murphy stayed back, leaving the room to players and coaches. Managing general partner Bill Neukom found him and handed him the World Series trophy, nudging him toward the clubhouse, where he would hand it to Matt Cain.

When the Giants won their second title and again gathered for a celebration at city hall, Murphy watched from a back corner of a large room as players and their families poured drinks and hit the overflowing buffet. When an onlooker suggested he belonged right in the middle of the action, he shook his head. "They're the ones that did everything," he said, nodding at the players.

That couldn't have been further from the truth. For more than half a century Murphy did anything and everything that was needed to help the team function behind the scenes. If you ask a former Giant to look back at some memorable tasks or asks, they might scrunch their face up. It all blends together. If a player needed help in any way, Murphy simply got it done.

That was that. And throughout it all, he said the same thing: "I don't bother nobody." "But," Will Clark pointed out, "everybody bothered him."

Murphy was there for everyone from Mays to Posey. He watched his beloved Giants almost leave town twice and then helped them settle into a new ballpark, where the home clubhouse is named after him, the club's longest-tenured employee. Occasionally, in quiet moments, Murphy would remind young Giants of that longevity. "I was here before you got here," he would say. "And I'll be here when you're gone."

Murphy was 13 years old when he caught the eye of Leo Hughes, who served as the San Francisco Seals trainer and equipment manager. Hughes noticed Murphy would throw baseballs back onto the field when he caught them during batting practice, and before a game he asked if he wanted to help out as a batboy. Murphy was an amateur catcher and first baseman at the time, but he embarked on a much different path, one that would keep him around the diamond longer than any player.

He remained the batboy when the Giants arrived at Seals Stadium and took over the visiting clubhouse in 1961. He held that job until 1980, when Eddie Logan—who had come over with the team from New York—retired. He was then moved to the home clubhouse and ran it until 2015, although there were a couple of close calls. Murphy had no intention of leaving his hometown, especially when it seemed the Giants were headed to Tampa Bay.

After a few years as a clubhouse advisor, Murphy finally stepped away for good in 2023, ending a career that spanned 65 years with the organization and allowed him to live out not just his childhood dream of being involved with baseball but also to experience things the young fan never could have imagined. His office at Oracle Park was across the hall from the manager's and became a green room with perhaps the greatest guest list the city has ever seen. Mays was a regular, holding court and telling stories as players stopped by to pay their respects and hopefully get a piece of advice or two. But the magic in Murphy's office was not limited to the sport of baseball.

He seemed to know everyone, and different generations of Giants gawked at the celebrities they would find sitting in that office. From Tony Bennett to Joe Montana to Robin Williams, it seemed there was no level of stardom with which Murphy had not connected. He was there the night in 1966 when the Beatles visited Candlestick Park and played their final show, and he was in the clubhouse when Pope John Paul II prepared for Mass in front of 70,000 people in 1987.

There might be more longevity in the Giants organization than anywhere else in professional sports, and Murphy outdates them all. He helped babysit a young Barry Bonds and was sitting at the ceremony when Bonds's number was retired. Mike Krukow and Duane Kuiper are in the midst of their fourth decade as broadcasters, and Murphy greeted Kuiper when he arrived via trade in 1982 and Krukow when he was acquired a few months later.

Murphy was even in the ballpark in 1962 when a young fan from Hayward, California, named Jon Miller attended his first game and watched Mays hit a homer. Decades later, when Murphy joined former owners Bob Lurie and Peter Magowan as the only nonplayers to go on the Wall of Fame, Miller found the perfect way to sum up his place in the franchise's lore. "Murph has been a Forever Giant since the first day," Miller said.

The plaque outside the home clubhouse at Oracle Park reads, WELCOME TO MIKE MURPHY'S CLUBHOUSE. But inside those walls, everybody knew him as Murph. No group loves a nickname more than a baseball clubhouse, although most of those nicknames involve simply shortening a last name or adding a letter or two. It's common to add an *er*, as in Cainer or Belter. Or you can take letters away, turning Crawford into Craw or Zito into Z. Madison Bumgarner became MadBum, or just Bum. Often—and this was particularly popular when Bruce Bochy gave out nicknames—a *y* will be added. Kelby Tomlinson was Tommy, Steven Duggar was Duggy, and Eli Whiteside was Whitey. Bochy at one point had too many Gomezes and room for just one Gomey, so young infielder Miguel Gomez became Go-Go.

Murphy was shortened to Murph, but he was also the man responsible for handing out dozens of nicknames. His most popular greeting was "Hey, kid," which could be used for anyone from a reporter fresh out of UCSB to trainer Dave Groeschner, who has been with the Giants for nearly three decades. Groeschner is Groesch, but sometimes he was just "Hey, kid" to Murph. Occasionally, though, Murph really hit on one he liked.

Italian shortstop Rich Aurilia was Richie Goomba. Marvin Benard was Marvelous Marv. Will Clark was Nuschler, which was his middle name. Juan Marichal was Popeye, with Murph joking that he was throwing so well he must have had his spinach. Jim Ray Hart was Old Crow because he liked to drink Old Crow bourbon. Gaylord Perry was the Greaser for obvious reasons. Hector Sanchez was George Clooney because Murph felt the 230-pound catcher kind of, sort of, looked like George Clooney. He sometimes would yell "Clooney!" when Sanchez was walking through a crowded space, knowing it would embarrass him. Bud Black was Tijuana Harry, a play on his birth name and the fact that he lived in San Diego in the off-season. When Brandon Belt became the Captain, Murph went all in, wearing a captain's hat as he went about his work and referring to the first baseman only as Captain.

One of Murph's best nicknames involved three generations of the Snow family. J. T. Snow was Snowball, so Murph referred to his dad, a former Los Angeles Rams wide receiver, as Snowman. J. T.'s son, Shane, became Snowflake. Like hundreds of other children of big leaguers, Snowflake quickly learned that hanging out with Murph was the best way to spend a game.

After getting ejected one night, Snow watched the rest of the game with his son and Murph, who were eating ice cream in the clubhouse. He was steaming about a bad call that cost him a homer, but that didn't last long. When you were around Murph, it was always about positivity. These days, the Giants have an entire mental skills staff to help players through tough times. But for decades, they simply had Murph. "If we lost, it was, 'You'll get them tomorrow' or 'Let's win the Series,'" Snow said. "He was like a second father to everyone, but he was also a psychologist and therapist. He was always so positive. I'd walk in, in a slump and be like, 'Murph, I can't fucking hit.' He'd go, 'You'll be all right, kid; you'll be all right. Just hang in there, kid.'"

Handing out nicknames was an unofficial duty, something to keep things light during a long season (or perhaps to make life easier for a man who often would have to keep an eye on more than 100 players and coaches from the start of the spring through the final game). But there was another task that was officially a big part of his job, and it was a very important one.

Murph was in charge of jersey numbers, making him the man behind some of the most popular ones in franchise history. Fans will never forget what 22 or 28 or 35 or 55 did in orange and black. Murph chose all of them, and he usually put great care into the decisions. Sometimes, however, it was simply the luck of the draw.

Rookies are often called up during the season, meaning most of the desirable numbers are already being worn. Posey had never been 28 before, but it was a low enough number, and Murph was rightfully confident that the catcher would be sticking around for a while, so he put that in his locker. Bumgarner didn't have a preference, so he got 40. Lincecum didn't mind having a high number and was happy with 55, which previously had belonged to a coach. Brandon Crawford got 35 because Murph had been fond of Chris Speier and Rich Aurilia, two shortstops who also wore the number. When Matt Cain debuted, he wore 43, but for the most part, Murph's early picks stood the test of time. They became synonymous with some of the most popular players in franchise history. "That's the way it should be," he said. "The Giants always had traditions here with their uniforms. Now they have four or five, but the way it always was, was they had two uniforms and you would see the same ones all the time."

The players who debuted during the championship era became such fan favorites that Brad Grems, Murph's successor, found himself in a tight spot. The main rule Murph passed down to him was that when a homegrown player did a lot for the organization, his number should be taken out of the rotation for a full year after he left. It was out of respect for the player but also for the fans. That was the case most recently with Cain and Belt, but other numbers have been put aside for much longer.

The only official request that has been passed down from the upper reaches of the organization has been to make sure nobody ever wears 15 again. At some point after Bochy retires, the organization will put his number on the wall. No hints are needed with 28, as Posey will join Bochy among the Hall of Famers from the Giants' championship years. After that, it gets a bit more complicated.

The Giants originally had a rule that only players in the Hall could have their numbers retired, but they made an exception for Bonds. His number retirement opened the door for Will Clark's 22 to go up on the wall. Coincidentally, 22 different players wore the number after Clark departed, but nobody wore 25 after Bonds. The same can be said of 35, 40, and 55, although at some point the Giants will have to make tough decisions. Crawford's status as the franchise's best shortstop would seem to put 35 on the wall, and Lincecum is one of the most iconic athletes in Bay Area history. But if you retire those two, don't you also have to retire Bumgarner's number? And if you do that, can you really draw a line before getting to Cain?

It's a puzzle that has left Giants clubhouse managers with the most difficult decisions in baseball. The organization already has retired 3 (Bill Terry), 4 (Mel Ott), 11 (Carl Hubbell), 20 (Monte Irvin), 22 (Clark), 24 (Mays), 25 (Bonds), 27 (Juan Marichal), 30 (Orlando Cepeda), 36 (Gaylord Perry), and 44 (Willie McCovey). Jackie Robinson's 42 is retired throughout all of Major League Baseball. Grems is running out of low numbers, and the situation was exacerbated when Gabe Kapler had the largest coaching staff in MLB history. As those kinds of staffs have become the norm around the game, the MLB Clubhouse Managers Association has petitioned league executives to change the rules and allow only the manager, bench coach, first-base coach, and third-base coach to wear numbers, leaving more options for players.

The Giants may eventually have to give out a popular number that leads to fan outcry, but if that happens, Grems will remember two other rules Murph passed along. He would never give a well-known number to a player who had the same position as a popular recent occupant, feeling that it added an unnecessary layer of pressure for the new guy. If 40 ever does go back into circulation, it won't be for a pitcher, and Bumgarner will get a call before it happens. Murph would always call the former player and give him a heads-up when his number was going back into a locker. "It's just a respect thing," Grems said. "It's what made Murph such an amazing person. He had the mindset to still think about these guys even after they were out of the organization or retired, which is a very cool thing. It's his care and love for every player that has put this uniform on, and that will always be there."

It took 13 minutes for Krukow and Duane Kuiper to introduce all of the guests and former players who descended upon Oracle Park in 2023 to pay tribute to Murph. Every decade of San Francisco Giants baseball was well represented, starting with infielder Joey Amalfitano, who played in New York in the 1950s and San Francisco in the 1960s. The Giants do pregame ceremonies better than anyone, but even by their high standards, this was an impressive red carpet, with Posey and Bonds sitting among rows and rows of former players and coaches. The one man missing was Mays, but he sent in a letter, which Kuiper read. "Murph took care of everybody and never asked for a thing. He just knew what to do for you," Mays wrote. "We speak our own language, Murph and me. He knows how I feel. There's nothing else to say. Well, except this: Congratulations, Murph. You deserve this honor. You've always been the best guy on this team!"

The size of the group was a testament to what Murph meant to his players. The diversity of the group exemplified what made Murph so good at his job. MVPs sat alongside middle relievers. Hall of Fame talents exchanged hugs with former Giants who could walk into a meeting of season ticket holders and have a hard time getting recognized. Murph had treated them all the same. The last man on the roster deserved the same respect as Mays. "That was his gift," Krukow said. "In his eyes, we all were royalty."

A higher pedestal was reserved for the children of players, which made for a fascinating reunion in 1993. Bonds first met Murph when he was four years old, and as he careened around the clubhouse at Candlestick Park, Murph would sneak him bubble gum and baseball cards. Bonds thought of Murph as his coolest babysitter, and when he returned years later to play for the Giants, Murph was still there, and he hadn't forgotten a thing. Bonds's locker was put right where Mays's had been, a subtle way to make the new superstar feel at home.

Like everyone else, Bonds soon became familiar with Sinatra Sundays, one of the organization's longest-running traditions. Frank Sinatra's songs would play softly in the clubhouse as the Giants got ready for Sunday games, and one year, Mays returned all the favors Murph had done for him by taking him to Sinatra's house for dinner.

The Major League Baseball season is unlike any other. When Hall of Famers would sit with rookies in Murph's office, they stressed the importance of staying even-keel, of not getting too high or low over 162 games. Routines are essential—the only way to make it through six weeks of spring training, six months of daily games, and potentially another month of the most intense baseball you have ever played.

Like the players he cared for, Murph found comfort in consistency. He went to Don & Charlie's every night during spring training, always sitting in the same booth, which was sent to the Giants clubhouse at Scottsdale Stadium after the restaurant closed. Sinatra Sundays brought him joy, but for the players, it also served a purpose. It didn't matter what had happened in Saturday's game. There was Murph on Sunday morning, bustling around with clean jerseys and fresh spikes as Ol' Blue Eyes crooned.

That commitment helped set the tone for decades, including for three groups of World Series champions. It's why Murph was an easy choice to be the first to receive a ring, and why so many former players showed up to celebrate him in 2023. During the Wall of Fame ceremony, Murph noted that he cared for about 2,500 players and coaches over the years, calling them a great group. And then he laughed, and just for a moment he allowed himself to embrace his special place in it all. "What a group that came out for me today," he said. "I guess I'm pretty good, huh?"

Acknowledgments

None of this would be possible without my parents, who saw their oldest child gravitate toward an unlikely career path and provided endless encouragement and patience. Thank you also to Andrej, Amir (a gifted editor), Daniel, Youseph, and Natalie. And to Yahya and Doug, who were incredibly supportive over the years.

Kirsten, thank you for convincing me to write this and taking on such an incredible workload as I finished it. Thank you for everything, really. Max, I hope this one day replaces *I Thought I Saw a Dinosaur* as your favorite book!

There is no shortage of people who have helped along the way, starting with Bud Geracie, who gave me a one-way ticket to Scottsdale and a chance to win a job. Thank you to everyone at NBC Sports Bay Area, and in particular David Tedla and his encyclopedic memory. I'm forever grateful to everyone at Triumph Books for giving me this opportunity and leading me through every step of this process.

Beat writers rely constantly on media relations staff, and Matt Chisholm and the Giants' group made this project much, much easier. Thank you to all the players, coaches, managers, executives, and Giants employees who so graciously gave their time and told their stories. Brandon Crawford was easily the first choice to write the foreword, and I'm appreciative for all of his help.

Finally, a shout-out to Robert, the world's best late-night writing partner, who brought the stress level down between naps and treats.

Sources

The Giants have had tremendous writers capture their history over the years, with a special debt owed to Andrew Baggarly, Chris Haft, Henry Schulman, and John Shea, who not only documented much of it but served as mentors to me. Marty Lurie and Missy Mikulecky were also extremely helpful.

Books:

Baggarly, Andrew. *A Band of Misfits: Tales of the 2010 San Francisco Giants.* Triumph Books, 2011.

Konte, Joe. *The Rivalry Heard 'Round the World: The Dodgers-Giants Feud from Coast to Coast.* Sports Publishing, 2013.

Mays, Willie, and John Shea. *24: Life Stories and Lessons from the Say Hey Kid.* St. Martin's Press, 2020.

Murphy, Brian. *The San Francisco Giants: 50 Years.* Insight Editions, 2008.

Murphy, Mike, and Chris Haft. *From the Stick to the Cove: My Six Decades with the San Francisco Giants.* Triumph Books, 2020.

Vaught, David. *Spitter: Baseball's Notorious Gaylord Perry.* Texas A&M University Press, 2022.

Zito, Barry, with Robert Noland. *Curveball: How I Discovered True Fulfillment after Chasing Fortune and Fame.* Thomas Nelson, 2019.

Newspapers:
Los Angeles Times
New York Times
San Francisco Chronicle
San Jose Mercury News

Websites:
Associated Press (apnews.com)
Baseball Reference (baseball-reference.com)
Major League Baseball (mlb.com)
NBC Sports Bay Area (nbcsportsbayarea.com)
Society for American Baseball Research (sabr.org)
YouTube (youtube.com)

Television:
NBC Sports Bay Area
San Francisco Giants
SFG Productions